MAGIC AND

MAGIC
Its Ritual, Power and Purpose

— & —

THE MAGICIAN
His Training and Work

W.E. BUTLER

Introduced by
Dolores Ashcroft-Nowicki

The Aquarian Press
An Imprint of HarperCollins*Publishers*

The Aquarian Press
An Imprint of HarperCollins*Publishers*
77–85 Fulham Palace Road,
Hammersmith, London W6 8JB

Magic first published 1952
The Magician first published 1959
This compilation volume published 1991
1 3 5 7 9 10 8 6 4 2

A catalogue record for this book
is available from the British Library

ISBN 1 85538 141 9

Printed in Great Britain by
Mackays of Chatham, Kent

CONTENTS

Introduction by Dolores Ashcroft-Nowicki   7

MAGIC: ITS RITUAL, POWER AND PURPOSE

	Foreword	II
I	Some Definitions and a General Survey	13
II	Human Personality	17
III	The Magical Thesis	23
IV	The Apparatus of Magic	27
V	The Kings of Edom	33
VI	Invocation and Evocation	39
VII	Magnetic Magic	46
VIII	The Magical Images	53
IX	Initiatory Magic	57

THE MAGICIAN: HIS TRAINING AND WORK

Preface   73

Part I: General

I	Why the Book was Written	77
II	The Basis of Magic	87
III	The Tree of Life	94

Part II: The Training of the Magician

IV	Preliminary Notes	109
V	The Astral Light	112
VI	The Invisible Body	118
VII	Visualisation and Audition	123
VIII	Words of Power: The Magical Use of Sound	133

IX	The Words and Names in Magical Working	138
X	The Flashing Colours	142
XI	The Vestments	148
XII	The Subconscious	150
XIII	The Interwoven Light	156

Part III: The Magical Keys

XIV	Magnetism	165
XV	The *Tattvic* Tides	172
XVI	The Body of Light	176
XVII	The Magical Personality	184

Part IV: Magical Rights

XVIII	The Construction and Use of Forms	193
XIX	Building a Ritual	201
XX	Talismanic Magic	208
XXI	The Way of *Magical* Attainment	213
XXII	L'Envoi	220

Appendices

A	Relaxation and Breathing Exercises	223
B	The Banishing Ritual	228
C	The Exercises of the Middle Pillar	232
	Bibliography	235

| | *Postscript from Magic* | 239 |

INTRODUCTION

SOMETIMES one comes across a book that changes one's life for ever. The size of the book has nothing whatsoever to do with it—it is what that particular book has to say to your inner self at that precise moment in your life. Its influence goes on and one returns to its pages again and again finding new levels of understanding each time. Such a book is *Magic: Its Ritual, Power and Purpose.* Its return after being out of print for so long is a joy to me, and it will be of great benefit for those who are coming to a serious study of the occult for the first time.

As I have already said, the size of the book bears no relation to its influence and, small though it is, within the pages of *Magic* can be found the essence of what a true magician is, and what he or she strives to become. The language may be old-fashioned and its views deceptively simple to those used to a plethora of books on occult subjects, but when it was first printed it broke new ground, setting before those who were hungry for information a set of principles that have never been equalled in their simplicity and directness. Here was a man, an ordained priest, calmly setting out the why's and wherefore's of magical training with utter sincerity.

I was one of those whose life was totally changed by this book. I bought it in a tiny bookshop-cum-publishers in Vauxhall Bridge Road in London, whose name was to become synonymous with occult publishing: The Aquarian Press. I was very new to this aspect of magic and the then owner put a small book into my hands and said '. . . this is the one for you.' I read it at one sitting on the plane home and the friend who met me at the airport said, '. . . you look quite different, as if you have found a new way of looking at things.' And so I had, as will anyone who reads this book in the right frame of mind and for the right reasons, which is why I often recommend it to people who write to me for advice concerning occult training.

The Magician: his Training and Work continues where that first all-important book ends. It was also one of the first of its kind, a *real* training book for the aspiring magician. Full of wisdom and down-to-earth common sense, it said, as Ernest Butler always did, 'Magic is not something for the weekend, the few special days in the year; it is for every day of your life.' He believed that with all his heart and trained his students accordingly. It is to my joy that I was one of them for ten marvellous years.

It is all to easy nowadays, when the would-be student is spoilt for choice, to take half a dozen assorted titles from a shelf and go on from there. Indeed, many do; but quantity is by no means quality, and the oldest is still sometimes the best. In the area of the occult, ethics are of paramount importance. Add to this self-discipline of the highest kind and a set of principles to act as a lamp on this the most difficult of paths, and all these must be thought about and accepted before anyone should place a single foot on the road to Adepthood. In the Nineties there are many schools offering tuition, some good, some bad, and many indifferent, but there will always be those who prefer to work alone. It was mainly for them that Ernest wrote this book, into which he poured his experience, his hard-won knowledge, and his unshakeable belief that only the best you had to give was worthy of the Path. It contains, even after the myriads of books written since it was first published, some of the best advice and basic self-training you will ever find. Look beyond the words and seek the man, the teacher, and the true Adept.

So now you hold in your hand those two books that made occult history. Issued in one volume you also hold a miniature course in workable, practical magic and, more importantly, a set of principles to work by and adhere to as you learn. Within these pages you will find a lifetime of carefully gathered knowledge, not only of magical instruction but of one man's enduring commitment to the Western Mystery Tradition.

Dolores Ashcroft-Nowicki
March 1991

MAGIC

Its Ritual, Power and Purpose

FOREWORD

I T is obviously impossible to fully cover such a vast subject as Magic in the small compass of these pages. I have therefore attempted to give a general idea of one aspect of the Magical Art in the hope that this little book may encourage my readers in the serious study of the Science of the Magi.

Acknowledgements are due to my wife, for her help and encouragement, and to Bishop Robert King of the Liberal Catholic Church and the late Dion Fortune, Founder and first Warden of the Fraternity of the Inner Light, for the teaching and advice I have received from them. It is fair to add that none of them are to be held responsible for the ideas herein expressed.

W. E. BUTLER.

February 16th, 1952.

CHAPTER I

SOME DEFINITIONS AND A GENERAL SURVEY

IN this imperfect world, where it is so easy to misunderstand or to be misunderstood, it is necessary, when writing upon such a subject as ceremonial magic, to define carefully one's terms. But before giving any definition, let us deal with the popularly accepted ideas of magic. By so doing we may cut away much of the obscuring undergrowth of thought, as one might clear away the tropical vegetation from around some hidden Aztec temple, and so reveal its true proportions and appearance.

The simile is apposite, for the temple of magic has been so overgrown with the lush growth of uninformed and superstitious thought throughout the ages that, in the Western world at least, its true appearance and nature has been lost. Only amongst the ignorant and superstitious on the one hand, and a certain nucleus of informed and instructed magicians on the other, has any idea of the true nature of magic been retained, and in the former case that idea has been sadly distorted and bears very little relationship to the actual facts.

As students of archæology and the learned exponents of comparative religion alike inform us, magic goes back to the very beginnings of human life on this planet. All systems of religion, with the exception, possibly of certain Protestant sects and the Southern Buddhists, have at some period or other in their history made use of ceremonial magic. Those who are interested in the historical aspect of the subject will find listed in the bibliography at the end of this book works by recognised experts in the field, foremost among them being Sir James Frazer, whose *Golden Bough* is a classic.

If these authorities be carefully studied, it will be observed that broadly speaking, each succeeding religion assimilates the best in the religion it supersedes, and the remainder is left to the ignorant populace and to those priests of the old religion who will not conform to the new. As the new religion organises itself it begins to persecute the remnant of the old, and this remnant is driven underground.

Such a state of affairs arose when Christianity emerged from its infancy and became the dominant religion of the West. The old religion disintegrated and the Christian Church absorbed much of its philosophy and ritual, gradually permeating all levels of society, until the only followers of the old faith were the rustics, the dwellers in outlying and isolated places. These rustics or *pagani*, untrained in the philosophy of their religion, handed down a distorted semblance of it. Always in the background, they were often cruelly persecuted, but their numbers were constantly recruited from many sources, including those who rebelled against the Papal claims.

When, however, the impulse of the Renaisance began to make it possible to break the yoke of Rome, the very godly Reformed Churches were as bitter as Rome had been in their persecution of the witches, wizards and magicians. The history of Europe from the XIth to the XVIIIth century makes harrowing reading. With the emergence of the " Age of Reason " popular belief in the malign power of the magician began to disappear. Concurrently, in Protestant circles at least, religious belief began to deteriorate into a formality which had very little driving force.

This dead level of mediocrity in England reached its high water mark in Victorian days, when physical science in the form of one of its greatest exponents declared " there is no room in the universe for ghosts," and the President of the Royal Society said, " In matter I see the promise and potency of all life." But with the increasing knowledge of the universe which modern developments in science have brought, such ideas have had to be considerably revised, and the modern physicist such as Jeans, Eddington or Einstein, has propounded an idea of the nature and purpose of the universe which can readily be accepted by the magician. Allowing for the difference

in terminology, he has been saying the same thing for
centuries past!

It is, however, with the modern school of psychology,
more particularly that presentation of it which is associated
with the name of C. G. Jung, that the magician finds his
closest link with modern thought. By that curious swing
of the mental pendulum, first noted by Heraclitus, termed
enantiodromia, that which has been repressed and driven
underground now begins to flourish in the open, to the
manifest dismay of the orthodox communions.

But although repressed and persecuted throughout the
ages, magic never ceased to exist in the Western world.
The Roman Church had skilfully adapted much of the old
magic to subserve her own purposes, but behind the scenes
the magical tradition ran like one of the underground rivers
of the Peak district, emerging now and then into the light
of day, and then disappearing again beneath the surface.

One such emergence was the Order of the Temple, whose
members, the Knights Templar have been cleared of much
of the odium cast upon them by their persecutors; the
Albigenses in France were another; the Brethren of the
Golden and Rosy Cross, the Illuminati, the Magnetists, the
Theosophists and the numerous magical Orders and
Fraternities which appeared in the latter half of the XIXth
century were others. Of these, the most famous and the
most illuminating from our point of view is the " Order of
the Golden Dawn." Founded upon an alleged Rosicrucian
foundation, it brought into one magnificent synthesis all
the floating magical threads and, in spite of many
vicissitudes and divisions, it still remains the fountain-head
of the Western magical tradition.

So much for our general survey of the magical field.
Now for our definitions.

My dictionary gives me the popular definition of magic
—"The art of applying natural causes to produce
surprising results." Such a definition covers too much
ground. It could be applied by a savage to the radio, the
telephone or the aeroplane, though such an one would
probably conclude that supernatural, not natural causes
were at work! A modern magician who has written

extensively upon the subject has defined magic as "the art of causing changes at will." Again, this is too wide a definition—it would include the operations of all workers, both manual and mental, who certainly produce changes at will.

In the present writer's opinion, the best definition of magic is that given by another modern magician who has defined it as "the art of causing changes in consciousness at will." This agrees with both the theory and practice of magic and we may profitably employ it here, with due acknowledgements to its originator, "Dion Fortune," who was amongst other things, the Warden of a well-organised magical fraternity.

Having arrived at a suitable definition, we are confronted with another difficulty. What do we mean by "changes in consciousness?" It will be necessary, then, for us to consider (a) what is consciousness, and (b) what is meant by changes in it. In the next chapter we will consider the modern psychological view of human personality. It must be remembered, however, that psychology is not yet sufficiently developed, as a science, to be hailed as a unified body of knowledge.

There are several schools of psychology, differing in their explanations of the observed facts. The followers of Freud place the greatest emphasis upon one aspect of life, the followers of Jung upon another, the pupils of Adler upon yet another. It will be seen that the bias of the present writer is in the direction of the Jungian school.

As a matter of fact, the writings of C. G. Jung are so much in line with the magical tradition that it is easy for us to understand the feeling of some of his more materialistic colleagues that he has "fallen away into mysticism." The results of this falling away seem to be satisfactory from the psycho-therapeutic point of view, anyway, and it is the considered opinion of the present writer that in Jung we have the Darwin of the New Psychology. One is aware that this is not an original opinion—others have said the same—but it bears repeating!

CHAPTER II

HUMAN PERSONALITY

THE problem of human personality is one that has remained unsolved for many centuries in the Western world. Eastern thought has evolved a classification of human personality which throws much light upon man's mental processes, but in the West dogmatic theology has up to recent times, limited any similar development of Occidental thought on the subject.

Within recent years, however, many factors over which dogmatic religion has no control have conspired together to put forward a truer view of the real nature of the personality than that hitherto held. The old academic psychology dealt purely with the waking consciousness, and its method of research was mainly by the conscious inturning of the mind upon itself. But many facts began to emerge which pointed to the possibility that the mind of man was greater than was realised. The observed phenomena of mesmerism and hypnotism, telepathy and the psychic marvels of the spiritualists, all began to show the necessity for a new psychology, based this time upon a much broader foundation than its academic predecessor.

F. W. H. Myers in his epoch-making book *Human Personality*, roughed out the general theory of what he termed the "subliminal mind." The general idea (which still remains valid) was that the conscious mind was that part of the mind which was above a certain level of consciousness which was known as the *limen* or *threshold*. This supra-liminal or above-threshold consciousness is not, however, the only level of consciousness. Below the threshold there exist other layers of consciousness, and these are termed the subliminal levels, or, generally, the "subconscious."

So the mind of man, according to this hypothesis is dual, having a conscious or waking level, and a subconscious, which remains below the threshold. Myers showed that all the various phenomena he was considering could be explained on the assumption that under certain conditions and through certain channels, the subconscious could thrust itself up and emerge into the waking life. He showed, too, that this subconscious level of the mind was much greater in its extent and potentialities than the conscious levels of the personality.

The simile which is usually employed is that of the iceberg, the greater part of which is hidden in the ocean. Such a simile is an excellent one, since the behaviour of such a berg closely parallels the behaviour of the mind. It often happens, for instance, that although the wind may be blowing from one point of the compass, the berg will move majestically against it, since its great submerged bulk is actuated by ocean currents far below the surface. So it is with the mind of man.

Upon this new concept a new psychology began to be built, and two men stand out as pioneers in the field. The first name is that of Sigmund Freud, and the second is that of his pupil, C. G. Jung. Freudian psychology is familiar to the general public because of its insistence upon the sexual element in psychological disease. With this extreme view, Jung disagreed, and gradually formed what is known as the "Zurich School." From the magical point of view, there can be no doubt that Jung's teachings are closer to the facts than those of Freud, and it is certain aspects of his system, therefore, which I will now briefly outline.

It is understood that behind the manifest life of both animals and humanity there is a driving force or energy which has been given many names. By the psychologists it is referred to as the *libido* or sometimes the *Id*. This basic urge manifests itself in what are termed the fundamental instincts, and in the usual classification these are held to be three in number, namely the Self-Preservation Instinct or Will-to-Live; the Sex Instinct, or Will-to-Create; the Herd Instinct or Social Urge.

To these three, Jung adds a fourth instinct which he claims as the prerogative of man alone, the Religious Instinct. This instinct is a counterpole to the three biological drives of the primitive instincts and is therefore an essential part of the constitution of man. Whatever system of psychology is built up, if it lack this essential point, will fail to cover fully the field of human personality.

Now in the early evolution of man, the three great instincts predominated though even then the religious instinct was definitely at work. As mankind began to advance, the gradually developing conscious mind began to cut down the intensity of some of the instinctive drives, and to divert their energies into new channels. But this was done in an unregulated and ignorant way, so that considerable friction occurred within man's mind.

With the appearance of Christianity, and the fierce reaction it evoked towards the degeneracy of the old faiths, this repression of the natural instincts became intensified and gradually became accepted as part of the Christian Faith itself until, in the Victorian period, it reached its culminating point. The conscious mind, it was affirmed, conforming to a certain ethical code, was the highest achievement of human evolution.

But this has resulted in the gradual increase of what is, in the main, a disease of the Western world, "psycho-neurosis." There are, of course, neurotics in all races, but by far the greater number are to be found in the Western civilizations. The powerful instincts being thrown back upon themselves become twisted and perverted and the energy they should bring to the workings of the conscious mind, were they properly directed, or "sublimated," is lost in internal mental friction, giving rise to that sense of frustration so common in the West.

This repression of the dynamic power of the individual has resulted in the establishment of a hard line of cleavage between the subconscious and the conscious levels of the mind. But it is obvious that only by bringing through into the conscious mind the dynamic power trapped below the threshold can the activities of man reach their true level. It is such a release of the subconscious which is aimed at in modern psycho-therapy, and this also is what is attempted in modern magic.

This does not mean that the primitive instincts have to be given full play in their crudest forms, but rather that the driving energy of such instincts is canalised and redirected into other channels. There must be, however, a natural similarity between the energy being redirected or "sublimated" and the new channel of expression which is offered it. An instance of this is the advice given so often to adolescents troubled with excessive sexual urges. They used to be told "Go in for sports, gymnastics, etc., and work it off." Sometimes the remedy succeeded—more often it failed—having apparently increased the urge rather than decreased it. This was because a channel for the first biological drive had been used for a force belonging to the second drive.

Sports are a splendid way of subliminating the Self-Preservation Instinct, and such group associations also form a good channel for the Herd Instinct, but they are unsuitable for the Sex Instinct, which is essentially individual and creative. Nowadays the general advice to such sufferers is to engage in the creative arts and crafts, to create, to make, even though it is only a rustic seat in their own garden. Such creative work affords an excellent channel of sublimination.

It must not be thought that the entire energy of such instincts can be—or indeed should be—sublimated but these basic energies should be available for the continued development of the spirit of man. It is here that the fourth instinct posited by Jung comes in, for it is the counterpole drawing the developing man up to greater heights and we might with advantage equate this fourth drive with what the occultists call the Superconscious or Higher Self, and the magician calls the Holy Guardian Angel.

Modern psycho-analytical research has pointed to the existence in the Unconscious or Subconscious of certain levels or layers of development, and the deeper of these levels link the individual not only with the minds of his immediate neighbours, but successively with the mental processes of all mankind down to a certain level, and below that again with the consciousness of the animal and vegetable kingdoms. It would seem that just as our physical bodies bear within their very structure the marks

of their evolutionary development from the lower kingdoms
of Nature, so our minds show a similar line of ascent.

There is what is termed the "personal subconscious"
consisting of ideas, emotions and memories, some of which
have been thrust down below the threshold because we
refused to acknowledge even to ourselves, that we were
capable of such thoughts. Such groups of thought charged
with emotional energy are known as "complexes" or
"constellations," and where they have been refused
acknowledgement they tend to break away from the
general unity of the mind and become semi-independent.
They are then said to be "dissociated," and it is these
dissociated complexes which result in the locking up of the
psychic energy of the self. The repressed complexes and
the dissociated complexes, together with all the host of
forgotten experience, memories and emotions make up this
"personal subconscious."

Deeper than this level we come to those emotions and
thoughts, those primordial images which we share with all
humanity, not only present humanity but past humanity
as well. This "collective unconscious" is as it were, the
conditioning background of our subconscious mind and the
images and memories buried in its depths exercise an
influence upon our lives which, though unknown to the
waking self, is exceedingly potent.

It is known that the Unconscious, whether personal or
collective works by means of pictures or images, speech
being a comparatively recent development. Therefore,
says Jung:

> Who speaks in primordial images speaks as with a
> thousand tongues; he grips and overpowers, and at the
> same time he elevates that which he treats out of the
> individual and personal transitory into the sphere of the
> eternal, he exalts the personal lot to the lot of Man and
> therewith he releases in us too, all those helpful forces
> which have ever enabled humanity to rescue itself from
> whatever distress and to live through the longest night.

Magic, with its roots in the immemorial past, does just
this, it speaks to the subconscious mind of man through
the archaic images of its symbols and rituals, and thereby
produces those "changes in consciousness" which the

magician seeks. So also it is recorded of the Lord Jesus that "without a parable spake He not unto them." (Mark iv, 34). It was as a Master-Psychologist that He added two positive affirmations which summed up the Mosaic Law.

We may sum up all that has been said in this chapter by saying that the best modern psychological school establishes the existence of four levels of the mind, namely

    (a)   The Conscious Waking Mind.
    (b)   The Personal Subconsciousness.
    (c)   The Collective Subconsciousness.
    (d)   The Superconsciousness.

All these are aspects of the one mind, but of this totality we are normally only aware of one, the waking mind. Nevertheless all the rest constantly affect us so that often we find that the hidden and mysterious currents of the deeper Self impel us along ways we have not consciously chosen.

To be able consciously to become aware of the set of the hidden currents, and turn them to the task of directing our life into the ways of wisdom and the paths of peace is the fervent desire of the magician, who, looking into the depths of his being and seeing therein the spark of eternal light which is his own true centre, exclaims in the name and power of that spark, "I have Omnipotence at my command and Eternity at my disposal."

CHAPTER III

THE MAGICAL THESIS

L EAVING aside all the multitudinous details which surround the subject, we will devote this chapter to a consideration of the magical theory of man and the universe. The magical tradition affirms that the universe is one, and that no part of that universe is *in esse* separate from any other part. As the poet writes, " All are but parts of one stupendous Whole." All that exists in the universe, therefore, is the expression of an underlying unity which subsists through all things. This may be condemned as mere " pantheism " but it is not so in reality, for behind the subsisting unity which expresses itself in the existing universe there is *That* of which the Universal Soul, the Collective Host of Life and Form is but an expression. " Having created the Universe with a Fragment of Myself, I remain," says Deity in the Hindu Scripture, the Bhagavad Gita. A God immanent yet also transcendent is the God of the magician.

The transcendental One, according to the magical teaching is reflected in the Waters of Chaos and Old Night, and that reflection of the Supreme, known as the Adam Kadmon brings order out of chaos. As one magical ritual describes it: " In the Beginning was Chaos and Darkness and the Gates of the Land of Night. And Chaos cried aloud for Unity. Then the Eternal arose. Before the Brightness of that Countenance, the Darkness rolled back, and the Shadows fled away." Now this indwelling reflection, the Adam Kadmon or Great Man of the Kabalah is the Logos " By Whom all things were made," the Brightness of His glory and the express Image of His person. Therefore, nothing in this universe exists except as an integral part of the Logos. All things subsist in that underlying unity, even as the Greek poet quoted by St. Paul affirms—" for we also are His offspring."

The soul of man is part of the greater universe and in

himself is a replica of it. So it is said in Magic that man is the Microcosm in the Macrocosm, the little universe in the greater universe. To the magician there is no such thing as "dead" matter in the Victorian sense. Indeed, he holds the view that it is only because it already *subsists* as part of the eternal life, that anything material can *exist* in time and space. That which we see "down here" as an inert block of metal is to the magician simply the material appearance of innumerable whirling centres of power, reaching back through the planes of the invisible worlds to the living heart of all. "The Spirit of the Lord filleth the Earth," and to the true magician nothing is common or unclean, for all subserve the purpose and are the expressions of the life of the eternal. This is declared in the ritual by the initiated adept who cries: "There is no part of me that is not a part of the Gods."

"The Gods." Does the magician believe in many gods? Yes, but his views on their nature are not quite what may be expected from him. He finds in the universe, visible and invisible, a mighty field in which innumerable forces play, each force being an aspect of the Supreme. And in these dancing and scintillant energies he sees units of the One Life, Sons of God evolved in previous universes, who as perfect channels of the supreme power act as living lenses through whom that power is brought down into manifestation. They are the "Dyan Chohans" of Eastern Scriptures, the "Ministers, Flames of Fire" of the Bible, and that Ray of Their essential being which flows from the unity and is refocussed in time and space is the "substance" in the theological sense which is the "real" universe and which manifests the secondary qualities that we call matter—the "accidents" of theology.

Thus, in the magical philosophy, there is no dichotomy between spirit and matter; there is no such thing as "dead" matter *per se*. All material existence, all manifestation is but the expression of the all-pervading Life—indeed, it *is that Life* in one of its innumerable modes of being. Believing thus in the life-structure of the universe, the magician holds that just as the power of the unity is manifest through those His ministers, so in the descending or densifying modes of His self-expression, innumerable hosts of lesser intelligences carry out His plan—"Angels and Archangels, Thrones, Dominations, Princedoms, Virtues, Powers; Cherubim and Seraphim, Ashim and all the Ageless Hosts of Heaven"—each in his degree.

The magician, seeing how the Supreme has "constituted the services of angels and men in a wondrous order" sees himself not as a stranger in the universe, not even as a separate being apart from it, but as part of that living diversity in unity, and says with the Greek initiate of old, "I am a Child of Earth, but my Race is from the Starry Heavens."

Turning from the vision of the Heavenly Places, he sees himself in Malkuth, the Kingdom of Earth, and realises that this imperfect, frustrated existence in the physical body, *is* imperfect and frustrated because, although he may know by the intellect of the realities behind the appearances, he has not yet been able to *realise* this truth in the physical world. "Know ye not that ye are gods," says the Christian Scripture, and a modern poet has sung, "Know this, O man, sole root of fault in thee, is not to know thine own divinity."

Over the Temple of the Oracle in ancient days was carved this inscription—*Gnothi Se Auton*—"Know Thyself." It is the realisation of the true nature of the Self which is the aim of the true magician. Following this principle and gazing within himself, the magician beholds a fallen world. He sees that the primal plan upon which man is formed is there, shining through the whole universe as the Supreme Harmony and Beauty, and in this light he sees the ideal in which his personal self is rooted and by which it is sustained.

Then, looking outwards, he sees in his own nature and in the natures of those around him the evidence of a Fall from the Potential Perfection. But in the midst of this Fall he sees the evidence of a Return, and through the sufferings of myriad lives he realises that the Way of Salvation is the Way of Sacrifice.

So he formulates the old Hermetic axiom *Solve et*

coagula, which may be rendered as "Dissolve and re-form," and so he uses the rites of the High Magic to effect both that dissolution and that reformation.

But what is dissolved, and what is reformed? Not that Eternal Spark which "lighteth every man"—rather it is the personal self which he has for so long regarded as his only real self, this personality which he has so tenaciously clung to and defended, has pampered and indulged—it is this *persona* this mask of the real man which must be dissolved and reformed. But how shall that which is itself imperfect produce perfection? "Nature unaided, fails," said the old alchemists, and in the Scriptures we read "Except the Lord build the House, the workman worketh in vain." So the magician in all humility seeks the Knowledge and Conversation of his Holy Guardian Angel —that True Self of which his earthly personality is but the mask.

This is the supreme aim of the magician. All else, spells and charms, rituals and circles, swords, wands and fumigations, all are but the means by which he may accomplish that end. Then, being united with that True Self—if only for a brief time—he is instructed by that Inner Ruler in that Higher Magic which will one day bring up his manhood into his Godhood and will achieve that which the True Mysteries have ever declared to be the true end of man—Deification.

CHAPTER IV

THE APPARATUS OF MAGIC

IT is only natural, perhaps, that the apparatus of the magical art should have caught the imagination of beholders, and it is in this word "imagination" that the key to the *use* of the various "props" employed by the magician is to be found. In this business of "causing changes in consciousness at will," the right use of the imagination is of the first importance. Let us then consider this faculty of imagination.

It may be defined as the power of the mind to form mental images. From this definition it will be seen that the strictures passed upon its use by the so-called "practical man of the world" are wide of the mark, for anything which is to be carried out into practical effect *must* start as an imaginative picture. What the "practical man" meant, of course, was that any imaginative effort which did not immediately result in material gain was a waste of time and effort. But here again, such an idea is far from the truth, for, many imaginations which have never brought gain directly, have nevertheless opened up channels whereby such advantages might accrue and have also resulted in lasting social and political achievements.

It is evident, therefore, that the "practical man" is not the best authority. What does the psychologist have to say? He deals with the mind in his daily work and may be able to give us a truer picture.

Let us revert for a moment to our consideration of the human personality. We divided it into three levels—the conscious subconscious and superconscious levels, and suggested that the latter two were of greater importance than the ordinary conscious mind. But nevertheless, the conscious mind is that part of the mind with which we are working and evolving upon this planet, and for this reason it must be the directing authority in any attempt at mental and magical work. Allowing it this authority we must also define the limits of its authority. It can and should direct, *but the actual work must be done at the subconscious level.*

The subconscious mind is older, in terms of evolutionary development than the conscious mind, and it retains one trait of its immemorial past in the fact that, as we have said before, it works by *images*, not words. Each of the five physical senses reporting to the brain sends in a series of images visual, tactile, audible, olfactory or gustatory, and these images are linked up in the subconscious mind with their appropriate emotions. If, therefore, one consciously introduces carefully selected images into the subconscious mind one can evoke the corresponding emotion.

Since the emotions are the subjective aspects of the driving energy which wells up from the deeper levels of the mind, it is evident that by the right use of such conscious evocation the " potential," or pressure of life in the personality, can be greatly enhanced. We see this in a perverted form in the abnormal strength shown by some lunatics during their insane periods, or again, in a higher and more admirable form in the way in which we rise to the occasion of a sudden peril and perform feats which would be impossible to us under ordinary conditions. The phenomena of hypnosis introduce us to the same thing under conditions which allow us to study it at will. In hypnosis we find that, once the barrier or "threshold" has been pierced, and the subconscious levels allowed to emerge above it, any images introduced at this time will have a direct effect upon the dynamism of the personality.

In many systems of mystical and occult thought appropriated from Eastern sources, great stress is laid upon the importance of meditation, and the Eastern Yoga systems are advocated as training methods. Whatever may be the advantages of Yoga, the disadvantage of the application of *Eastern Yoga* to *Western* bodies is found in practice to be considerable, and for that reason, if the Western magician uses the Yoga technique, he employs a modified system which has been adapted to Western use.

In the purely mental methods of meditation there is an insistance upon the control and inhibition of the bodily senses—one is told that it is necessary to be able to shut

out unwanted thoughts, to keep the mind unwaveringly
fixed upon one thought only, and to refuse to allow any
sense impressions to distract one from the chosen object
of thought.

In the magical system, however, the images pouring
into the mind from the various senses are used as
"suggestions" to the conscious mind, which, because of
the particularly sensitive condition that has been induced
in it by the ritual itself, continues to follow the line upon
which it is concentrating. It is a form of psychic *ju-jitsu,*
in which the very power of the sense-impressions is used to
render the conscious mind immune to their distractions.

Before, however, such images can produce such an
effect, two things must be done. The mind must first be
"conditioned" to the image. Consciously and persistently
the image must be held in the mind and the appropriate
emotion associated with it, until, the image being held in
the mind, the emotion automatically wells up from the
subconscious level. Secondly, either by the actual
performance of the ritual, or by some form of auto-
hypnosis, the threshold of consciousness must be lowered,
so that the subconscious levels emerge into consciousness
and become available to the suggestive power of the chosen
thought.

So with all magical "props"—the sword, the wand, the
pentacle, the cup, the circles, triangles and sigils, the
lights, the robes, the incense, the sonorous words of
invocation and the "barbarous names" of evocation—all
work by a cumulative suggestive process upon the
subconscious mind. Such a cumulative suggestion results
in what may be termed a mental change of gear, and
therefore conforms to our earlier definition of magic as the
"Art of causing changes in consciousness at will."

The levels of consciousness reached will depend upon the
symbols, etc., used, and also on the amount of conscious
association of ideas which the student has put into it.
Magic, far from being an irrational superstition is based,
as will be observed, upon profound psychological laws,
and possesses its own special technique. With Eastern
magical systems we are not here concerned, since this book

is written for Western people, and is based upon the
theory and practice of the Western Schools.

The "Western Tradition," to give it its technical name,
is a composite thing, embracing the magical techniques of
all the countries of the Mediterranean Basin on the one
hand, and the indigenous system of the Norse and Keltic
peoples. The average man, if he takes the trouble to
discuss magic, usually has a preconceived idea based upon
the fragments of magical practice of the Middle Ages in
Europe. Such fragments from the magical "Grimoires"
give a very imperfect picture of what the Western Magic
is, but they are usually used by our critics as proof of the
foolishness and superstition of the practitioners of Magic.
However, the same line of argument could be followed
by any critic of, say, the Roman Church, and, in fact,
the very contemptuous term "Hocus Pocus" which is
generally directed against magical practices is the
Protestant distortion of the most solemn part of the
Christian Eucharist—*Hoc Est Enim Corpus Meum*—"This
is My Body." It was because of certain abuses and
superstitions that this word of approbrium was directed
alike against Romas Catholic priest and magical adept.

It is, however, a truer and more equable criterion if we
consider the best, and not the worst, in any human
institution. Quite apart from any claim which might be
made by the Catholic Church to be a supernaturally
organised body, or by the magical adepts that they possess
a wisdom which has been handed down "from time
immemorial," it is evident that their respective organisations are composed of fallible human beings, whose
failings and imperfections must inevitably affect the
presentation of their beliefs and doctrines.

The Western Tradition affirms of itself that it is the heir
to a body of teaching and practice which has been handed
down from remote antiquity, and that the central
philosophy around which it is organised is the body of
Hebrew mystical teaching known as the Qabalah. This
word in itself conveys the idea of secrecy, since it signifies
the oral transmission of knowledge "from mouth to ear,"
and indeed, this oral tradition long antedated the public

compilation and appearance of such works as the *Sepher Yetzirah,* one of the standard Qabalistic works.

In all the ancient systems of mystical and magical training we find that together with certain philosophical teachings there is to be found a symbol or group of symbols, which has a specialised significance for the followers of that system. Such symbols are known in the East as " Mandalas," and some are exceedingly intricate.

In the Western Tradition, the glyph or composite symbol which is the basis of all its mystical teaching is the diagram known as the Tree of Life and this glyph is described as " The mighty all-embracing Glyph of the Universe and the Soul of Man." It is upon the Tree of Life that the whole of the elaborate detail of ceremonial magic in the West is based. If, for example, the magician is attempting an operation of Jupiter. he will use such properties as are associated with Jupiter on the Tree. He will, for instance, wear a light-blue robe, burn cedar in his censer, have four lighted candles, and use the Hebrew name of the Sphere of Jupiter.

It will be noticed that the magician is using the principle of " association of ideas " but it is necessary to point out that such association of ideas depends in the first place upon a mental link between the various details and the central idea. Now this link may be made voluntarily or involuntarily. In the first case it is made by consciously and deliberately associating the ideas; in the second, the association is immediate and subconscious. Tying a knot in one's handkerchief as a reminder that one has to buy some particular thing, is an example of the first class, whilst the association between, say, sausages and airships is a natural example of the second class. Such involuntary associations often appear to be far more powerful than the deliberately willed ones, for they represent the direct workings of the subconscious mind.

But the willed-association links can be just as powerful if they are correctly built up, and it is this deliberate training of the pictorial imagination which is the basis of the practice of the magician. By this deliberate training it becomes possible for him to link. certain pictorial or

sensory images with their corresponding emotions, and
the consciously directed association causes the appropriate
emotional response to appear whenever the sensory images
are received. All this, however, is still on the surface
of consciousness.

If we wish our association-train to work with the power
of magical evocation, then we must use some device to
imprint it upon the deeper levels of the subconscious, where
it will be able to produce definite results. For this
purpose some auto-hypnotic device may be employed,
such as, for instance, the use of a rosary or even the
meditative repetition of the ritual itself. The rosary, of
course, is usually associated with the Roman Catholic
Church, but both Mohammedans and Buddhists use the
rosary as a device for concentration. Another technical
auto-hypnotic device is the use of what are known as the
" Flashing Colours."

But before evocation of the subconscious can be safely
performed, it is necessary that some work should have been
put in on the foundation of character, and this work will
be discussed in our next chapter.

CHAPTER V

THE KINGS OF EDOM

CHARACTER training, to the magician, is something very different from that which the ordinary man considers it to be, for the magical character-training involves the willed and purposive re-education of both the conscious and subconscious minds. Ordinary methods of character building usually concentrate almost entirely upon the conscious mind, the subconscious levels being affected only slightly, if at all. It must not be thought, however, that the magician is biassed in the opposite direction. He cultivates conscious and subconscious levels alike, but since he realises that the subconscious is the greater part of the mind, he naturally tends to give it the greater part of his attention.

When, following the occult maxim, the magician turns his mental gaze inwards upon his own personality, he finds, as we said before, that this personality is imperfect and to a large extent inchoate, and he realizes that before a true superstructure can be built it will be necessary to pull down much of the present edifice. The question then arises how much can safely be demolished, and what shall be the test as to which part shall be broken down, and which part retained?

This involves the consideration of what constitutes evil, since it is evident that it is the evil aspects of the personality which have to be broken down. But how shall we be able to define evil? Many things which are regarded by some people as "evil" are not so regarded by others! Is there any basic test by which we may judge? The answer is that there is such a test, which is set forth in the Qabalistic systems in the story of Abram and the Kings of Edom. The legend is to be found in Genesis, Chapter XIV, and for the purpose of this book we may briefly summarise it here. Those who prefer to do so, may then read the fuller account.

Briefly, Abram was leagued with certain kings in their fight against four other tribal rulers, and on learning that his nephew had been captured by the enemy, Abram fitted out a punitive expedition of his own and defeated the opposing forces, releasing his nephew in the process. Those against whom he fought are termed the ' Kings of Edom,'' and in the Qabalistic books are referred to as "those who reigned before there was a King in Israel."

On his return from the slaughter of the Kings, Abram was met by that mysterious being Melchizedek, King of Salem, Priest of the Most High God, who administered to him the mystic Eucharist of Bread and Wine and blessed him. In the Epistle to the Hebrews, this Melchizedek is described as "without father or mother, having neither beginning of days nor ending of life, he abideth a Priest forever." In all probability the story can be taken at its face value. The nomadic chieftain Abram in alliance with others, defeats the common enemy, and is blessed by the local priest.

The Qabalists, however, regarded the books of the Old Testament in a somewhat different way. The Torah, the Divine "Nemos," as it was written, was the Body of the Law, but just as the body is inert and useless unless it is ensouled, so the written Law was useless without its informing spirit—the Qabalah. So in this story of Abram and the Kings of Edom, each character represents some part of the human personality, and the action of the story shows the interplay of those parts of the mind.

Before considering the esoteric and magical application of the story let us consider the problem of evil in itself, What is " evil "? The magical doctrine is that there are several kinds of evil, some of which, to use a paradox, are not evil! The first type of evil is the innate resistance of form to force. Organised form imposes restrictions upon free-moving force, but this very restriction and opposition enables the force to be controlled and directed. In physical life we observe that the friction between the foot and the ground enables us to move forward—in a frictionless world walking would be impossible and force ineffective—and this principle of restriction works in other fields. By the restriction of boiler and cylinder and piston, steam is harnessed and made to do useful work. So this evil of "inertia" is in reality no true evil, but part of the machinery of this evolving universe.

There is, however, a form of inertia which goes beyond this normal and beneficial one, and this form may truly be called evil. It is the inertia of formlessness and chaos—the "Abortion of Space," the Cosmic Quicksands. Here there is no definite resistance—no springboard from which life can climb to greater heights. But just as the shifting sands of the quicksands though providing no "take-off" yet will cling to, and impede and finally draw down into their depths whatever trusts to them, so is it with the cosmic chaos. Evolving life, finding no resistance, no fulcrum for its lever, may be absorbed and rendered impotent in this "Chaos and Darkness and the Gates of the Land of Night."

A third form of "evil" is that which is termed "unbalanced force." Here a perfectly good and useful force or energy is displaced in space or time and the resulting out-of-balance is definitely evil. Let us consider one or two examples of such unbalanced force.

The coal in the grate is serving a useful and beneficial purpose, giving warmth to the room. Should it fall out upon the carpet, however, it immediately becomes evil. It sets the room alight, damages property, possibly causes loss of life. The water in the bath is good, but the same water escaping from the bath and cascading down the stairway, is evil. These two instances may serve as illustrations of displacement in space. There is also displacement in time. This may be of two kinds, reversion to the past, or anticipation of the future.

Reversion to the moral and ethical standards of a lower and primitive level of human culture is, to the modern civilized man "evil," since it is a definite regression in evolution. But it is equally evil if, with the limitations and mental outlook of the present day, a person reaches out too far into the future, and attempts to materialise in the conditions of the twentieth century, the state of civilization which will possibly be the norm of the peoples of, say, ten thousand years hence. To use an expressive remark the present writer heard the other day, "the lion may lie down with the lamb, ultimately—but he will need his digestive arrangements radically altered! "

This over-anticipation of the future is the fallacy underlying the pacifist attitude. Since the pacifist attitude is only practicable in a well-policed community, it is clearly untenable as a working policy at the present time. Those who may feel that this is a cynical condemnation of what has been taught by the great religious teachers we would refer to the Catholic "Counsels of Perfection." Always the ideal of the future must be pointed to, but although that vision will be the inspiring force tending towards its own realization, the premature establishment of such conditions is evil.

These types of evil may be termed positive evil, but there is also what may be called positive positive evil. Here we come to a point which in these modern days is often overlooked—the existence of *organised* evil. It seems as though the materialistic "hang-over" from the last century has raised some unconscious inhibition in the minds of modern men, so that it is extremely difficult for them to realise that organised evil can and does exist, both on the physical and superphysical levels.

The calculated beastliness revealed during the war should have opened the eyes of some of our idealists to the possibility of organised evil. We say "should have," advisedly, since some friends of our—idealists to the core— told us recently that *all* the stories of atrocities were absolutely without foundation, all were merely propaganda, since " no one could be so evil as to do such things! " It was suggested that they should attend the courts and listen to a little of the evidence given there in some of the more sordid cases which come up for trial in this country. The suggestion was declined with a display of emotion which suggested that the Old Adam was not entirely extinct in even their pacifist breasts!

All the old religions have taught of organised spiritual evil, and the Christian Faith has personified it as Satan. St. Paul speaks of such organised evil on the superphysical levels when he says "For we wrestle not against flesh and blood, but against Principalities, against Powers, against the Rulers of the Darkness of this present world, against the Spirits of Wickedness in the Exalted Places" (Eph.: Chapter VI, verse 12).

In the process of the evolution of the Universe energy of various types has been mis-placed and has been added to the mis-directed thought of the whole of evolving humanity, throughout the ages. So the psychic atmosphere of this planet periodically becomes charged and over-clouded by the "evil" vibrations until at certain points in time, the evolving life is checked. It is then that great souls come to earth to recall the minds of men to the ways of wisdom and the paths of peace, and to "lift a little of the heavy burden of the sin and suffering of the world."

The most momentous and significant of these evolutionary cycles came some two thousand years ago, when the nadir of the descent of life into form was reached, and the whole of the manifesting life was in danger of being totally checked and thwarted. Then came He, the incarnate manifestation of the Logos, the Lord of Light, and through His identification of Himself with the whole human race, He gathered up into Himself all the evil conditions of the planet, and by the Power that was His, He transmuted them into higher conditions and influences—a World Alchemy!

So, too, by His life and death, He established a line of direct contact between the Transcendent God and evolving humanity, along which there might flow into the world-soul the regenerating divine forces, and thus "a new and living way" was made, whereby mankind might enter into the Most Holy Place.

In the parable of the Prodigal Son, we find that not only did the Prodigal set out on his long and painful journey home, but that when he was yet a long way off, his Father saw him, and ran to meet him. So the transcendent Logos hastens to His evolving children as they tread the path that all humanity must tread, and so the Lord of Love, Who is also the Lord of the Balance, gives equilibrium to the unbalanced forces of the universe. So is it also in the heart of each individual, and for this reason the magical student is told in one ritual that he may receive the holy Bread of Life Everlasting and the Chalice of Eternal Salvation " when you shall have slain the Kings of Unbalanced Force in your own nature."

This acquisition of balance is of paramount importance for anyone who desires to operate the Higher Magic whereby his indwelling spirit may manifest itself through the veil of the earthly tabernacle, and it is for this reason, too, that in the Eastern Tradition it is said that " Discrimination is the first virtue of the Path." For the power of the indwelling light, pouring through into the lower personality energises and activates all its levels, good and bad; dissociated complexes explode, as it were, and the whole psychic and mental nature is thrown into ferment. So, therefore, whosoever unworthily and with unbalanced personality drinks of the Grail of the Holy Guardian Angel drinks to his own condemnation, as the mighty forces he has invoked tear through him, inflating his false egoic sense, intensifying his unbalanced passions and finally commencing the disintegration of the personality itself. For such a one, his symbol is " The Blasted Tower," for the house of his life is destroyed by the Fire of Heaven and he goes forth, " fleeing where none pursueth," a Son of Perdition, a Wandering Star, for whom is reserved the Blackness of Darkness for the Ages of the Ages.

That such a fate awaits *all* who essay the magical art, is, of course, untrue, and as a matter of observation, the magical rituals, properly used can be of the greatest assistance in producing that state of inner equilibrium which is the basis of the Great Work. The neophyte is cautioned that above all things he must cultivate true humility—not the humility of Uriah Heep—but the humility of Him who said " I am amongst you as One who serves." In the first grade of certain Mysteries, the neophyte approaches the East in the ritual position of humility, head bowed and palms outwards turned, and he is instructed that only by self-less service of the Light can he gain power to go forward into the Most Holy Place.

CHAPTER VI

INVOCATION AND EVOCATION

" I CAN call spirits from the vasty deep," exclaimed one of Shakespeare's characters, to which his friend replied, "Why, so can I, and so can any man; but will they come when they are called?" This is, of course, the crux of the matter. The average man in the street has a very sceptical approach to the subject and would unhesitatingly answer the question with an emphatic "No!" and regard the attempts of the misguided magician as vanity. Popular superstition has also envisaged the magician as one who conjured, or claimed to conjure the inhabitants of the invisible worlds.

Bearing in mind our definition of Magic as the art of causing changes in consciousness at will, it becomes evident that we must first consider the whole question of invocation and evocation from the subjective viewpoint. In other words, assuming for a moment that it *is* possible for the magician to "conjure to visible appearance" beings of another order of existence, we must attempt to show that it is the personality of the magician himself which is the channel through which such manifestation is brought about.

It is a cardinal principle in the Western esoteric schools, that the planes of nature are *discrete,* not continuous, i.e., that each plane of existence has its own laws and its own peculiar method of working, and does not exert a direct influence upon any other plane. Whatever influence is exerted is of indirect or "inductive" nature. The phenomena of electrical induction furnishes a very close parallel to this statement. If a coil of wire carrying an alternating current or a varying current is brought close to, but not touching, a similar coil of wire, which is connected to a galvanometer and is not carrying any current, it will be found that as the current-carrying coil is brought near the other, the meter will record that a current of electricity has been generated in the latter.

Furthermore it will be found, if a galvanometer be placed
in the current-carrying coil, that if the second coil has its
resistance to electricity altered, the free flow of the current
in the first or "primary" coil will be either checked or
increased, showing that both coils act upon each other. So
it is with the planes of existence. The higher is negative
or *receptive* to that which is higher than itself, and positive
or *dynamic* towards that which is lower. But equally, the
lower reacts upon the higher, and this is the justification
for the Biblical statement that the Kingdom of Heaven
" suffereth violence, and is taken by storm."

Now it has been found by experience that the levels can
come into direct contact with each other through the lens
of an organised consciousness of some kind or other. The
best point of contact that can be found is a trained and
balanced human consciousness. The human mind contains
within itself the vibration-rates of all the planes, and by
tapping it at certain points a link-up may be made with
the existence of that level. It is a process of "tuning-in"
such as is used in wireless, and once again the electrical
analogy is very close. When we tune in to our favourite
radio programme, whatever it may be, we do not hear the
actual voice of the singer, or the actual sound of the
instrument. What we hear is a *reproduction*, a projected
reproduction of the actual voice or sound.

So it is in evocation and invocation. We make contact
through our own energised consciousness with the
consciousness of the beings we seek to evoke and the
" visible appearance" we conjure up is a *projection* from
our own mind. (So, for the matter of that, is the visible
image we form when we use our physical eyes! The light
vibrations strike the retina, set up nervous impulses in the
optic centre and we project a mental image answering to
those impulses.)

In both cases, however, this reaction is caused by an
objective reality of some kind, whether physical or
superphysical, and here we come to what may be termed
the "objective" viewpoint. The magical tradition
declares that all these existences exist *per se* and have their
own place in Nature. But—and this is important—the

appearances which are seen are conditioned by the
subjective mental machinery of the magician himself.
Through this machinery also, the actual power and energy
of the invisibles is brought through into the waking
consciousness. (Not that the *identical* power of the
invisibles is brought through, but rather the effect of the
contact of the consciousness of the magician with that of
the being invoked or evoked arouses into activity the
corresponding force within himself, and it is this
corresponding power which is projected and which
produces the results desired.)

It is important to note the difference between
"invocation" and "evocation." In invocation we act in
such a way as to attract the attention of some Being of a
superior nature to our own, or some cosmic force of a
higher order. In evocation we impose our will upon beings
of a lesser order of existence and compel them to execute
our wishes. In both cases the actual contact takes place
through our own mental channel, but a magical technique
has been devised whereby the essential difference between
the two sets of influences—the higher and the lower—is
kept before the magician. The reason for this is that
should there be any confusion in the mind of the magician,
the results may be disastrous.

For a moment let us consider this from the psychological
point of view. If the forces, or Beings, summoned by
invocation represent the super-conscious part of the mind,
then the Beings who answer the evocatory commands of the
adept represent—or rather work through—the subconscious
levels. But whilst the supraconscious contacts tend
towards a greater and more effective integration of the
mind, the subconscious ones tend, if not controlled, to bring
about its partial or total disintegration, as C. G. Jung has
pointed out. So the Magical Tradition has evolved the
technical devices known as the "Circle of Safety" and the
"Triangle of Art," the whole being termed the "Place of
Working."

By certain rituals, the place where the magical work is
to be performed is purified etherically on the objective
plane, and psychologically on the subjective one, and the

Circle of Safety is drawn upon the floor as a kind of fortress from within which the magician may work. Then the Triangle of Art is drawn outside the Circle, for in the case of evocation it is necessary that the objective manifestation of the beings evoked should be kept within its limits and under rigid control, and in the mind of the operator there should be a clear-cut psychological distinction between himself as the positive or dominant and the lesser forces or beings which are negative to him.

The purification of the Place of Working is done in the Western Magic by what is known as the Banishing Ritual of the Lesser Pentagram, or in other cases by the Ritual of the Hexagram. The Lesser Pentagram ritual is more often used, and its efficiency can be vouched for by the present writer, who has performed it on many occasions. It is a combination of geometric signs made by the operator, Names of Power which are intoned by him, certain mental images which are visualised very strongly, and the definite invocation of certain Arch-Angelic Powers.

Again, looking at this from the psychological angle, we are asserting by word and sign the sovereignty of the Higher Self, whilst by the invocations, we draw down upon ourselves certain of its powers—powers which are released by the action of existences of another order upon it.

In the greater number of cases the invocation or evocation " to visible appearance " is to psychic vision only, and nothing is seen upon the physical plane. Where material visibility ensues, we have another process at work, and this is the process of "materialisation." For such materialisation to take place, it is necessary that there should be present some source of the peculiar substance termed by the spiritualists, "ectoplasm." One such source, and that the most effective, is the bodily organism of one of the people known to the spiritualists as "materialisation mediums." They are people who possess a certain little-understood power which enables them to give out this ectoplasm in large quantities. Ectoplasm is so named because it is a peculiar plasma or living substance which is exuded from, and manifests outside of the physical organism of the medium.

It appears to be capable of being moulded by thought and desire into forms—in fact, one of its characteristics is an innate tendency towards organisation. The data so far obtained by the spiritualists and by open-minded observers such as Sir William Crookes, Baron Shrenck-Notzing and Dr. W. J. Crawford suggest that this ectoplasm is the basic substance of living protoplasm, and as such is the matrix of the physical organism.

We find, however, that there are other sources of ectoplasm, though it is of a different type and is given off in small quantities only. Before passing on to these sources, we may briefly mention one method of obtaining sufficient ectoplasm for a materialisation to take place. This method is the use of fresh animal blood. It is a method known throughout history and is referred to by Homer. There is an obscure Gnostic legend which says that the golden bells worn upon the dress of the Jewish High-Priest were designed to warn the beings evoked by the blood sacrifices of the Temple to assume human shape instead of their own grotesque forms. Anyone who takes the trouble to study the details of the temple sacrifices will appreciate the force of this legend, and will also become convinced that there was sufficient blood for any materialisation.

One can vouch for the efficacy of freshly spilt blood as a basis of such materialisation. Quite recently a case of "haunting" investigated by the present writer proved to have, as its basis of manifestation just such blood emanations. Once the material basis was removed, the manifestations ceased to be objective and the subjective psychic atmosphere was easily cleared by a banishing ritual. We may note in passing that many cases of hauntings are due to the efforts of a so-called "dead" person to make contact with the world he or she has left behind, and the spiritualists have developed a very effective technique which allows the discarnate person an opportunity to make a conscious contact with those on the earth who are able, by their knowledge of psychic matters, to help in the necessary adjustment of the new conditions of life.

Returning to our consideration of the sources of ectoplasm other than materialisation mediums or the emanations of blood, the one commonly used in magical rites is a peculiar incense known as Dittany of Crete. Fresh flowers also give off an appreciable amount of this substance in a rarified form, as do also the naked flames of candles. In normal magical work, the blood rites are never used, and the use of a medium is also eschewed because of the depletion of vitality which may result. The use of the incense is free from the disadvantages of these two methods, but the forms which are "evoked to visible appearance," although clearly perceptible to normal vision do not possess the solidity of those produced by the former methods.

Although the evocation to visible appearance is one of the more spectacular feats of the magical art, it is not often resorted to, as for the majority of purposes it is sufficient if the "visible appearance" is to psychic vision only. It is sufficient if the operator is enabled to perceive objectively the beings evoked—conscious comprehension and direct perception of them giving the magician power over them. Once again we find a parallel in the psychological field, the dissociated or repressed "complexes" in the mind are controlled by the conscious realisation of them. Moreover, when spirits of a "good" nature are evoked, we can again resort to the psychological clue, for it is a fact that the clear realisation of a mental faculty results in the rapid development of that faculty in the individual concerned. And such a subjective realisation means also that by virtue of a law of sympathetic induction, we come into contact with objective beings and forces of a similar type existing in the inner worlds. It is this which gives validity to such statements in the mediæval "grimoires" or magical books as "The Spirits of Mercury give understanding of science."

Having completed the evocation, it becomes necessary to dismiss the beings evoked. We may employ an electrical analogy here and say that it is necessary to discharge our charged circle, to "earth" it, and so return our evoked force to its normal place in the natural economy. This

dismissal is performed by " The license to depart." Here
is a typical charge of dismissal. The magician makes upon
himself the Kabbalistic Cross, and addresses the beings he
has invoked thus : —

" Because ye have duly appeared unto us, and
performed that with which ye were charged ; depart now in
peace to your own habitations. Peace be between us ; be
ye very ready to again obey the summons, and may the
blessing of Adonai be upon you as ye may be able to
receive it."

The magician then proceeds, by the technical device of
the " Closing of the Gate," to withdraw his attention both
conscious and subconscious from the inner plane levels and
to re-focus upon the physical plane. This is most
important, as it prevents the disintegration of the mind
which results from the habitual uncontrolled evocation of
the subconscious. Where the magician has been invoking
higher intelligences, the license to depart is unnecessary,
but the Closing of the Gates is important just the same. It
is stated by certain authorities that in the Eucharist the
words *Ita missa est* at the end of the service are, in
effect, not a license to depart, but a statement to the angelic
Beings who have taken part in the service that their work
is now concluded. It is not a peremptory dismissal.

CHAPTER VII

MAGNETIC MAGIC

WHEN Dr. Mesmer first attracted international attention in the Eighteenth century by his remarkable cures and his peculiar doctrines, the Western world was just beginning the serious study of the more recondite forces of Nature such as electricity, magnetism and gravity.

Mesmer, in the thesis which gained for him his doctorate, outlined a theory of the universe which was, and still is, that of the Western Esoteric Tradition, though in its public form it had of necessity only a shadow of its real content. Briefly, Mesmer saw the whole universe as a living unity, wherein each part was affected by and in its turn affected every other part. The universe was a living organism of balancing forces. Health, therefore, lay in each part so adjusting itself to every other part that it received to the fullest of its capacity the directing, controlling and sustaining life of the whole.

He taught that this formative life could be transmitted from one being to another, and he claimed also that its force was operative behind and apart from the physical plane energies which were being studied by the scientific world. Particularly, asserted Mesmer, did this universal force manifest behind and through the phenomena of magnetism. He used bar magnets which he claimed possessed curative power because of this universal force, but later both he and his followers taught that it was also thrown off freely from the human organism. It was therefore named " animal magnetism," and the school of the animal magnetists, chief amongst them being such men as de Puysegar and Baron du Potet developed their theories and practice along this line.

When Dr. James Braid put forward his own theory of " Hypnotism,"* and later when the followers of Charcot

*A modern investigation into this subject is to be found in *Proceedings of the Society for Psychical Research*, Vol. XXXII, July, 1921, in a paper " Problems of Hypnotism " by Dr. Sidney Alrutz, Lecturer on Psychology at the University of Upsala.

and the members of the so-called "Nancy School" put forward the theory of "Suggestion," Mesmer's "fluid" theory was discarded and the very idea of animal magnetism was deemed ridiculous. But though it was respectable to deny the existence of the magnetic fluid, there were many who quietly worked along the lines indicated by Mesmer and du Potet. One of the notable names in this connection is that of Baron Reichenbach who conducted an exhaustive enquiry into what he called "Odic Force," or, more briefly, "Od." His researches clearly established the existence of a force which underlies all natural forces.

Thus, the sensitive people who acted as his observers could see, in total darkness, a "flame" as they called it, emanating from the end of a wire the other end of which was exposed to strong sunlight or moonlight. Experiment showed that if the exposed end of the wire was shielded the observers noted the disappearance of the odic flame. though they were entirely unaware of any change in the conditions of the experiment. It was observed that similar odic flames were associated with the poles of both electro-magnets and permanent magnets. The human body was seen to be radiating this same force. A touch of humour is to be found in the observation that the human lips also radiated odic energy, and a possible reason was thus suggested for the efficacy of lovers' kisses!

To-day, with the researches of Dr. Kilner and the use of very sensitive electrical measuring instruments, the existence of this odic force is being more and more accepted. We may use the name "magnetism," providing that we make it clear that this "magnetism" has nothing to do with the magnetism studied by physicists and electricians, even though it may be associated with it. This animal magnetism, therefore, is an actual force or energy thrown off automatically by the healthy animal and the healthy human alike, but it is capable of being consciously developed and intensified, and it is this intensified and directed power which is the basis of the branch of magic with which we are now dealing.

It will help the reader to understand the magnetic

phenomena if he thinks of this force as the "magnetic
fluid," remembering that the French term is more
comprehensive than the English word "fluid." Perhaps
the phenomena of radium may afford some analogy. It is
known that from a small speck of radium there are
innumerable small particles radiating in a constant stream,
and this stream is measurable as a definite force, though it
is composed of these extremely small particles.

So the magnetic force is also of the nature of an
emanation of extremely refined substance which is directed
and controlled by the will and thought of the magnetist.
It can be stored—can be attached to or absorbed by
certain material objects, whilst other objects will act as
insulators to it. Herein it seems to have some indirect
relationship to electricity, for most of the *electrical*
insulators are also *magnetic* insulators, though there are
some puzzling exceptions. All metals are good magnetic
conductors, oil and water absorb it readily, though oil
retains it for a longer period. Wool and paper, wood, brick
and stone absorb it slightly, but silk will neither conduct
nor absorb it.

It has been established by careful experiment that the
magnetic force tends to reproduce in the object to which it
is directed its own particular "vibration or note," and the
object will then come into close psychic sympathy or
"rapport" with the person who projected the magnetism.
Thus, animal magnetism is the basic power in many forms
of psychic and spiritual healing, being as it were, a
healing power in itself and also acting as a carrier for more
subtle forces which through its agency are enabled to
affect the physical body.

It will be remembered that one of the miracles* attributed
to Jesus was the healing of the woman with an issue of
blood. The Gospel story gives a clear picture of the
occurrence, the Teacher standing in the centre of a crowd
of people who press in upon Him, pushing past His
disciples who are trying to keep an open space around

*Cf the definition of "miracles" given by St. Augustine,
" Miracles are not contrary to Nature, but only contrary to what
we know about Nature."

Him, and everyone trying to touch even the hem of His robe. The East does not change rapidly, and the present writer has often witnessed similar scenes in India. The Master asks, "Who touched Me?" The amazement of the disciples is pardonable. Who touched Him? They might well exclaim, "Who didn't touch Him?" But the record goes on to say that He perceived that virtue had gone forth from Him.

We have, perhaps, been mislead by this word "virtue," thinking of it only as an ethical thing—"A virtuous woman is above rubies." But the true meaning of this word is that of power, so that we also say such-and-such a thing has virtue in it. (In the Middle Ages, and to-day in the East, the virgin and the child without sin are held to possess a power which is the result of their purity.) When the word which is translated "virtue" in the Authorised Version of the Bible is studied, we find that it is the root-word from which are derived such words as "dynamo," "dynamic" and "dynamite," all words implying powerful active energy. So the Master's query is clear. The woman who had touched Him had, through the conditions established within her by her faith become a conductor, or rather an absorbant of the healing virtue or vital dynamic energy which was radiating from Him. Many a magnetic healer at the present day can echo that statement in the Gospel, for they, too, perceive that virtue has gone forth from them. Father John of Cronstadt and Father Mathew, an Irish priest, both died prematurely as a result of their excessive work. It is interesting to note that Father Mathew received an annuity of £300 per year from Queen Victoria, in recognition of his services.*

In magical work, this magnetic power is made use of in many ways. It is used for healing by charging or impregnating a handkerchief or other article with healing power, this "charged" object being worn or used by the sick person. Sometimes, water is similarly charged, or oil; sometimes crosses, pendants or other personally worn articles are charged or "magnetised" to use the technical

---

* Cf Dr. Percy Dearmer's *Body and Soul* for a learned study of this form of healing.

term. In the New Testament we read of people taking cloths which had been in the vicinity of St. Paul to sick people, and the practice of charging or "blessing" objects has never ceased in the Catholic Churches of both the Western and Eastern Obediences

It is important to remember that the magnetic fluid is neutral in itself, and will take upon itself the impress of the mind and will that sent it forth. Like all the bodily forces, it is manipulated by the subconscious mind, and since the subconscious responds most readily to pictorial suggestion from the conscious mind, the magician has to have a stock of clear-cut mental images to which the subconscious mind has already been emotionally linked or "conditioned." Such a stock of images is found, for instance, in the Qabalistic Tree of Life, which is the training glyph of the Western magician; in the East, other glyphs or composite symbols are used.

The process of magnetising an object falls into two divisions, de-magnetising or "exorcising," and magnetising or "blessing." A third process is what is known as "consecration," but this involves other factors, as will be seen. The de-magnetisation is performed by holding in the mind the intention to purify the object, and the magnetism of the operator is directed upon it by one or other of the traditional signs of power. In the Catholic Church exorcism is performed through the sign of the cross. The Qabalist also uses the Cross, but it is important to notice that this is the *equal-armed Cross of the Elements*, not the Latin form. A traditional form of words is used, and the general formulæ of the Catholic priest and the Qabalist are very similar—probably due to the influence of mediæval times, when it often happened that the priest carried on a certain amount of magical work in addition to his ordinary clerical duties. Lapsed priests who followed the magical tradition would almost of necessity adapt their familiar formulæ to the new work, and the educated magician altered such formulæ to suit his own purposes. In any case, the Roman Church, with its amazing versatility absorbed much of the magical traditions of the cults it superseded, and, as Evelyn Underhill points out in her valuable work *Mysticism,* the truly Hermetic employment of lights and salt and water and oil in the baptismal service is far removed from the simple lustrations of St. John the Baptist.

Having demagnetised or exorcised the object, we have it now in a neutral condition, ready to absorb any magnetic force which may be impressed upon it. Now the process of magnetisation begins. Again the operator must have in his mind a certain "intention," and this intention must be expressed in words and manual acts which are linked in his mind with the desired action of the charged object. Together with this, the magician employs a certain technical mental device known as "commemoration." This consists of a recital of similar work performed by others in the past, and serves to link the operator with the archetypal images in the collective consciousness of the race, thus reinforcing the individual powers of the magician. Whether the events commemorated actually occurred or not makes no difference to their efficacy if they are part of the folk-lore or mythology of the race.

It is important to note that the ideas and images which are held in the operator's mind must be positive, *never* negative. Thus, if we were charging or blessing an object for the purpose of reinforcing the courage of the person using it, we should fill our minds with the pictures of courage, not fear. We should not say, "Let the wearer of this cease from being afraid," but rather, "Let the wearer of this be strong and of good courage," and we should use a form of words which would reiterate this idea. In fact we should proceed as if we were giving suggestion to the person concerned directly.

We spoke of consecration as a technical method embodying other factors. In the normal magnetisation of objects the powers and forces of the personality of the operator are utilised, but in consecration, after the object has been de-magnetised it is re-magnetised with a special intention that it may be the vehicle or channel of a higher force or being apart altogether from the operator. A typical consecration ritual is the Mass of the Catholic Church. Here we have all the elements we have mentioned, the purification of the bread and wine, their solemn blessing and setting-apart, and then in the Prayer of Consecration, the commemoration of the first Eucharist of the Christian Church, and the invocation of the Presence of Christ in and through the offered elements.

In treating of this talismanic magic, and of the much greater "Magic of the Mass," it may be thought that we have departed from our original definition of magic as the art of causing changes of consciousness at will. This is not the case. The effect of the talisman is to effect a change of consciousness—usually in a gradual fashion—in the person using it, and the same applies to the power of the Blessed Sacrament. That the change of consciousness may not be observed by the user matters not. Man's consciousness, as we have seen, is greater than his surface waking mind.

It is possible that the linking-up of the Eucharist with the subject of magic may cause some disquiet. This should not be the case if the objectors hold sincerely the central doctrine of Christianity. For what was the Incarnation but an act of supreme magic whereby the Word was made flesh and dwelt among us, His transcendent Power flooding the planet on which we live, and, like the leaven in the lump, working throughout the ages to effect a change of consciousness in the whole of humanity!

Talismanic magic was very popular during the Middle Ages, and even the consecrated Host was used for magical purposes. In the first reformed Prayer Book of Edward VI, in 1549, there is a rubric which runs as follows:—"And although . . . the people these many years past received at the priest's hands the Sacrament of the Body of Christ in their own hands . . . yet as they many times conveyed the same secretly away, kept it with them, and diversely abused it to superstition and wickedness . . . it is thought convenient the people commonly receive the Sacrament of Christ's body in their mouths at the priest's hands."

CHAPTER VIII

The Magical Images

THE technical methods of the magical tradition are based, as we have already seen, upon a deep knowledge of the human mind, and in the use of what are called the "magical images" this is clearly seen.

Two very different men have introduced the concept of the magical image to the Western world, St. Ignatius Loyola and C. G. Jung. The first of these in order of time is, of course, St. Ignatius, whose *Spiritual Exercises* are the foundation of the system of mind training and discipline which has produced one of the most effective of the Catholic Orders—the Society of Jesus. Whatever may be ones private opinion of the Jesuits, one thing is certain, they form one of the most effective communities in the Church.

It is sometimes objected to the Jesuit system of training that it is "anthropocentric" in contradistinction to the Sulpician method which is "theocentric." It is really a matter of temperament—one type turns inward and seeks through knowledge of the self to know the One, the other type seeks through knowledge of the One to understand the self. If one is permitted to use a physical simile, one type is centrifugal and the other centripetal. Just as these two opposing forces produce as their resultant the balanced system of a sun and its planets, so the magical tradition makes use of both the Ignatian and Sulpician methods—in point of fact it was using them long before they were introduced into the Catholic Church.

In modern days, the psychologist Carl G. Jung has shown how important to everyone are what are termed the "archaic images" of the collective unconscious. It will be remembered that in our study of the mind, we spoke of the stratum of the mind that is common to all humanity—a Race Consciousness from which our individual personal consciousnesses rise like mountains from their surrounding ranges. Jung points out that if the normal consciousness "regresses" or turns inward upon itself, it turns the psychic energy loose upon the vast storehouse of the subconscious levels. Now in the magical tradition these subconscious levels are known as "The Treasure-House of Images," and it is upon these images that the inward turned energy proceeds to work.

As these images become active, they tend to rise past the censor at the threshold of the mind and emerge in the conscious levels as dreams and visions and intuitions, moreover they "project" special meanings upon objects and images which have affinity with them. Now it is obvious that the involuntary and pathological regression of neurosis is detrimental to the mental unity which constitutes normal health, though even the regression of the neurotic is an attempt by the deeper levels of the mind to re-establish balanced conditions. But the regression of the magical technique is a voluntary, willed activity whereby the normal mental polarity is deliberately reversed and the stream of psychic energy redirected in accordance with a certain well-defined plan. We may describe this as a system of evocation. But not only is the psychic energy directed into the subconscious levels, it emerges therefrom carrying upon its stream the potent images of the Collective Unconscious, or rather, the "lines of force" of those images.

Perhaps an illustration will make this clear. If a solution of some salt is allowed to crystallise we observe that the substance forms crystals of a certain type, and it is evident that in the solution itself there must already exist the pre-disposing "lines of force" along which the peculiar crystals of the substance form. We may say, therefore, that although six-sided or eight-sided crystals did not *exist* in the solution, there nevertheless was a system of stresses *subsisting* therein, whose manifestation is seen in the solid crystals formed later. So the archaic images of the collective unconscious *subsist* in the deeper levels of the mind, as *systems of stresses*, not *objective* images.

But if the "dead" images of the immemorial past are thus resurrected, with what body do they come? The answer is that that which is "sown" in the conscious mind is not that image which shall arise, but is the link whereby the archaic lines of force are clothed upon and appear in a new "body." But this new body is charged with the power of the regions wherein it had its origin, and the psychic energy which has evoked it is reinforced by this primordial force emanating from spaceless and timeless regions. So mortality puts on immortality and the image, arising in consciousness brings a new power to bear upon the personal self. This resurrection of the Deeper Self results in the regeneration and reconstitution of the personal self. It is the *coagula* portion of the alchemists' formula, and this power is, in Christian terminology the power of the Holy Ghost.

In the psychological technique of Jung and his disciples there are several methods whereby this resurgence may be effected. The magical tradition has also evolved a detailed system of training whereby this evocation of the Images may take place. "Deep calls to Deep," and this is the key to the magical method. It is one of *induction*.

In those magical ceremonials wherein this evocation of the primordial forces is aimed at, carefully selected images are employed. These are chosen from the mass of symbolic images which are to be found in the Qabalistic books, and are used by the magician to build up the mental atmosphere which will evoke from the deeper levels of the mind those archaic images and powers which are desired. Now the archaic images of the collective unconscious tend to group around certain definite centres. As Jung teaches, the motives of the archtypes (archaic images) are the same in all cultures. We find them repeated in all mythologies and fairy-tales, in all religious traditions and mysteries. Prometheus the stealer of fire, Hercules the slayer of dragons, the numerous myths of creation, the fall from Paradise, the sacrificial mysteries, the virgin birth, the betrayal of the hero, the dismembering of Osiris and many other myths and tales portray psychic processes in symbolic-imaginary forms.

Likewise the forms of the snake, the fish, the sphinx, the helpful animals, the World-Tree, the Great Mother, the Enchanted Prince, the mage, the *puer eternus*, stand for certain figures and contents of the collective unconscious. Myths and fairy-tales are the day-dreams of the race, and each race has its own particular forms of the common myths. Being aware of this racial selectivity, the magician therefore endeavours to use such images as may be in affinity with the collective mind of the race with which he is dealing. As we have said before, the Western Tradition is a composite one and the Western magician uses one or other of the subordinate systems which it contains.

For example, in this country he works with the Keltic contact and the images of the Grail legend if he desires to avail himself of the power of the Rosicrucian Order. There are very many images which may be used without stepping outside our racial boundaries, and though it is of the greatest advantage to us to be able to avail ourselves of the Eastern systems of philosophy, when it comes to a question of practical magical work, it is best to restrict ones efforts to Western methods. This is not to deprecate Eastern methods which are sound and efficacious—for Easterns and for those few who, though born in the West are spiritually of the East.

In conjunction with the glyph which is used by the Qabalists, there are ten magical images which represent the working of the universal energy in all its aspects, and these are used to "tune in" to that energy on the particular level required. This energy, however, is not a blind mechanical force, but a living, pulsating, energy-consciousness, so that if a thought-form or magical image is built up in the conscious mind and linked up with its corresponding archetype in the deeper consciousness, the image that emerges from the depths and floods the waking consciousness with power is a living thing.

If, now, many people over a prolonged period of time build such a mental image, then the individual images appear to coalesce, and we have one image, charged with the Divine Life in one of its aspects. This is what the ancients termed a "god." It is important to note that the objectivisation of such a "god" is through the minds of the worshippers, and what is really happening is that the form or image consciously visualised acts as a line of contact with the collectively-built form, and this in its turn is linked with the cosmic energy it symbolises. The result is that cosmic energy flowing through the mind of the worshipper stimulates the appropriate archetype which rises into consciousness and acts as a transmitter of that energy to all levels of the personality of the worshipper.

That which is done by faith and devotion alone, the magician does with the added knowledge of the mechanism whereby this energy is brought through for the strengthening and refreshing of his soul, and for that willed change in consciousness which we have agreed upon as our definition of magic.

It is important to note that there are two ways of working with the magical images. One of these methods is not to be recommended, as it tends to reduce the power which may be obtained from them. These vast collective thought-forms are "charged" with the emotional energy of their makers, and this stored energy is available for any individual member of the group. We may liken the magical image to the charged batteries of a private house lighting-plant. If the batteries are constantly being drawn upon there comes a point when they fail to deliver power —they are, as we say, discharged. So it is with the magical images. If they are used inexpertly they tend to lose their charge of energy. But no skilled electrician would allow his batteries to become totally discharged, but would start up the dynamo and allow the drain of energy to come upon what is, for practical purposes, an inexhaustible source of power. Neither would the skilled magician use the images as sources of power *in themselves*. He uses them as temporary sources of energy, but always links up *through* them with the infinite power behind all manifestation. This marks the difference between the amateur and the skilled magician, and is one of the reasons why the detailed descriptions of the magical images used in the occult Lodges are kept secret.

Some of the magical images are of great antiquity and are highly charged with psychic energy. They have been built up and used by generations of initiates. Outside the occult Lodges, the great images built by generations of

worshippers of the major religions possess great potency
and because of their evocative power over the archaic
images in the subconscious minds of the people, they are
of the greatest possible value to organised religious
systems, and those sects which attempt to dispense
altogether with ceremonial and imagery are giving up a
very valuable weapon in the spiritual armoury.

This brings us to the consideration of the practice of the
Catholic Church known as the Invocation of the Saints.
Before going any further, it may be pointed out that in the
Roman Church three grades of " worship " are recognised.
First we have *dulia*, the reverence paid to Saints because
of their spiritual greatness; *hyperdulia*, the reverence paid
to the Virgin Mary, and *Latria*, the worship paid to
Almighty God alone. This by way of disposing of the silly
Protestant idea that Catholics give to the Saints and the
Lady Mary the worship due to God alone. If we consult
the official documents of the Church, we find that there is
a point which is of interest to us in our study of the magical
images. The Council of Trent, which removed many of
the mediæval abuses of the Roman Church defines the
Invocation of the Saints in the following manner:—

> To worship the Saints means to worship God, for their
> blessedness and sanctity are really His. And to pray with
> the Saints means to adore God together with the hierarchies
> of Angels, with the spirits of the just men made perfect,
> and with the Church invisible of those who are first-born
> unto the heaven world. *(Concilium Tridentinum, Sessio
> XXV. De Invocatione Sanctorum.)*

The point of interest in this passage of the proceedings
of the Council is the statement that to worship the saints
is to worship God, i.e., it is the power of God shining
through the saints which is, shall we say, canalised or
concentrated by the personality of the saint. This is, of
course, the doctrine of the magical image. But the
personality which is used as the channel is a *true*
personality, a human being who with us worships the same
God. So it is that the Saint of the Catholic Church, still
remaining a distinct being, nevertheless acts as a psychic
lens, focussing and concentrating that ray of the eternal
light of which he or she is an especial channel. All who

by innate temperament are on this particular ray will be able to draw upon this saint for that power.

This applies not only to the saints of the Church, but to the heroes of folk-lore. In our own native tradition pagan and Christian heroes and saints are intertwined in the Grail and Arthurian legends. It was the custom at one time, tc reduce all these hero figures to myth-personifications and to deny their existence as real men and women. At a later date it was held that they really had existed and that popular thought had clothed them with the garments of myth.

The initiated magician holds that both views are partly right, right that is, in what they affirm, wrong in what they deny, and he believes that the full truth is to be found in a combination of both ideas. When the magical images are being employed in lodges of ceremonial magic, the impersonal cosmic images are used, but by the technical device known as Commemoration, the archetypal images are linked up with the personalities who in their earth-life in the past have exemplified the particular power symbolised and canalised by the magical image concerned.

In order that this power may be brought still further into physical plane conditions, each member of the magical team performs the operation known as "assuming the God-form." He or she "plays the part" of the personality, or Being commemorated as forming the channel of the power of their particular office in the lodge, at the same time attempting to link up through that personality with the cosmic power. Now the method of assuming the God-form is a certain technical method of auto-hypnosis. When by this operation a lesser change of consciousness has been effected, it is as though a self-starting mechanism has been switched on. The personality of the magician is overshadowed and flooded by the power of his deeper Self, and this is illuminated and charged through the entity who has been commemorated, and through the channel of the linked personalities the cosmic energy rushes down into the psychic and magnetic conditions of the magician. The effect of this downrush of power is to cause the buried archaic images to rise into his temporarily exalted

consciousness, and these images allow the invoked power
to effect definite and far-reaching changes in the character
of the initiate.

Around the ten basic magical images of the Tree of Life
there are grouped the gods and goddesses of the pagan
pantheons as well as the saints and heroes of myth and
legend, and the choice of a particular image depends upon
the effect desired. In passing it may be said that each
group of Images has a certain affinity with one or other
of the great psycho-physiological centres of the human
body, and with the particular mental "control-centre"
governing each one. The vibrational key-note of each
centre determines the traditional words of power connected
with the images linked with it. The whole subject of
"words of power" is one of great complexity and can
only be touched upon briefly here.

A variation of the assumption of the God-form is that
curious "illusion technique" referred to in the magical
books as "making oneself invisible" and "transforma-
tion." Such "glamour" has to be experienced to be
realised. A typical instance is given in Col. H. S. Olcott's
book *Old Diary Leaves*.* Here the protagonists were
Madame H. P. Blavatsky and a certain Qabalist.

If this study of the magical images seems a little
disjointed, it must be remembered that although one may
discuss general principles, it is difficult to be precise
without saying too much.

Old Diary Leaves. Vol. I.

CHAPTER IX

INITIATORY MAGIC

IN the religious rites of all nations from time immemorial, we find certain ceremonies of admission into the tribal membership or the religious life of the nation, and these initiations have certain common elements, whether it be the induction of a boy into the tribe by Australian aborigines or the reception of a postulant into the Catholic Church. Sir James Frazer, in his *Golden Bough*, has brought together many examples of initiatory rites from all over the world, and these, together with such present-day forms of initiation as that of the Masonic Craft and the baptismal rites of the Church all show an underlying similarity.

The word "initiation" is derived from a root signifying "a first step or beginning," and this, of course, is just what initiation is. It is the first step in a new life, whether that life be the tribal life of the clan, the religious life of the monk, the ethical and benevolent life of the modern mason, or the generally benevolent and brotherly activities of the Royal and Antediluvian Order of Buffaloes. All these have their initiatory rites, through which the neophyte is introduced to and linked up with a new life. We may add to these examples two others—the initiatory ceremonies of knighthood and the coronation of the British King.

It is obvious that all initiations will not have the same power—that some will affect the candidate at entirely different levels to others—but, and this is a point to be stressed, even the most innocuous and naive of initiatory ceremonies may, if it is built upon true foundations and is worked by men of knowledge, be the means whereby radical and far-reaching changes of consciousness in the postulant may be brought about.

It is a remarkable fact that practically all organised societies sooner or later develop some form of initiatory ceremony, and although this may be considered as due to

the natural desire to make a clean break between the old
life and the new, it has yet to be explained why the basis
of all such initiations seems to be the same. Associated also
with these rites we find the " laying on of hands " or some
similar act, and it would appear from anthropological
research that where such rites commenced without the
laying on of hands, the process was nevertheless introduced
at an early date.

It will be seen therefore, that there are two essential
components of a true initiatory rite. First the severance
from the old life dramatised in certain symbolic forms, and
secondly the transmission of power to the neophyte. The
former is built upon the idea of a departure from blind
wanderings in the chaotic and darkened conditions of
ignorance into the realms of light and order—the " Coming
Forth by Day " of the Egyptian *Book of the Dead,* the
" Entrance into the Clear Light " of the Thibetan *Bardo
Thödol,* the Royal Transmutation of the Alchemists, the
New Birth of the Christian mystics. But each in its degree.
For obviously the masonic initiation has rarely such
thaumaturgic effect. Neither have many of the formal
initiations of East or West.

Yet some effect is produced, and some power conferred,
but it is " under the veil of earthly things." For these
formal initiations, valid and valuable though they may be.
are the earthly shadows of the true initiations which are
conferred in the timeless and spaceless eternities. In the
words of the Qabalah, they are " reflections into Malkuth,"
i.e., the representation in earth terms of supersensible
realities. Thus, we are not made adepts by the ceremonial
initiations in lodge (though certain powers, as we shall see,
do acrue to us as a result of the ceremony), but we become
initiated when we have ourselves voluntarily changed our
habitual consciousness and begun to look at all things from
a different point of view. The word which is translated in
the Authorised Version of the Bible as " conversion," is a
word which can best be described as meaning " the turning
the mind around and regarding of things from another
point of view." This, of course, is just what initiation
—and conversion—really is.

Here we come to one of the points at issue between the Catholic and Non-conformist. The Church teaches that infant baptism is efficaceous and sufficient, the Non-conformists look for a conscious change of heart, taking place in youth or adult life, which brings the person concerned into the true fold. From the occult point of view, both sides are again right in what they affirm and wrong in what they deny.

Baptismal regeneration and conversion are both valid and efficaceous and should be complementary to each other. The magical tradition gives a clear explanation of this, and it is reinforced by the findings of the psycho-analysts. In order to understand the magical tradition it will be necessary to study what is known in psychology as "the group mind."

When a number of people associate themselves together in pursuit of a common object, their minds link up together and form—for the purpose they have in mind—a composite or group mind. The more emotional the object of their combined thought, the stronger and more clearly built becomes the group mind. The permanence of the group-mind depends upon many factors; for instance, some group-minds formed by the impassioned oratory of some demagogue may last only a few minutes or hours. Others, formed by united thought over a period of years may have a life of many centuries. Even though they may seem to cease to exist, they will again recur when conditions are suitable, for quite apart from the original mental impulses, the combined mental action of the group builds a " form " in the inner worlds, as we have seen when discussing the magical images. Each age sows in the inner worlds the seeds that, even if they do not immediately take objective being, will ultimately come to germination and fruitation in a later age. And, the esoteric teaching avers, those who originally started the group form will find themselves back in reincarnate life at the period when the results of their former group thinking are becoming objectivised on the physical plane, and they will have to work and possibly suffer under the conditions they themselves originated in the past.

There are four types of emotion which may energise such group-minds. Power, Sex, Herd and Religious emotions. Most of these are interblended in varying proportions in every group-mind, but one is predominant. Now the great religions of the world, with their more or less stereo-typed rituals, their common emotion and their long life, have built up very definite group-minds, as have the systems of government which have stood for many centuries, as, for example, the British Monarchy. Chivalric Orders, and initiatory fraternities such as the Masons, the Rosicrucians and many others, all have built up very definite and very powerful group minds in the inner worlds.

The strongest religious group in the Western world is the Christian Church and here we have a closely-knit and vitally charged group-mind going back for nearly two thousand years. But in the case of Christianity we have to deal with much more than the sum total of the mental and emotional activity and aspiration of its members. It may help if we consider our physical body. It consists of myriads of cells, constantly growing, reproducing and disintegrating, but retaining a common relationship the result of which we term our physical body. But each cell has its own psychic life, and the combined cell-life forms the *Nephesch* or Animal Soul of the Qabalists. Moreover the co-ordinate psychic lives of the many cells form a receptacle or vehicle by means of which the Ego or self may come into contact with the material plane.

So the common group thought, emotion and idealism of all the members of the Christian Church forms a vehicle or body through which and by means of which the head of the Christian religion may come into close contact with all the material world. In theological terms, the Church is the extension of the Incarnation. Just as the psychic health of each cell in the body depends upon its co-ordination with all the others, and just as certain groups of cells are specialised within the general group for special duties, e.g., organs, nerves and sense organs, so in the body which is the Church we find a similar specialisation and functionalism. Entrance into the corporate cell-life of the body is possible by an identification of the psychic life of the individual substance ingested into the system with the common life, and herein, incidentally, is the key to the varying problems of bodily nutrition.

In exactly the same way, the individual becomes part of the group by a similar identification of his psychic self with the common life of the group, and this mental and psychic process is almost invariably accomplished by some rite of admission, such as baptism. Possibly the only exceptions to this are the Society of Friends or Quakers, as they are more commonly known, and the Salvation Army.

Now in the baptismal service the individual is linked mentally with the group mind of the whole Church, and this link is made through the agency of one who is a member of that group and acts by its authority. Even in cases where baptism is performed in emergency by a layman or even a non-Christian, their mental "intention" to link up the newcomer with the group is sufficient. But, it may be objected, in the rite of the Infant Baptism the child cannot consciously identify itself with the Church. Consciously, no, but man is greater than his conscious mind, as we have seen, and the child links itself subconsciously through the officiating minister, with the life of the whole. The god-parents should also provide extra links between the child and the Church—though it is very doubtful whether many do, or even realise they can!

Now what is the result of this piece of initiatory magic? The child is put into the circulation of the Life of the Divine Head of the Church, and the conditions are provided whereby he or she may begin the journey from the chaos of the past, which is built into the subconsciousness, and become in posse what they have always been in esse, a child of God. So the Anglican Catechism says that baptism is " a death unto sin and a new birth unto righteousness," and this is the formula of all true initiations. Water is used as a symbol of cleansing and is blessed with that intention, using the Christian sign of power, the cross. In the old Mystery religions the initiation was preceded by cleansing lustrations and the waters of baptism are the Christian counterpart of the lustrations of the Mysteries.

Although the child has been initiated into the Christian community, and has begun to partake of the spiritual life thereof, this baptismal initiation is but the earthly shadow of the true Christian initiation of New Birth. The true initiation takes place when the personal self is for a moment caught up to and united with its Greater Self of which it is the earthly expression, and through that Greater Self with the Logos in whom it lives and moves and has its being. So a great mystic, Angelus Silesius has written:—

> Though Christ a thousand times in Bethlehem be born,
> And not within thy heart, thou art left forlorn.
> The Cross on Calvary thou lookest to in vain,
> Except within thy heart it be set up again.

The experience of " conversion " is an unregulated form of this Christian initiation, hence its importance from the Non-conformist point of view.

To return to the general question of initiatory rites, all true ceremonies link up the neophyte with the life of the group mind and also implant within him the seeds of power which it is hoped will at a future time bring him to a conscious " realisation " of his true nature.

A friend possessing psychic vision made the following report upon an initiatory rite which was worked in his presence:—

" When the minor Officers in the Lodge made their ceremonial contact with the candidate, his aura became luminous, each portion of the aura corresponding to the particular Office shone brilliantly. Observation of the new member at a later date showed that the effect is relatively permanent—at least in this case.

" When, however, the magus of the lodge made his contact it appeared as if a minute portion of his subtle body was detached from the region of the heart centre; a brilliant minute seed of golden white light seemed to pass down through the aura of the candidate until it came to rest in the region of the solar plexus. Later observation suggests that this is a permanent effect."

A similar, though far more intense phenomena has been recorded by other clairvoyants studying the ordination of a priest in those sections of the Church which have retained the "Apostolic Succession." Perhaps after all, it may fall to the lot of the despised magician to confirm the claims of the Church concerning its priesthood!

In this chapter the Christian baptism has been used as an illustration, but the principles involved are not peculiar to Christianity. The Mystery religions of the Mediterranean basin in the classical period used the same symbolism and very similar rites. In the Mithraic rites the "washing in the Blood of the Lamb (or Bull)" was realistically performed in the "kriobolium" or "taurobolium," where the initiate, robed in white, stood under a grating upon which a lamb or bull was slain, and was thus literally washed in the sacrificial blood. Some of the parallels with Christian symbolism are very close, so much so, in fact, that some of the Christian Fathers explained them by saying that the Devil, knowing what Christianity would be, had guided the heathen to copy what would later be revealed! Others, not Christian apologists, have said that this similarity proves that Christianity borrowed its sacramental system from the preceding religions.

The magical tradition avers that the Christian religion, founded on certain principles, expressed itself in similar forms to those of the pagan world around, but redeemed them from the corruption into which they had fallen. It also suggests that the Christian Church had no need to borrow its rites and forms, since it had its roots in the secret tradition of the Hebrews, and what is infinitely more, it was founded and directed by the Supreme Master of all the Mysteries. The "Mysteries of Jesus" of the early Church could hold their own against any of the surounding Mystery religions. In any case, a religion manifests its vitality in just this assimilation of the best elements in other systems. The Church, like the wise householder of the parable, brings forth from her treasure store things both old and new.

THE MAGICIAN
His Training and Work

TO MY WIFE

"Through Wisdom is an house builded: and by
understanding it is established."
(Prov. 24, *v* 3.)

PREFACE

THIS book is really a continuation, though in greater detail, of my former book *Magic: its Ritual, Power and Purpose*. So many questions were asked by readers of that little work, that it was thought that a more detailed treatment of the subject would help to meet the evident need for information on this subject.

I recognise, of course, that my efforts do not reach the standard of those who are the acknowledged stars of the magical firmament —Eliphas Levi, Dion Fortune, Israel Regardie and many others— but it may be that, from the standpoint that is mine, I may be able to help those who are "desirous of knowing in order to serve" to take the first step along the road of magical achievement.

My thanks are due to many who have helped me in magical work throughout the past forty years. Catholic priests, Free Church ministers, occultists of both the Western and Eastern Traditions, doctors and psychologists, all have helped in various ways, and to them all I am most grateful.

Particularly in connection with the writing of this book am I indebted to the late Bishop Robert King (who was my first teacher in these things) and another, a true Master of Magic, who by his own wish must remain anonymous.

i also wish to gratefully acknowledge the help afforded me by Mrs. Hilda Eastburn of Peaslake, who, amid the duties of a busy life so kindly made time to voluntarily and freely type the manuscript of this book.

As in my former book, so in this, I have endeavoured to give the principles involved in such a way as to encourage the reader to do some constructive thinking in applying them in actual practice —my distaste for "tabloid information" being as strong as ever!

THE AUTHOR.

PART I. GENERAL

Chapter I

WHY THE BOOK WAS WRITTEN

THE question may be asked, "why another book on Magic? Surely there are too many already written. In any case, they are all cut from the same piece—they are all descriptive of other peoples' experience—and simply mean that their respective authors take in each others' literary washing."

This particular question was, in point of fact, put by a friend of many years standing. Although, of course, it is an exaggerated description of the situation, there is an element of truth in it, and it made the present writer endeavour to think the matter out.

The trouble is that magic has lain so long under a cloud of superstition, ignorance and fear on the one hand, and on the other, been obscured by a smoke-screen of secrecy engineered by those who feared loss of power and prestige if the subject was brought into the light, that it is very difficult for the average writer to do more than give a general outline of the subject. He is compelled to draw his material from the published work of others, who were also under the same limitation.

The position was further complicated by the fact that those who could have given a first-hand account were muzzled by terrible oaths of secrecy, and the breaking of an initiation oath is no light matter. Of course, some did break their oath of silence and loyalty, but as a general rule they did so, not to enlighten the general public, but to enhance their own power, and although they purported to give out all the secrets, yet they retained certain essential keys. They then formed around themselves groups, sworn to secrecy and obedience, and the whole story was repeated.

Now, the breaking of an oath is a serious matter, and involves the honour of the individual concerned. *But the exaction of oaths of secrecy where no secrecy should be present, is also dishonourable.* It was Aleister Crowley, who gained considerable notoriety, both as a magician (black variety), and as an oath breaker, who bitterly wrote that his initiators swore him to silence by dreadful oaths, and then revealed to him the Hebrew Alphabet and the names of the planets!

The general body of magical knowledge can be roughly divided into two groups. The first, in quantity if not in quality, is the general body of ceremonies and magical practices which is the stock-in-trade of the average "occult" organisation. All of this, with few exceptions, is composed of material already existing in books which are accessible to the public. The Bible, the Qabalistic "Book of Formation," the "Wisdom literature" of the Hebrews, and the many Apocalypses both pagan and Christian which appeared in the first centuries of our era, together with the fragments of the Gnostic books, all provide inexhaustible quarries from which we may obtain the material we need. Nor, as that great occultist, Dion Fortune once wrote, are we tied by any ordinance to one region alone, but may bring gold from Ophir or cedar from Lebanon, as it suits our purpose. There are innumerable books and manuscripts in both East and West, from which we may draw; such books, for instance, as *Nature's Finer Forces*, by Rama Prasad, M.A., and the works of the Roman Catholic Sir John Woodroffe ("Arthur Avalon") *The Serpent Power, Shakti and Skakta*, etc. Or, to come nearer home, in a later section of this book mention is made of the Elizabethan astrologer and occultist, Dr. John Dee, and the curious communications received by him. Now this Enochian tongue, as it was termed, is employed in the rituals of one very powerful magical order, but it is well to note that it already existed in published form under the title of *Concerning Dr. Dee and some spirits*, by Edward Casaubon.

The question arises, why should the various magical orders have sworn their initiates to secrecy concerning these things which are of common knowledge? The answer is, that in those orders and fraternities which were genuine the information given in these various sources *was combined in a particular pattern*, and it was this *pattern* which was the real object of secrecy.

The ritual-patterns used in any particular magical order, are kept secret for a very good reason. The power of thought is little realised by the ordinary person, but in the magical workings of a lodge, constructive visualisation is practiced, and definite "thought-forms" are created. If any of my readers should be inclined to query the idea of thought-forms, I would refer them to *Yoga and Western Psychology*, by Dr. Geraldine Coster, and another book by one of the most erudite of the members of the Society for Psychical Research, the late G. N. M. Tyrell, entitled *Grades of Significance*. The clairvoyant observations of Dr. Annie Besant, Bishop C. W. Leadbeater, Geoffrey Hodson and Mrs. L. J. Bendit (Phoebe Payne) may also be mentioned in this connection.

However, without entering into any argument on the matter, it is an article of faith in the occult lodges, based upon repeated clairvoyant observation, that these thought-forms may be built by the use of correct ritual. But because they are thought-built, they can be affected by thought, and for that reason they are kept secret in order that the work which is being done by their aid may not be interfered with.

We may say that the component parts of the ritual-patterns resemble various metal strips and pieces and following a certain plan they are welded together to form a metaphysical lock. Into this lock certain keys are inserted and turned, and the door of superphysical consciousness and power swings open. Since the construction of the lock gives some idea as to the type of key which will open it, the lodges jealously guard the pattern-rituals with which they work. Apart from this, too, as I have already said in my former book,* inexpert use of the magical images renders them useless. At the same time it should be kept in mind that it *is* possible to make and use magical images quite openly without such deterioration. All depends upon whether the *keys* are in the hands of the rulers of the order or fraternity.

These keys are of two kinds, the major and the minor keys. With the major keys we will deal presently. The minor keys consist of physiological, psychological and psychic techniques which have been handed down from the past, or have been built up by a process of experimental work. The various yoga exercises are such techniques. A good deal is "public domain," but there are various technical devices which are very powerful in their effects, and which require due preparation on the part of the person using them. These keys are therefore kept secret. The present writer doubts whether this secrecy is always advisable. It may prevent certain people from rushing into unwise experiments, but generally speaking, those who are liable to come to harm along these lines usually have not enough perseverance and power of concentration to do much harm, either to themselves or others. Possible exceptions are mediumistic sensitives, who should not "dabble" in these matters. With them, it is a matter of thorough training in the technique, under careful supervision, or of leaving it severely alone. There is, of course, no reason why a *properly developed and stabilised* psychic should not follow the path of ritual magic, if he sincerely wishes to do so.

These minor keys constitute the main keys in the hands of the rulers of the lodges. But the major keys are an entirely different proposition. The minor keys may be communicated to others, who may practise the technique and acquire dexterity therein, but with these major keys such a process is impossible. Again quoting Dion

* *Magic: Its Ritual, Power and Purpose* (Aquarian Press).

Fortune, I am of the opinion that the *real secrets* of occultism could be proclaimed from the housetops without anyone being the wiser except those who were ready to receive them. "He that hath ears to hear, let him hear!"

But if the major keys cannot be communicated from initiator to neophyte, how then can the pupil receive them? Well, though they cannot be communicated, they can be implanted within the pupil by a process of "induced realisation" or "impactation," as it is sometimes termed.

This may be effected by the use of certain of the minor keys, and is, in fact so done where a lodge or order is working on "true contact." It must be remembered, however, that such "apostolic succession" of the major keys depends entirely upon the grade of the initiator and the preparedness of the pupil.

When this method, an outline of which can be found in Paul Brunton's book *A Search in Secret India,* is used, there is always some effect, but whether that initial "seed" grows, as it should, into a new type of consciousness, depends upon the nature of the soil wherein it is implanted.

Enough has been said to give some idea of the reasons for the secrecy of the magical orders and fraternities, and it now remains for the present writer to indicate his own position in the matter. For this purpose, a certain amount of autobiography is needed. He has been, in his opinion at least, exceptionally fortunate in having had, at the two crucial periods of his occult experience, the guidance of wise and experienced teachers. From the age of seventeen until the present day, he has been instructed and advised by his first teacher, a man who possesses both occult knowledge and power. During a later period, when in India, he came into contact and worked with a group of Hindu occultists, again people who not only knew, but had power in these matters.

Later, following a mystic "leading," he came to the doors of the Western Mysteries, and was helped and taught by one who herself has the reputation of being one of the most upright and fearless occultists of the West, the late Mrs. Penry-Evans, better known in the occult world as Dion Fortune.

In the course of his wanderings during some forty years since his first contact with these matters, the writer gained experience in many fields, and it is this experience, plus the framework of the instruction given him by his teachers, which is written herein. His first teacher has never exacted from him any oath of secrecy, nor did the oriental occultists with whom he worked. As a member of

Dion Fortune's Fraternity, he gave the usual oath of secrecy concerning its teaching and rituals, and this oath he still respects. Nothing herein is in any way part of that which he swore to keep secret and inviolate.

But from his first teacher and his Eastern associates, and from Dion Fortune herself, he received a considerable body of knowledge, without any restrictions upon its use except, of course, the general warning which is well expressed by the notice which was placed above an American sawmill "Don't monkey with the Buzz-saw!"

Having upon at least one occasion "monkeyed about" with one buzz-saw, he now appreciates the force of the injunction. Therefore, the practical instructions herein given are prefaced by the warning that in these matters one must realise one's limitations. This is really the only warning necessary. As one occult writer, Israel Regardie, says very truly* "here is no place to utter portenteous warnings about the use and abuse of magical powers and spiritual knowledge. Within the psyche itself is a sentinel who never sleeps. It is a guardian of the moral law whose punishment is so dire and devastating that there is no appeal, save by expiation of the crime. From the dicta and judgements of this inner Self, there is no escape, except through the admission and the acceptance of the abuse, followed by a grim determination forever to avoid a similar deed."

This warning will seem to some readers to be insufficient, so we had better, perhaps, give some explanation of our point of view. In so many esoteric groups and fraternities one hears such portentous warnings given against magic that it is as well if we try to discuss the subject in the light of day.

Is there any danger in the practice of magic? The answer is "Why, yes; of course there is. Anything can be abused, and the more powerful for good the thing is, the greater the evil if it should be misused." But this is true of many things we meet in daily life, and one should preserve a sense of proportion in these matters. The dangers of magical work may be divided into spiritual, mental-emotional and physical dangers. Let us briefly study them in this order. Spiritual danger! What do we mean by this? Simply that overweening and Satanic *pride*, by which, as the poet says "the angels fell." This is the characteristic vice of the follower of the *occult* path, and by far the greater number of magical students follow that path. The intellectual aloofness and cold contempt for the "ignorant herd" is very common in occult circles, and since

* *The Middle Pillar*, page 77.

the magical rites demand a very concentrated and continuous application, the student begins to feel himself in some way superior to the others around him. So he is, but that should make him very humble, since he should be beginning to realise that the only justification for the practice of the magical art is in order that he may be better able to help his fellow men. "I desire to know in order to serve," says the neophyte of the Mysteries, and this is the only reason why we should train ourselves along these lines. One who disregards this advice and does not subscribe to this undertaking has taken the first step on the downward path, and though great power and knowledge may be gained by him, yet is he in danger of becoming one of the Sons of Perdition, a Wandering Star, for whom is reserved the blackness of darkness for the Ages of the Ages. But this is the destiny of but few, for the Christs of Evil are as rare as the Christs of Good. Nevertheless, the "inflation of the false or empiric ego" as the psychologists term it, does mean that at one point or another spiritual disaster awaits the one who has attempted to isolate himself in proud contempt from his brethren.

What are the mental-emotional dangers? To answer this question it is necessary to remember that the personality is built up during earth life by the experience it meets, and its reactions thereto. Since these experiences are many and varied, and since the personality reactions are exceedingly complex, we usually arrive at middle-age with a personality which has been built up without any definite plan. Here we have fought circumstances, there we have given in to them. Here we have faced adverse conditions and learnt the lesson they had to teach, their power being thus obtained for ourselves, there we have attempted to escape from such conditions and from the necessity of having to make a decision concerning them. And so it goes on, so that it will be seen that the temple of our personality is usually a very curious structure, built with ill-assorted materials, and showing very little trace of any coherent plan. Into this structure we draw down the forces and powers of the universe, and it is small wonder if it happens that this house of the personality is overthrown by the lightning-flash of the forces invoked. In simple language, the presence of the power invoked acts upon all parts of our "psyche," and the repressed "complexes" as well as the integrated consciousness feel that pressure. So it sometimes happens that a student of magic begins to show signs of mental instability. Under the supervision of a wise teacher, such a condition may become what is known in psychology as a mental "catharsis" or purification, and the repressed material, having been driven up into the conscious levels, becomes integrated with the normal consciousness. The symptoms of unbalance disappear, and the student has definitely gained by the experience. But sometimes such a happening as this cannot take place. The buried complexes are charged with power, but cannot emerge into, and be integrated with consciousness. The result is a more or less complete disruption of the mind. But is must be remembered that this is a very rare occurrence, though when it happens, it seems to justify the parrot-cry that magical study makes one go insane.

Magical study may make some people psychopathic cases, but it must be kept in mind that the psychopathology *was already there* before the student commenced his magical work. All that magic did was to bring it into active manifestation. The study of things mysterious attracts a certain class of psychotic, and it does not much matter whether the attraction be to magic, spiritualism, or Seventh-Day Adventism. Spiritualism has been most unfairly credited, along with magic, as a *cause* of insanity. The statistics issued by the authorities of the mental hospitals in this country give the lie to this. Indeed, doctors, lawyers and clergymen would appear to be far more predisposed to mental disease, if the figures given are any guide. It is important here to point out that all such statistics can be mis-read, or distorted. If, for instance, three out of every twelve spiritualists became insane, there would seem to be a case to be made out against the subject, even though, in the total number of psycho-pathological cases, the figure for spiritualists would be low, as the spiritualists form but a relatively small section of the entire population of the country.

It is upon the insanity percentages *within* the spiritualists or occult or magical organisations that the verdict should be given, and judging by this all three of the above-mentioned emerge triumphantly.

But there is one thing which causes some difficulty in assessing the tendency of any of these movements to cause mental unbalance. What was the mental condition of the person *before* he entered the movement? It is a commonplace idea for the general public that mediums and psychic sensitives "hear" and "see" things which are not visible to those around them. But so do certain mentally-unbalanced individuals, and it does happen that these unfortunates, hearing of the visions and voices of psychics, will gravitate to the psychic organisations. If they are recognised for what they are, mentally sick people, then all is well. They can be steered out of

the organisation concerned, and it may be that through an understanding of their case, they may receive healing treatment which,
although unorthodox from the medical point of view, may be very
effective. For not all psychopathologies can be explained in the
terms of orthodox medicine, and not *all* "alternating personalities"
are splits in the patient's mind.

Where, however, such unbalanced people are allowed to attempt
psychic or magical work, then the responsibility rests fairly and
squarely on the shoulders of those who are the leaders in such
work, and they must not grumble if, when the unbalanced one
finally breaks down and has to be removed, people say "There!
That's what comes from dabbling in spiritualism—or magic." Incidentally, anyone who "dabbles" with anything along these lines
is asking for trouble, but I have yet to read in the daily press that
Mr. So-and-so has been removed to the mental home as a result
of "dabbling" in the Salvation Army or Anglo-Catholicism; yet
members of both do, on occasion "go slightly off the hooks," to
use the phrase of the learned Doctor Hooker, the writer of the
Anglican classic, *The Laws of Ecclesiastical Polity*. No, there is
a definite press bias against the spiritualist, the occultist and the
magician, and as the general public forms its opinions in these
matters largely from the daily press, the misunderstanding is likely
to persist for some long time yet. So anyone who tries to assess
the psychological dangers of magic and psychism, does well to
remember this bias, and to rely only on definite facts and figures.
One of the most courageous men of his time, the late Dr. Forbes-
Winslow, once publicly asserted that there were forty-thousand
spiritualists in the asylums. Challenged by the spiritualists to prove
this, he began a careful investigation of the subject, and finally
announced, again in public, that his former statement was entirely
erroneous.

But although one has seen him quoted many times as making
the original statement, one has yet to see in the press any reference
to his retraction of that statement. So much for fair-play in these
matters.

So when the would-be magical student receives grave warnings
of possible mental unbalance if he takes part in magical work, it
is useful if he immediately asks for chapter and verse; not an
account given by one whose cousin's friend knew someone who
went insane because they practised magic. Usually, such a frontal
attack reveals the baselessness of the warning.

We come now to the psycho-physical dangers of magic. There

again are dangers which can be avoided by anyone who uses com-
monsense. It must be remembered that one of the direct results of
magical work is a tremendous enhancement of the vital energies,
and this enhanced power, as we have already said, affects all the
personality. Now part of the personality is the physical body, and
its nerve-systems and nerve-centres. Closely associated with the
nerve-plexi are those very wonderful chemists' laboratories of the
body, the endocrine or ductless glands. Also associated with them
are the various instinctive and emotional factors of the mind, and
we know that the secretions of the endocrine glands, the "hormones"
or "messengers" conveyed by the blood stream to all parts of the
body, do cause far-reaching effects on both body and mind. If by
magical practices we increase the vital energies, and if by concentration upon the various psychic centres (which are situated near
the physical nerve-plexi) we direct an excessive amount of this in-
coming energy to them, then we may expect that the increased
activity of the nerve-centre and gland concerned will result in the
excessive release into the blood-stream of its hormones. Just as the
mind can thus affect the body processes, so these can affect the
mind. There is a "psycho-physical arc," and under such conditions
it is easy for a definite out-of-balance activity to be set up. The
way in which this may be avoided will be given later in this book,
in the section dealing with the training of the magician.

Another psycho-physical danger comes when magical practices,
mystic-meditations and psychic techniques are jumbled together
without any real knowledge on the part of those concerned. It is
as if a child were to say, "here is some black stuff the grown-ups
call charcoal, here is some yellow dust they call sulphur, and here
is some white salt they call saltpetre. I'll mix them together and see
what happens." If by chance he should mix them in a certain proportion, and should then set light to the resulting mixture, the results
might well be disastrous. So one of the first rules is "don't mix the
techniques, unless you know what you are doing." Even, then, don't
mix them until you have brought each particular technique under
your conscious, positive control.

There is another danger, the pseudo-magical lodge or group.
Here a little knowledge is dressed up in grandiloquent terms, and
certain psychological or physical "tricks" are employed by the
leaders of the group. To take one thing only. Incense, as we shall
show in another section, has a very powerful psychic effect on the
consciousness. But there are many kinds of incense, and not all
produce a beneficial psychic result. Hashish produces curious

dream-visions, as do also *marihuana* and *peyotl*. All these are noxious and illegal drugs, though *Anhalonium Lewinii*, the Mexican cactus bean is *not* a habit-forming drug. Nevertheless, the use of any such drugs is not only an offence in law, but also an extremely unwise thing to do.

In one such lodge, known to the writer, hemp seeds (containing the hashish drug) were separated from parrot-food and burnt with the incense. The results were startling, but definitely bad. In the magical groups wherein these practices take place, the use of drugs and sex-attraction is one of the principal methods employed, and the effects of such practices are thoroughly and completely evil.

In the accounts of the witchcraft trials of the middle ages and later, the use of ointments to produce supernormal results is mentioned. Such ointments (the recipes of several are known) usually contained drugs which have a strong effect on the heart and nervous system, as well as producing hallucinatory effects. The use of such drugs is as old as humanity. In all cultures we find them used, but always the effects, when assessed over a long enough period, are seen to be so deleterious, that in all civilizations their use has been banned. As we have said, they are still used by some occult groups, but any group using them as sensational adjuncts to the rites, does, by that very fact, proclaim its indifference to the moral standards laid down by the Lodges of the Light. Well informed and careful research by trained seers into the properties of these drugs is another matter, but such researches are not carried out in the general lodge work. So the would-be magician, if he is wise, will shun any group or fraternity when such things are offered as inducements to join it. Such inducement sometimes takes very subtle forms, and it is easy to become involved before one is aware of it.

For this reason, it is wise to have a standard of reference to which one may turn in times of doubt. The writer's standard of reference is the Lord Jesus. It is not necessary to accept all or any dogmatic views of Him, but His life and teachings do give us a standard against which we may set the teachings or practices of whose nature we are in doubt. Others may prefer other standards, and "to each man his own master." But some standard should be adopted *before* the seeker joins any occult or magical group.

Chapter II

THE BASIS OF MAGIC

AS we have said books on magic seem to be largely made up of quotations from and comments on other books on magic, and this, in the end gives very little enlightenment. People who enquire into the subject are disappointed by this negative result. They want to know not merely what magic is, but how it may be practised. To be able to do a thing oneself is much more satisfying to many of us than simply to hear or read about what other people have seen or done. Kipling, in "The Ballad of Tomlinson" indicates, from another angle, the futility of second-hand knowledge and experience.

In his former book, the writer tried to show some of the general principles governing the Magical Art, and as a result of the reception of that book, he now feels that it may be as well if he provides whatever practical instructions may safely be given out openly. Obviously, there are increasingly complex depths in magic, and *for one who is unprepared* to try to plunge into those depths is the sheerest of follies. But for anyone who is prepared to work steadily and to avoid unnecessary risks, there is everything to be said in favour of such general instruction. In any case it carries implicit within it a perfectly satisfactory regulating mechanism, as anyone misusing it will find by personal experience. Others, who follow the system given will be rewarded by an increasing sense of fulfilment and satisfaction, with wider and deeper insight into life and destiny, and with increased powers with which to serve their fellows. Arcane knowledge and power give great responsibility, but also great joy and happiness as one begins to take part in the Great Work which ever goes on in the souls of men.

"I desire to know, in order to serve"—such is the password which admits to the arcane knowledge, and those of my readers who can honestly affirm this can safely essay the way of magic. Safely, that is, if they obey instructions. One of the many traps that beset the student of these matters is the temptation to experiment with "bits and pieces," adding something here, subtracting something there, "taking a chance" somewhere else. Such behaviour is silly and dangerous.

The enquirer desires to learn the Magic Art. What guarantee can we give him that he will be successful? Can *anyone* be a magician? What are the qualifications? How can he make a start?

What are the signs that he is gaining proficiency? All these, and many more questions have been put to the writer since the publication of his first book. The present work is by way of an answer to some at least of these questions.

One of the most cogent of these is "Can *anyone* be a magician?" The answer is yes, anyone can become a magician, but there are phases of magic which are not within the capabilities of some people, though they are in others. The Victorian novelist, Bulwer-Lytton, in one of his stories* which gives its title to the book of the same name, quotes from Albertus Magnus† to the effect that the description of the magical process he describes "will instruct and avail only to the few . . . that a man must be born a magician!", that is, born with a peculiar physical temperament, as a man is born a poet. Now this is very true, but it is not the whole of the truth. Poets *are* born, not made; that is great poets. But many minor poets spring up, and though their verse is not of the quality of that of the great immortals, yet do they find satisfaction in the exercise of their modest powers, and so do they also add to the enjoyment of many.

There are two aspects of magic which appertain to the spectacular. One, "Evoking to Visible Appearance" is the high-light of phenomenal magic,—the other, the "Transmutation of Consciousness," though less objectively spectacular is equally important. It is found in practice that certain people are expert in one or the other of these aspects, whilst others seem to have little or no power in either of them. On investigation it will be found that invariably the successful evokers to visible appearance possess the peculiar psycho-physical type of body which characterises what the spiritualists term the materialisation medium. A classic example is Madame Blavatsky. This does not mean, however, that the magician is a medium in the ordinary sense of the word. This is not the place to discuss the merits or demerits of mediumship, but put briefly the difference between the magician and the medium is that the one is controlled and influenced by his *own spirit self*, the other is the channel for the forces and influences of others. Of course, there are no cut and dried lines in these matters, in many mediums the inner spirit-self is working through their mediumship. In the case of Madame Blavatsky, the unregulated "physical phenomena" of her

---

* *The Haunters and the Haunted*, page 122.
† Albertus Magnus (1193-1280) was one of the teachers of St. Thomas Aquinus. He was one of the leaders of Dominican thought in Germany.

early years were brought under her conscious control, as Sinnett records in *Incidents in the life of Madame Blavatsky.*

The other type of magical work is perfectly illustrated by Dr. Paul Brunton in his book *A Search in Secret India.*

Between these two extremes of objective and subjective magical phenomena, there are many grades, and every sincere student who is willing to obey instructions and to persevere, can find some aspect of magical power which he can develop and use for the common good.

Many books on our subject give exhaustive lists of magical practices (indeed, that is all that many of them seem able to give) but in this book we shall only touch briefly upon the various practices which are included under the name of magic. We have already shown the basic division of the magical art—"objective" and "subjective" phenomena. All feats of magic combine the two, and, in fact, the main difference between the various magical happenings is the proportion of "objective" to "subjective." Always there is definite interaction between the magician and his environment, and here we come to one of the fundamental principles of magic.

The modern world, with its increasing use of scientific knowledge, and its lack of faith in anything except matter, as it is commonly thought of, has divorced man from his environment and made him simply a fortuitous form of life on a second-rate planet revolving around a second-rate sun. It has become the fashion to think with kindly contempt of the ancients who regarded Man and Nature as parts of one living universe. "Great is Science of the Modern World" is their cry, as their predecessors cried in similar terms "Great is Diana of the Ephesians." It is true, of course, that solitary members of the race have risen up and protested against this deification of modern science, and it is true also that the more advanced scientists of our day, when unhampered by political ideologies, are beginning to regard man and the universe in a different light. But popular opinion has been said, quite rightly, to be always fifty years behind the growing point of knowledge; even though it uses the latest terms and symbols of that knowledge. By a process of unconscious "rationalisation," as the psychologists call it, popular opinion charges the new word-symbols and ideas with the old interpretations of fifty years ago, and fondly regards itself as being up-to-date in scientific knowledge!

Deep within humanity there is a desire for stability, for security and for safety, and this desire operates always in the direction of maintaining whatever *status quo* it regards as embodying that state of safety, of stability and security. Whatever intellectual, philosophical or religious system they may adopt, it will be found that *for them* this is a veritable ark amidst the roar and turmoil of the tempest of the world. But those there are who in divine desire for "Light —more Light" scorn the safe refuge, and press fearlessly onwards into the Unknown—to find, in the words of a great scientist of today, that "the universe is friendly."

If it is in this direction that true and unfettered science is today moving, then perhaps we may look back to those ancients and briefly consider the philosophy which underlies the whole of their teaching. We in the Western world, having had our main philosophical systems mediated to us through the Schoolmen of the Great Western Church, tend to think in terms of what may be described as "dualism." Always we are setting the Eternal Source, God, over against Its manifest creation.

But the philosophy which underlies magic is the philosophy which appears in the Indian "Vedanta" the philosophy of "Monism." In this philosophy God and His Universe are seen to be one and the same. But this, it will be said, is Pantheism pure and simple. It would be if we were so foolish as to regard Nature as the whole of God. We do not only hold the idea of His being in and through His Universe, but also we believe He transcends it.*

An Immanent, and Transcendent Being is the God of the magical philosophers. But both these terms can easily be misunderstood. If, by "immanent" we think of "something" behind manifestation as we see it, then we are beginning to use the philosophic counters of Aquinas, "substance" and "accident." Though this is a perfectly valid distinction, the magical philosopher would go further and say that all manifestation exists as an expression of that substantial Being, and *because of that* it possesses Reality after its own kind. It has been said that the touchstone of a philosophic system lies in its use of the word "Real." In one Eastern prayer it is said "From the Unreal lead me to the Real," and those monistic philosophies which stem from the Eastern teachings are mainly based upon such an idea.

In the early Christian Church certain Gnostic "heretics" taught such things, and for this reason were repudiated by the great councils. Such heretics were the Docetae and the Manichees. One of the greatest figures of the early Church, St. Augustine of Hippo,

---

* "With a fragment of Myself, I create the Universe . . . and remain." (The Bhagavad Gita).

had followed the Manichean philosophy before his conversion to Christianity, and traces of it are to be found in his teachings. As he later became a great authority for the Roman Catholic Church, some of his views distorted the Christian philosophy, and even today they cloud the teachings of some of the sects. But the doctrine of the evil nature of matter is not a part of the Christian philosophy or, indeed, of any of the great philosophic systems of East and West. The doctrine of the unreality of material manifestation, however, is part of several Eastern systems, and in certain Western systems which owe their inspiration to the East it is also to be found.

It is *not*, however, an essential part of the true magical philosophy. It has sometimes been said that the magical doctrines are doctrines of "emanation," and in one sense this is so. But if by this it is thought that they teach that (in all reverence) God emanates the universe from Himself as a kind of Cosmic Spider spinning His Web from Himself, then such a conception is entirely foreign to the magical scheme.

The magi teach that the whole universe of matter in all its grades, physical and non-physical, *is* the manifestation of the very Essence and substantial Being of the Eternal.*

So the physical universe, so far from being evil or "low," as so many "spiritually minded" folk would have us believe it to be, is as holy as any other plane of being—there is nothing common or unclean. "The ignorant man gazeth upon the face of Nature, and it is to him darkness of darkness. But the initiated and illumined man gazeth thereon and seeth the features of God."

So it is not *matter* which is unreal, only the appearances it presents to our consciousness, and as that consciousness is evoked and expanded, so do we begin to see in all things the Presence and very Being of God. Thus the magical path is no mere way of escapism, even though many try to use it as such. It is an adventurous, God-seeking quest, as true and as holy as any Mystic Quest of the Grail. Indeed, it is that Quest, undertaken "after another manner."

The basic ideas of this magical philosophy are embodied in a very wonderful "glyph" or composite symbol known as "The Tree of Life," *Otz Chiim*, and this is the meditation symbol or *mandala* which is used by the Western magician, since it is the philosophical symbol of that system of Hebrew thought which is known as the Quabalah. This is that body of esoteric teaching which was im-

---

* Cf. The Liberal Catholic Liturgy of the Mass. " . . . Who abiding unchangeable within Thyself, didst nevertheless in the mystery of Thy boundless Love and Thine eternal Sacrifice, breathe forth Thy own divine Life into Thy Universe . . . "

parted "from mouth to ear" as its very name implies.* It was regarded by the Rabbis as the inner spirit of their religion, even as the *Torah* or Law was its body, and the *Talmud* its soul. It is this basic Hebrew theosophy, enriched as it is by the Egyptian, Chaldean, Greek, Persian and Arabian elements, together with the mystical stream of the inner Christian Schools, that forms the tradition to which the magical student is heir.

It is therefore necessary to consider the Tree of Life in some detail, though, of course, we can give it but very elementary treatment here. There are, however, several books which deal with the Tree very fully. They will be found listed in the Bibliography at the end of this book, and it is only fair to the student to say that *some* grasp of the philosophy of the Qabalah is essential to the Western magician if he is to do successful work in his chosen field.

Now the first principle of the Qabalah is the Unity of All. Here, as we have said, the modern scientist and the ancient initiate stand side by side on common ground. The philosophy of the Qabalah treats of the relationship of the part of the Whole, and the glyph of the Tree shows this relationship in its design.

Man is termed the "microcosm," or small universe in the macrocosm, or greater universe around him, and it is taught that in his nature there are potentially present all the powers and forces of that greater universe. He is, in fact, an epitome of the macrocosm As the initiate of the Mysteries declared, "There is no part of me that is not part of the Gods."

It follows, then, that all the Beings and Intelligences of that greater universe have their aspects within the consciousness of man, the microcosm. If he evokes the elemental beings, he does so by virtue of their correspondences within him, for his physical, emotional and mental vehicles or bodies are built up by the action of countless elemental "lives." If he invokes the Mighty Ones, the Spiritual Lords and Vice-Regents of the Eternal, then through their correspondences within his own nature do they descend into his consciousness. If he invokes the Lord of the Roses, then through the indwelling Light within does that Lord answer him, and if he invokes the Eternal, then the Power of the Eternal rays down upon him through that within him which is the separate manifestation of the One.

So, and this is of the utmost importance, *all magical work begins within and is projected outwardly*. This is one of the first principles of magic, and it must *always* be kept in mind. It must be so built

---

* The word "Q B L" has the meaning "from mouth to ear."

into the magician's consciousness that nothing can obliterate it, for it is a true touchstone of safety. It will be seen that this is a very far-reaching principle, in fact some of its implications are as yet beyond the grasp of any embodied consciousness. Here we come up against one of the knotty problems of both philosophy and theology, the question of "objectivity." Berkely and Kant have had their say on one side of the problem, Schopenhauer on the other. Perhaps it will be as well if the would-be magician steers a midway course between the extremists, and holds to a belief in the reality of both the objective, and the subjective, remembering that both of them are aspects of the true Reality, which exists and subsists "after another manner."

For the practical work of magic, the idea which we must keep ever before us is that we are all like the Lady of Shalot in Tennyson's poem, we are all engaged in viewing *in a mirror* the universe in which we live, and a mirror, moreover, which is constantly changing. This mirror is our own personal unconscious or "subconscious mind," and was known to the older occultists as the "Sphere of Sensation." In modern terms it is the "auric egg" or psychic atmosphere which surrounds everyone. That Sphere of Sensation is the glass in which all things are mirrored and the first tasks of the apprentice-magician are designed to give him control over this magic mirror. He may not, except indirectly, work upon the outer world, but he can directly alter and remould his own subjective world, and this will cause him to come into such new relationships with the outer world, that he finds it shaping itself in accordance with his new point of view, since these deeper aspects of himself are part of the corresponding depths of the collective unconscious of the race, and of the universal consciousness.

This being the case, it is imperative that the magician should have some key to the forces and powers of that under-lying sea of consciousness—some idea of the tides that ebb and flow therein, and the living creatures to be found within its depths. Different cultures have used different glyphs, but the Western magical glyph is the Tree of Life which we will now discuss briefly in the next chapter.

To those who are acquainted with the standard books on the subject, the exposition given by the present writer may seem strange, but if they will try to translate the ideas therein given into their own terms, they will find that they have not wandered from the standard explanations. The Tree has only been described from another point of view.

Chapter III

THE TREE OF LIFE

ALL occult traditions worthy of the name employ certain diagrams and pictorial devices in the training of their members. As we have already pointed out, the Western Tradition is a composite one, embracing the mystery teachings of Greece, Egypt, Chaldea and Israel, and because of this it has a large store of such *mandalas*, as they are termed in the East.

But the *mandala par excellence* is that which is known as "The Tree of Life," and this comes from the Chaldean and Hebrew esoteric schools. It has been referred to as "The mighty, all-embracing glyph of the universe and the soul of man," and this is a very good description of it. It is, in itself, a complete diagram of a philosophy which is known as the Qabalah, and at the same time it can be used in connection with the various pantheons and philosophies of Egypt and Greece, as well as those of the Northlands and the Middle East.

It is an occult Rosetta Stone, which like the original Rosetta Stone, enables us to translate languages previously unknown to us into one with which we are familiar. As the reader will be aware, it was the fact that the original Rosetta Stone contained a decree which had been written in three languages; one of which was the Egyptian (which at the time when one of Napoleon's officers found the Stone, was an unknown language, the key to it having been lost). By deciphering the Latin and Greek inscriptions which were identical in meaning, it became possible to commence the translation of the Ancient Egyptian characters, and from this start, the work has gone on until the language of ancient Khemi is no longer unknown.

So with the Tree of Life. Once we have found the meaning of the Hebrew names upon it, we can "place on the Tree," to use a technical term, any other system of philosophy and be able to see how it will work out. This in itself is of great importance, but there are many other uses which may be made of the Tree.

It is essential to realise, however, that the Tree is *not* a *map* of the undiscovered country of either the soul of man or the universe in which he lives, but is rather a diagram of the mutual relationship of the underlying forces of both. Together with the Tree we have inherited a large body of philosophy based thereon, and it was the mutilated fragments of this philosophy which formed the back-ground of mediæval magic.

Several books on the Tree of Life have been published in recent years. The most important of these are mentioned in the bibliography at the end of this book. For this reason, it is not proposed to give a detailed exposition of the Tree in these pages. But what is intended is to give the magical apprentice *another point of view* with regard to this ancient glyph.

Briefly stated, the Tree is a wonderful diagram of *forces;* not things. If we consider the universe in which we live, and then con-sider the nature of our own immediate contact with it, we come to see we are living in a universe in which one of the supreme manifestations of the underlying reality is that phenomenon which we term "vibration." All things, all forces and all beings are finding expression in the universe by means of vibrations. When anyone speaks, the vibrations of his voice are carried by the air. When we see, the light vibrations are affecting our optical machinery. The vibrations of sound affect our ear, and there is cause to believe that the sense of smell does not entirely depend on the wide diffusion of small particles of the substance smelt. When we consider both light and sound we find they have an ascending scale of frequency, and into this scale all manifestations of light* and sound can be fitted. So the whole universe in which we live is the theatre of an infinity of interweaving forces, and these forces are at work in both the objective and the subjective levels of both the universe and the soul of man. The Qabalah declares there is an enormous field of acting and reacting *forces and lives,* and this field of the concourse of forces is generally known as "The Adam Kadmon," the Heavenly Man.

In the body of this Heavenly Man, we literally live and move and have our being, though we must be careful not to identify the the *Body* of the Heavenly Man with *His essential Nature.* Truly, in the midst of the Concourse of Forces, we exist, and equally truly in that Immanent Spirit which is the Heavenly Man Himself, we human spirits subsist; since, as the Greek poet wrote, "we are also His offspring."

We are living parts of a living organism; an organism which is pervaded, and is actually created, by the Eternal Spirit who is at the same time immanent in it, and transcendent to it.

---

* This is not to dismiss the "Quantum" hypothesis of light. It has its value both in physics and in magic, but a consideration of it here would carry us too far from our chosen field.

By experience over thousands of years the illuminated mystics of Egypt and Chaldea, from whom this system is derived, worked out a system of notation which would enable them to classify some of the forces with which they had come in contact, and so gradually a body of knowledge was formed which could be handed down to succeeding generations of students. The very name Q B L signifies "from mouth to ear," i.e. it was an oral tradition, never written down until the School of Moses de Leon first gave the *Sepher Yetzirah*, the "Book of Formation," and the *Zohar*, the "Book of Splendour" to the outer world.

But although the arcane knowledge was passed down in oral form, there was also elaborated a diagram by means of which the *relationships* existing between the various forces of the universe could be deduced. The diagram or glyph is known as *Otz Chiim*, the Tree of Life.

A cynic once said that words were used not to convey our thoughts, but to conceal them. Up to a certain point, of course, he was correct, but the purpose for which spoken language evolved was to convey information from one individual to another.

In the infancy of the race, a certain unconscious exercise of telepathy was the basis of communication, but with the evolution of the cerebro-spinal nerve system the images which had hitherto been transmitted by telepathic means were now linked with certain sounds. So arose the sequence of thought which we now use: perception, concept, word. Where it is a question of passing on information, then the process is concept and then word. But it was perception by one or other of the physical senses which gave rise to the concept. Let us explain this in more detail. The little grandson of the present writer is now just beginning to talk, and his efforts give a good indication of the process at work in his mind. He has evidently one or two pretty clear concepts which have been built up by his sense-perception, but they are very comprehensive. All living animals are "Sals" (the name of the household dog being "Sallie"). All men are "dads," and all plants are "flo-flos" (flowers). It is evident that each of these very comprehensive concepts will have to be split up into many more subdivisions, but the general concept has been built and linked with a particular word sound.

Now, all our lives we are constantly varying the mental concepts which we have built up throughout our existence, either expanding their meaning, or narrowing down according to custom, temperament or conditions. But it must be clearly kept in mind that the *bases* of all these concepts are the perceptions of the five physical senses. They provide the "imagery" which defines and forms the various concepts.

Even when we come to so-called "abstract" thinking the same process is at work, though the connection is more difficult to observe.

Now it used to be a dictum of the psychologists (and still is for some of them) that nothing exists in the mind which has not come in by the gateways of the *physical* senses. This we now know to be incorrect, but if we alter the statement to read "there is nothing in the mind which has not come in through *the senses*," then we are nearer the truth. For the superphysical senses are also recording their perceptions in the mind.

There is, however, one great difference between the physical and the superphysical senses. The first group derive their images from the external world, the second from the Inner Worlds. Since the personality has been built up by reaction to physical stimuli, all its concepts are in terms of physical objects and beings, and concepts which are built in terms of the Inner Planes are meaningless to it. One often meets people who bewail their lack of power to "bring through" into consciousness the knowledge gained on the levels of the Inner Planes. Yet, curiously enough, it very often happens that they have actually brought through a great deal of such knowledge, but because the concepts so built up are of a different order to those built up through the physical senses they remain unnoticed by the conscious self.

Now the levels of the Astral Light have been worked upon by the mind of man, and the earth imagery has been imposed upon that sensitive astral substance, and so it happens that general descriptions of the Inner Planes, such as are given by clairvoyants or communicated through mediumistic sensitives, are relatively true, since they describe what we may term the "humanity-conditioned" levels of the Astral Light.

But if we wish to study the basic Forces of the Astral Light, then we have to use some form of concept based, not upon optical or sensory properties, such as size, weight, hardness, colour or sound, but upon *pure relationship*. It must of course be remembered that the mind will always use images of some kind or other, and if the waking consciousness has no stock images by which it may realise such a form of perception, it will use some of the sensory images derived from the action of the physical senses.

This is quite all right, so long as we clearly understand that such images are being used in a *representative* capacity, and are not the

AIN
AIN SOPH
AIN SOPH AUR

KETHER

1

12   11

13

BINAH   **3**   14   **2**   CHOKMAH

18   17   16   15

GEBURAH   **5**   19   **4**   CHESED

22   20

6   TIPHARETH

23   26   25   24

HOD   **8**   27   **7**   NETZACH

30   28

9   YESOD

31   29

32

THE TREE
AND
THE PATHS

10   MALKUTH

actual things perceived by the inner senses. Of course, a great deal in the Astral Light that concerns the more or less immediate after-death conditions of humanity is capable of being fairly accurately expressed through such physical plane images, since the action of human minds, incarnate and discarnate, upon the plastic astral substance has resulted in the building-up of forms very similar to those of the physical plane. This is done more or less automatically by both incarnate and discarnate minds, but it may also be done consciously and deliberately, and this is what has been done by generations of occult students working on the glyph of the Tree of Life. The various forces of the Astral Light have been assigned to their own particular symbolic images, and when a certain astral force is perceived by the clairvoyant who has been trained along these lines, it is seen as a being of a certain type. Now many of these representative images are arbitrary and do not afford any true picture of the reality. Such for instance are the "Deva-forms" seen by Hindu psychics, and the "Angel-forms" seen by many Western psychics. Such too are the traditional gnomes, sylphs, salamanders and undines of mediæval magic. In the same class are all the "spirits" personified by the ancient Greeks as oreads, nymphs, dryads, etc., and when the astral beings concerned are perceived by a psychic who sees in *the Greek mode*, because of some temperamental bias thereto, then those beings will be seen in that mode. The same applies to those in whom the mediæval mode is strong. They will see the astral beings and forces under the appearance of the gnomes, salamanders, etc.

It must be borne in mind, too, that the tendency of all elemental life (descending, as it is, *into* more material forms of substance) is to take any available form presented to it, and such forms are to be found by the million in the rolling billows of energy which we know of as the Astral Light. In this book, unless it is otherwise stated, the term Astral Light refers to those levels of the basic Astral Ether which have been modified by the action of the minds of all living creatures upon this planet, including the mind-consciousness of the planet itself, and which present to the observer certain definite forms. Forms as such are not native to that realm of living energy-substance which we have termed the Astral Ether, and the forms to be found in it are the results of the creative activities of minds working downwards from the higher mental levels, or upwards from the material levels. So the Astral Light divides naturally into the Upper Astral with its background of mind and spirit, and the Lower Astral with its background of physical matter.

But apart from the forms, the true Astral world continues to manifest under its own laws, and the genius of the adepts of the Qabalah has been to devise forms which may be used as *indicating symbols* of the particular forces concerned. So a mighty and complex system of living imagery has been built up around the central glyph of the Tree of Life, and generations of students, through hundreds of years, have used and meditated upon this root system of metaphysical symbolism. This has built up in the Astral Light what may be termed the *Egregore* of the Tree; the composite living "soul" of which the glyph of the Tree is the physical body.*

Those who "work with the Tree," come into sympathetic relationship with this *Egregore,* and may gain from it, by a species of telepathic action, light on their present-day problems, and knowledge of the inner realities which transcends that which they could reach without such assistance.

All magical operations, when carried out by those who have been trained in the Schools of the Qabalah, are based on, and utilise, the store of images in the *Egregore* of the Tree. All astral forces which may be used in such magic have their own symbolic personifications in that group of associated images, and by consciously manipulating these representative images, the forces of which they are an expression are likewise manipulated.

Since the level of the mind which deals with such images is the so-called "sub-conscious" mind, it is an axiom in magic *that it is the subconscious mind which is the magical agent* (the High Priestess of the Tarot) whilst the conscious mind is the directing and controlling factor (the Magician of the Tarot).

Thus, all magical operations by the personal consciousness are indirect. The actual operation is performed by the subconscious level of the mind, working through the appropriate images. This is one of the most important laws of Magic.

As the reader will see at a later stage, it is possible to make our own Tree. In fact we must do so if we are to do any real work with this system. But this does not mean that we should blindly accept the classifications handed down to us from our more ancient brethren. In this matter we should be ourselves originators. It must be remembered that with the increasing knowledge which is such a feature of our present times, there are so many new avenues of thought which were closed to our predecessors, and from those new

---

* Of course, the *Egregore* of the Tree is also built in realms far above the Astral Light, but the same law holds good. The higher realms we may term the "Divine Astral."

thought-images we may construct, what might be termed, an "up-to-date" Tree of Life. Indeed, it is necessary that we should do this, but the true apprentice of magic learns also to follow the example given in the New Testament, of the "wise householder, who brings forth from his treasure-house, things *old* and new."

Although our forefathers were ignorant of much that is elementary knowledge to us, they still had keen minds and still encountered the same basic human problems that perplex and worry their clever descendants of today. In the established system of relationships which is the Tree of Life, they found a key to open the door of Wisdom, and their meditations thereon have built up into the *Egregore* of the Tree much that still has a value today. So when we make our very modern Tree, it is well to realise that if we in this way make our contribution to that group-thought-form, it, in its turn, can work through the archaic images within our deeper minds.

The glyph of the Tree may be used for meditation purposes and also as a plan upon which practical, objective work may be done, but these two aspects of work upon the Tree (we may term them the subjective and the objective aspects) use different diagrams. Different in colour, that is, for the method of using the forces in meditation is different from that of using them in practical magical work, and this difference is shown in the colours of the Tree.

When considering the colours used for the Tree diagrams, it should be remembered that for objective magical work and ritual initiation, the psychic structures which are built up are linked with the appropriate Sephiroth, and these are coloured in a higher scale than the connecting Paths between them. But for meditation work concerned with action upon our own weaknesses, the psychic structure, or Astral Temple, should be in the same colour scale as the connecting Paths. This enables one to work upon the corresponding centre in ones own aura. In this connection, it will be seen that the cards of the Tarot pack are alloted to the Paths of the Tree, and by meditation on the card concerned, the appropriate centre may be stimulated. Direct concentration upon the psychic centres is inadvisable; the conscious mind can so easily upset their delicate equilibrium.

Careful study of the books already written upon the Tree of Life will enable the student to use the Tree in its different colour-scales, and for this reason we will not here give detailed instructions.

If we indicate the principles, then the practical use of them can be essayed by the student, and it is far better that he should be allowed to make his own approach, even though it may be faulty in its initial stages, than simply follow blindly the instructions of another. At least, so we think.

When using the glyph of the Tree of Life, whether for meditation or for magical purposes, it is important to remember that the symbols must be used systematically, in accordance with their functional relationship, for this relationship is the very essence of the Tree, as we have already pointed out. The Tree is a diagram of relationships. It is also advisable to work with the opposites, i.e. meditation or magical operation using the Sphere of Mars* should be followed by one using the symbolism of Jupiter.† In this way a balanced developement is assured, and we are told that "Equilibrium is the basis of the Great Work."

This is particularly important when we attempt to use the Tree for such things as psychic diagnosis. Dream interpretation by the use of the Tree is a most promising line of work, since the forces portrayed by the symbolism of the Sephiroth are to be found in the microcosm of the soul of man as well as in the macrocosm of the outer universe. As the Life-force descends into manifestation in the personality it may be deflected or thwarted at any level, and the type of symbolism shown in the prevailing dreams of the patient will show which Sephirothic level is at fault.

When considering this matter of the colour-scales, it must be realised that the colours are not purely arbitrary but are based upon a real relationship between them and the forces they represent. This relationship may be based upon a common identity, or may be one which has been given by the meditations of generations of students, and which, thereby, is built into the *Egregore* of the Tree. The same is true of all the symbols used on the Tree. They have this two-fold nature.

The student will have perceived that the Tree of Life is a stupendous memnonic system; a system which makes use of *the natural modes of action of the conscious*, subconscious and superconscious levels of the soul. He may, therefore, ask why could we not make up a Tree of our own and use it for auto-suggestive purposes? Why bother with the symbolism of the past? It is, of course, quite possible as we have already said, to make such an up-to-date Tree, but as we already possess, in our deep Unconscious, all the archaic symbols of the racial past, we may as well use them in our conscious work, thus linking our conscious and subconscious mental levels.

---

* The Sephirah *Geburah*.
† The Sephirah *Gedulah*.

Since the appeal of any system of suggestion is to the subconscious, it is evident that a system which uses the archaic symbols will be far better able to affect the subconscious levels, since it speaks in their language, than any arbitrary conscious, symbol-system could do.

We come now to a very important point. When we study the various forms of musical instrument, (apart from percussion instruments) we find there is a clear division into two classes. In the one, which includes the piano, the organ and the various wood-wind instruments, the notes are already made for the musician. He depresses the keys of the organ, or the stops of the wood-wind, and the corresponding musical notes are sounded. In the second class, which is composed of the stringed instruments, the musician makes his own notes by his fingering, i.e. he shortens or lengthens the effective vibratory length of the string, thus causing it to emit the chosen notes when put into vibration by the bow or plectrum.

When working with the Tree in practical magic, we are in the position of the musician of the second class, we first learn how to produce the right psychic "notes" as required. This is done by using the symbols of the Tree as objects in our meditation. Unless we have done this properly, our magic will usually be ineffective.

So, in our meditation we take the various symbols of the Tree, and consider them in their two aspects, for all these symbols have two sides to their nature. There is the "form" side, i.e. the actual pictorial symbol itself, and there is also the "force" side, which is the energy of which the symbol is an expression. This energy exists under its appropriate aspect on all levels of the soul and the universe, but on the plane of the Astral Light it is manifest as *emotional energy*.

In building up our symbol-system in meditation we have to learn to link, deliberately and consciously, a symbol with its appropriate force, and to become so expert at it that the mere fact of the symbol arising in consciousness brings with it a surge of emotional energy of the type associated with that symbol on the Tree. Equally, we must be able, by opening ourselves to a certain aspect of emotional energy to perceive inwardly with the "minds eye," the symbol which represents that energy.

In this technical meditation work, the linking-up of the astral energies with their corresponding forms is best done by building a "phantasy scene" based upon the emotional significance of the symbol. The more clearly the phantasy is built, the more closely do you come into contact with the energy concerned. This is one aspect of the work* The complementary aspect is developed by consciously linking the symbol with the energy by meditating upon the emotional charge behind it, and then allowing various emotional states to develop within our minds, visualising the appropriate symbol-forms at the same time. After steady practice on this, there will come a time when the mere thought of the emotion will throw up into the waking consciousness the symbol-form concerned.

When this has been attained, we have begun to work with the alphabet of a new language, and we learn to put together the various energised symbols in such a way as to build up what might be described as the language of the Mysteries. When these images and their corresponding forces have been so linked, we may use them in two ways. In the receptive mode, if we have learnt the psychological "trick" of allowing the images to rise, which we discussed earlier on, we may use these linked symbols to indicate to our waking consciousness the fluctuating pressures and tides of the emotional self, and since this emotional side of our nature is continually being affected by the forces and intelligences of the Astral Light, our symbols as they rise on the mental screen will be a translation into physical terms of the awareness on its own plane, of the astral body. In other words, we have a controlled and disciplined psychism. Such a system of psychic perception has the great advantage of being capable of check, since the sudden emergence of symbols of another type will show that the vision is mixed. With practise, this type of psychic perception becomes very accurate indeed, and merges into a form of direct perception of the astral levels without symbols.

This form of psychic training is one of great value and has the advantage of being entirely under the control of the waking self. It is important to make this clear. In the Qabalistic systems of psychic training, the various "planes" or vibration-levels are kept isolated from one another. To use the expression coined by Swedenborg, they are "discrete and not continuous." This means that the Qabalistically-trained psychic does not suffer from any sudden eruption of astral vision into his daily waking life. *Only when he deliberately wills it* are the veils between the physical and the inner levels removed.

On the objective side, the discipline of the "linking-meditation" allows the magician to construct his astral temple and charge it

---

* *The Spiritual Exercises of Ignatius Loyola*, who was the founder of the Jesuit Society, are a good example of what is wanted, though they are purely Christian—and Roman Christian at that.

with the corresponding forces through the conscious manipulation
of the symbols concerned.

It will be seen, then, that steady and prolonged meditation on
the Tree is necessary if any practical use is to be made of it. It may
also be pointed out that since all the manifold objects of physical
life can be placed on their appropriate level on the Tree, that the
relationships existing between the various Sephirothic groupings
will gradually build up an innate philosophic system within the
mind of the magician.

This process is assisted by the use of what are known as "seed-
meditations." In using these seed-meditations, the particular
statement is meditated upon, and then passed down into the Unconscious. It disappears, but at a later date it reappears quite suddenly in consciousness together with a host of associated ideas, plus
a realisation of its true meaning which would never have been
obtained by mere conscious meditation upon it. All the symbols on
the Tree, and more particularly the curious and cryptic "Yetziratic
texts" which are attributed to each Path, can be used in seed-
meditations in this way.

PART II

THE TRAINING OF THE MAGICIAN

Chapter IV

PRELIMINARY NOTES

IN this section of the book, it is intended that the student should be given some idea of the training which he must undergo if he would be a practical magician. It will be seen as the instruction unfolds, that it is no light task; indeed to attain the higher stages of magical power demands an application, an intensity of effort, and a perseverance greater than those required for any other pursuit in life. For indeed this is a Magnum Opus, a Great Work, nothing else in fact than the disintegration and reintegration of the student's own personality.

Since our personality has been built up in this earthly life by our general appreciation of the principles of pleasure and pain, it will be seen that it presents a rather untidy appearance. Our house of life has been built of material selected haphazardly from the workshop of the Architect, and because we ourselves did the selecting, we tend to overrate the results of our selection. The student has to gain the power to rid his personality of those things which are not true to plan, and to substitute those which are. This calls for what has been termed "The first virtue of the Path": Discrimination. It is evident, of course, that he needs guidance in the early stages, in order to develop this quality of Discrimination, and the best guidance, apart from personal supervision by his teacher, is to read and meditate upon some one of the many manuals of mystical devotion and thought. Some such are *Spiritual Exercises, God Calling, The Practise of the Presence of God, Interior Castles, Christ in You, Light on the Path, The Voice of the Silence, The Ascent of Mount Carmel*, the Gospel of St. John, *The Cloud of Unknowing, A Serious Call*, and many more.

The reading of these books and meditation thereon will serve to "key" the student to a certain level of spiritual thought, and he will find that they will give him a touchstone which will help him to see those things in himself which are out of place in the true plan of his personality, and also see with what other materials he may correctly replace them.

In attempting such alterations to the personality the student must remember that it is necessary to proceed with caution. It may be that some particular thing in the personality is a keystone which supports the weight of much of the personal self. To attempt to remove this *before* the correct substitute has been lifted into position is to risk the ruin of one's house of life. As we have expressed it in the motto on the title page of this book, "Through *Wisdom* is an house builded; and by *Understanding* it is established." "Wisdom" and "Understanding" are two of the three topmost Sephiroth of the Qabalistic Tree of Life.

Let us for a moment consider what happens when we do certain things. We are moved to action by two types of stimuli. The first is the stimulus we gain from our own self-initiated will and desire. We desire certain things to happen, and we determine that they *shall* happen. The sequence is desire—will—act, working from within.

The second type of stimulus comes from persons or conditions outside ourselves. The sequence here is stimulus—thought—feeling—and resultant action. This sequence we may term *reaction*. Reaction may be voluntary or involuntary. Usually it is involuntary, and our house of life is enriched(?) by a stone selected for us by someone or something not ourselves. In the unregenerate man, such instinctive reaction is the usual order of things, and by a wise use of this, it is possible to lead the average man into all kinds of queer paths. It will be evident that the more passionate and involuntary the reaction may be, the easier it becomes to guide the person concerned into good or evil ways. The classic instance of the Irishman who got all his pigs to market in record time by pulling them in the opposite direction is a very good illustration of this tendency of the human mind, and the tendency is used by the occult student in his training. When we come to the building of the Magical Personality it will be seen how this is effected, but it is necessary to mention it here. In some Eastern systems of training, great stress is laid upon *Ekagrata* or one-pointedness of mind, and the Yoga *Aphorisms* of Patanjali describe Yoga as the *conscious* modification of the thinking principle. The student must learn how to inhibit the *irrational reaction* which his personal self offers to stimuli from other people or other events, and be himself the conscious originator and modifier of whatever changes of consciousness he decides to bring about. So we have come to the definition of magic given in the writer's first book* "Magic is the art of effecting changes in consciousness at will."

Now we come to a point where the best and most detailed instructions lapse. There is a peculiar and personal interaction between the personalities of the magician and his apprentice, and it is in the atmosphere of that interaction that the best work can be done. This

* *Magic: Its Ritual, Power and Purpose* (Aquarian Press).

atmosphere cannot be given in a book, but the book may help the apprentice to train himself to the point where such a personal link with one of the Craftsmen of the Spirit becomes possible. Then, by an eternal law, when the apprentice is ready, the Teacher appears. But long before this, *he will have met that Teacher through the personalities who have successively guided him along the path*, for whenever he is ready for the next stage of his training, the necessary teacher *for that stage* comes to him. If this was more fully understood, there would be less "self-bamboozlement" amongst occult students, less seeking after "masters" and "initiates." The true masters and initiates exist, *but they do not advertise*.

Finally the apprentice must remember that in the end, there is only *one* master for him, the indwelling "Being of Light," whose persona or mask he is.

That Higher Self, itself a facet of the Eternal, one with all other facets, is the ultimate court of appeal, the True Master, and indeed the True Magician.

Chapter V

THE ASTRAL LIGHT

THE next phase of existence beyond this physical world is usually known to the Spiritualists as "The Spirit World." The Theosophists term it "The Astral Plane" and the Hindus speak of it as *Kamaloka*. We are using the old name current in the Western Schools, "The Astral Light," and we do this for a very definite reason.

Both the Spiritualistic and Theosophical names give the idea of a "place," and this is somewhat misleading. Although, to a certain extent it is correct to speak of the next phase of existence as a place, yet this obscures its most salient point. The more important aspect of this Astral Light is its aspect *as a state of consciousness*. By using the term Astral *Light*, we avoid the rigid limitation of the idea of "place."

The name "astral" comes from the Latin, relating to the stars. This name was used by the old occultists and it aptly describes the substance of the higher astral levels. There is another interesting point here. The old Anglo-Saxon word *steran*, which is based on the same root as the word "astral," means "to steer," and is itself the root of our present-day word. So the astral is the steering or directing level, and this is very true.

We have referred to the "substance" of the astral levels; what is really meant by that term? Is the matter of the astral light real? Yes, but its reality is of another order. It is taught that there are two aspects to everything: that which a thing really is, and that which it appears to be. Since the appearances or "accidents," as they are termed, are the manifestations of the realities, they have a reality of their own, but this "reality" is a dependent and not a primary one.

Now each level of existence has its own type of "substance," and each grade of substance has its own appearance or "accident." We distinguish here between the basic reality of the particular level, and the appearances it presents to the consciousnesses of those dwelling on it. But there is another definite division which affects us more directly. Every level of substance manifests under the dual aspects of Force and Form. In the great glyph of the Tree of Life, these two aspects are symbolised as the Right and Left-Hand Pillars, and in the Masonic Order, as the Pillars of King Solomon's Temple, Jachin and Boaz.

On the physical plane we are accustomed to its type of matter manifesting mainly under the form-aspect. It is stable and fixed; in fact it is difficult to make it obey any force brought to bear upon it.

Once moulded into a form, it persists in that form (we are now referring to what we term "solid" matter). Thus, when we wish to build a house or make a dress, we have laboriously to piece together our material, we have to have our material made, and we have to employ tools of all kinds to shape and build our house or make our dress. This is because that type of matter which we term "physical" manifests mainly under the "form" aspect. There are certain forms of dense matter which are also manifest to some extent under the force aspect. Such are radio-active elements of which radium is the chief. But even here, though the radio-active elements emit force and themselves change in the process, such change is towards more stable and inert types of matter—the form aspect becoming more powerful than the force aspect.

But the substance of the astral levels manifests chiefly under the force aspect of its nature, and for this reason, the "accidents" or appearances of the astral are quite different from those of our physical level. Since astral substance thus manifests, it does not take any *form* naturally. It may be pictured as an interpenetrating atmosphere of "energy—substance" reflecting like a mirror the forms impressed upon it either from the spiritual realms above it, or from the etheric and physical realms below it.

Thus we have a natural point of division in the Astral Light, and these two divisions are known as the "Higher Astral" and the "Lower Astral."

We have, therefore, two distinct types of "appearances," the one which is the natural expression of the astral substance and the other which is the expression of the consciousnesses of all living beings, including those who are the true natives and fauna of the Astral Light, and those who are sojourning there either temporarily or semi-permanently, but whose origin and true home is elsewhere.

It may be said, "But surely the descriptions given through psychics portray a very material and definite state." This is true, but always these appearances are the "creations of the created"; they are formed by the power of thought by the dwellers in the Astral Light. There are, it must be remembered, many kinds of dwellers in the Astral Light.

Here we must digress slightly, and consider the "body" or "vehicle" which is our natural expression in the Astral Light.

Ordinarily, we express ourselves through both thought and emotion, even though their relative proportions may vary according to the particular circumstances and temperament of our personality.

So this *persona* or "mask" is built up by us, through thought and emotion. According to our level of thought and emotion will be the particular grade of astral and mental substance which we are building into it. But only a small part of our habitual thinking is really conscious and deliberate. All our lives we are building up subconscious thought-habits, and these are always affecting our conscious thinking, even as they are always building into our astro-mental bodies types of astral substance which are in tune with the general sum of our subconscious activity. It will be seen that attendance at Church on Sunday is very definitely off-set by our daily thought activity during the rest of the week, for this daily thought is always working towards the establishment of subconscious thought-habits. So the type of astral body we possess is determined by the majority vote of our subconscious complexes. When we terminate our incarnation on the earth, and the "silver cord" is loosened, then we pass into the astral realms which correspond, in their grade of astral matter, with the matter which during our life-days we have built into the *Ruach* or astro-mental body.

Thus, as the Scriptures say, "Every man goeth to his own place." Moreover, because of the law of sympathetic vibration, we find ourselves in the company of those who also have built into their astral bodies similar grades of astral matter.

If, then, our habitual thoughts and emotions have been mainly on the level of the good, the beautiful and the true, then we find ourselves in most congenial company and our thoughts, working in their habitual subconscious fashion, form the plastic astral substance around us into the forms which, to our earth-developed minds represent such goodness, beauty and truth. So we find ourselves in a place of hills and mountains, of trees and rivers, a land of natural beauty—the "Summerland" of the early Spiritualists. It may be thought that even the grouped minds of many people thinking along such lines could not produce such stupendous appearances. The human mind is capable of much greater feats than at present appear possible to it, but we are not dealing with human minds alone. We have said that the Upper Astral reflects the mental and spiritual realms beyond, where dwell those great Intelligences who have gained that relative perfection which is the goal of the earthly pilgrimage. In that realm dwell also the Shining Ones of another order of being, whose thoughts, materialised down here on the earth plane by the hosts of their subordinate servants, give to all the phenomena of earthly beauty that atmosphere of ecstatic awe which affects all who are in tune with it.

So in these higher realms these thoughts of the Shining Ones are nearer to their source in the Infinite, and hence evoke in the minds of the dwellers there, the same ecstasy but in far greater degree, and this is reflected in their minds by the corresponding earth-images, and so the indescribable thought-forms of the Shining Ones are given "a local habitation and a name"; are imaged and seen under the forms of earth. Not yet is the soul ready or capable of seeing these things in the terms of their own nature—for we must walk before we can run.

It will be seen that we are not dealing only with the thoughts of discarnate man when we are dealing with the Astral Light. We are also concerned with the thoughts and feelings of man in the physical body as well as with those of the Lords of Light and the Shining Ones.

The great formative and creative forces of the Universe pour down through the Astral Light towards their materialisation in dense physical matter, and it is in the Lower Astral that these divine forces are most *powerful*.

These forces, too, are working through our subconsciousness, and therefore those instincts and passions which we are inclined to regard as low and earthly are in reality divine; it is only when they are out of balance that they become evil. The emotions and passions should be so governed by the Self that they may be used temperately in the service of the God within. This attitude of the magician is poles asunder from that which would regard the divinely working instincts as evil, and to be trodden underfoot.

They provide the basic elemental force which can be directed into the true channels of creation, not only on physical, but on spiritual levels also.

Now the "creations of the created," the great thought systems of the minds of men incarnate and discarnate are the "appearances" of the Astral Light. But in itself the basic Astral Ether is far different. It is not a realm of forms, except as these forms are built up out of its substance, and beyond and through the phantasmagoria of the Astral Light, the great tides of force in the Astral Ether ebb and flow.

The ever-fluctuating billows and currents of the Astral Light engender, by sympathetic induction, definite states of mind and emotion in all who dwell in the sphere of Earth. These induced emotions and thoughts are again imaged in the rolling tides of the Light, and reinforce those images and currents which brought them into being. So action and reaction are set up and intensify their rhythmic swing, until finally the accumulated and intensified power is discharged and materialised in earth conditions. From the lower realms of the Astral Light proceed those moral and psychic epi-demics which astonish the world, and from its higher realms come those spiritual impulses which make for the regeneration of the race.

For the Astral Light is dual. Like a glittering fiery serpent the lower levels of the Light wind their evil coils around the earth; they inspire earth's wickedness, they contaminate its inhabitants, and gain in a vicious circle by the perverted power and energy which is poured out in response to their stimulus.

This is the terrestial dragon, "earthly, sensual and devilish," and within its realms are to be found the darkest abortions of the human and animal-human mind. Here are the matrices of evolu-tionary time, here are the discarded moulds of early days, the "dog-faced demons of the Pit."

Here, too, acting as channels for the influences of the Lords of Unbalanced Force, are the astral simulacra-ideas of the "gods" of death and destruction, of lust and wanton evil; the tribal gods and fetishes of primitive tribes; and here also are the powers of darkness in whose image ignorant man has made his gods.

So the human race peoples its "current in space," and its thoughts and emotions, coalescing with the semi-intelligent forces of the lower astral, assume a semi-independent life of their own.

But there is also a Celestial Dragon, the Upper Astral, whose glittering radiance encircles the earth. From her flow harmony, peace, happiness; although far below the Supreme Nature, yet of her also it may be said that "her ways are ways of pleasantness and all her paths are peace."

Within her realm are to be found the heroic images of the past. Here are those mighty ones of past epochs, their traditional forms still imprinted in the Astral Light, and to this region there ascend all images of the good, the beautiful and the true.

But forms *as forms*, are not native to the Astral Light. Just as in our minds the latent memories persist as "tendencies," *not definite images*, but may gather around them and build up appropriate images, so in the Astral Light the forms perceived therein are due to the image-building power of the mind.

But if the mind provides the images, the astral energies vivify and make potent those images, bringing them a stage nearer their materialisation in the physical world.

So the Astral Light, in and through which the magician works, must be thought of as an interpenetrating atmosphere of pure energy-substance, fluidic and plastic, reflecting like a mirror the forms impressed upon it either from mental and spiritual realms above it, or from the physical realms below it.

Such is the Astral Light, and in this Light exist forces and powers which may lift us to the eternal stars, or drag us down to abysmal slime.

Chapter VI

THE INVISIBLE BODY

WHEN the average person begins to take an interest in magic, he is very often discouraged by what he feels to be the complexity of the magical systems. But this is simply because he is without any guiding principles which, like Ariadne's thread would lead him through the maze. When, however, these principles have been understood, then the whole magical complex becomes relatively simple. It is an essential law of the true magical tradition, that the neophyte should start with the study of certain definite laws and principles which underlie the whole subject. When these have been mastered, the various details of magic fall into place, and the whole magical system can be viewed as a unity. For behind all the various systems there is one philosophical thought-form, based upon that particular philosophy known as Monism. Briefly, this philosophy teaches that all things, manifest or hidden, are "parts of one stupendous Whole," and that there can be nothing which is outside that Whole. "By Him (the Logos) were all things made; yea all things both in heaven and earth; with Him as the indwelling Life do all things exist, and in Him as the transcendent Glory do all things live and move and have their being."*

We do not propose here to discuss the thorny problem of the existence of evil, etc., except in so far as it directly affects our subject. In any case, it is the faith of the magician that our three-dimensional brain-consciousness is unable *at the present time* to apprehend the realities behind the veil of appearances. That form of mystical consciousness which develops from the magical work gives an illumination which enables the personal consciousness to rise above the "pairs of opposites," and to see the cosmic scheme from another point of view. At first this higher perception will only show itself in very brief flashes, but as the magical training proceeds, these flashes of illumination increase in duration, until finally, it is possible for the trained magician to live entirely on the higher ranges of his spiritual nature. Since, however, the brain-consciousness is under a heavy strain when this higher perception is active, we find that all the great occultists recommend a rhythmic "approach-and-withdrawal" in order to check spiritual "lopsidedness" or "out-of-balance."

This concept of the unity of all life is a background against

---

* Part of the Eucharistic Liturgy of the Liberal Catholic Church.

which all else must be judged, and it is therefore a cardinal—indeed the primary—principle of the Magical Art. For a fuller consideration of the monistic philosophy, the reader is referred to the works on the subject listed in the bibliography at the end of this book. Though this is the cardinal principle of magic, there is another which is a very close second. This is the "Hermetic axiom," said to have been engraved on the famous Emerald Tablet of Hermes: "As above, so below." We must, however, be careful not to reverse it when we consider its applications, since we "below" can have but an imperfect comprehension of the nature of anything, and therefore our mental concepts will of necessity fall far short of the reality.

But "above" is the Reality, of which "below" is an expression, a true expression and correspondence under its own mode, but *not* the Reality in itself.

Although the "below" is necessarily imperfect, nevertheless it is one aspect of the Whole, of the "above," and therefore any action in the phenomenal worlds (whether those worlds are physical or superphysical) which is a true "correspondence" with some aspect of the "above," will tend to link up the levels of consciousness, and "draw through" the Cosmic Energy, or Grace of God. It is stated in the Qabalah that the physical plane, *Malkuth* on the Tree of Life, causes an influence to descend from *Kether*, the highest Sephirah on the Tree.

In a magical rite, therefore, apart from the psychological effects it may produce subjectively within the mind of the magician, there is a "drawing through" of power, and this power may be used in many ways.

Now, the closer the "correspondence" between any magical act and the realities "above," the more effective such an act will be, and for this reason, it is very necessary for the magical student so to construct his magical ritual, that it may effectively draw through the maximum amount of power *he is able to handle without risk*. This must be emphasised. It is no part of the magical work to take unnecessary risks, either alone or in company.

The next principle with which we must deal is that of the *Egregore*, or group-consciousness. When two or three or many people gather together in one place to perform certain actions, to think along certain lines, and to experience emotional influences, there is built up, in connection with that group, what may be termed a composite group-consciousness, wherein the emotional and mental forces of all the members of the group are temporarily united in

what is known in occultism as a group-thought-form, or "artificial
elemental." This group consciousness seems to have a much greater
power than the simple sum of the objective minds in the group
would suggest. This is because, not only is it a group-thought form
built up by the *conscious* minds of those concerned; it is also formed
through a linking-up between what we may call the "free-floating"
parts of the subconscious minds of all who help to build it up.
Since those subconscious minds reach back on the one hand into
the Collective Unconscious and on the other reach upwards into
the realms of the superconscious, the group-thought-form is psychi-
cally linked with, or contacted on to, many aspects of thought and
many forms of psychic-mental energy. Thus it is greater than any
sum of its parts.

When the group ceases to meet, this artificial elemental tends
to become passive and quiescent, but when once more a group is
founded, whether it be the original group or not, then the overshadowing group-thought-form makes contact with it, and works
through its members. Now, the use of any form of ritual and
ceremonial tends to make a stereotyped form, which will, if the same
ritual and ceremonial be used, as was used by its founders, manifest
itself in the same way. Where such ritual and ceremonial work has
been carried out for many years, or even centuries, the resultant artificial elemental is built up into a very powerful centre of consciousness, and one which has had built into it the powers, faculties and
ideals of all those who through the years have used those forms of
words and actions. Not only those in the body, but the group working behind the *Egregore* on the Inner Planes, will also contribute to
the building up of the form; for, as the *Yetziratic* text has informed
us, *Malkuth* causes an influence to flow from the Prince of Countenances which is in *Kether*. In other words, we form a group on the
physical plane, and simultaneously we draw into union with ourselves a similar group on the Inner Planes. Upon each level of the
Inner Planes is a similar group built, until we come to the realms
where the primal impulses which first began the work of creation
are still to be found, vibrating their notes, which are the realities
behind all phenomenal appearances on all the planes of life.

Now, according to the type of group will be the impulse under
which it works,* this is that upon which the group-thought-form is
built, and by which it is maintained. Now, upon this primary structure there have been formed what correspond to the flesh and blood
of the body, and this "body" is a thing of slow growth. When the

* Such impulses are personified in the "Lords of the Rays" Archangels, etc.

great archaic rituals are used, the growth has been in progress for many, many centuries, in some cases for many thousands of years, and much has been built into them which is not in true correspondence with the overshadowing impulse. At the same time it must be remembered that where such a psychic attribution is made over many years, it has become a true channel for the energy of the *Egregore*, though a *secondary* one. An instance is the attribution of the lily to the Virgin Mary. This is a secondary attribution, whereas Her blue robe is a primary one, linking up in the Christian *Egregore* with primordial cosmic Archetypal images. In the Christian religion, the Church is regarded as the "mystical Body" of Christ, and it must be remembered that the Church, according to its own authorities, includes the Church Militant here on earth, the Church Expectant in the After Life, and the Church Triumphant in the Heavenly Places. Also it extends through all time, since as St. Augustine puts it, "That which is now called Christianity has never at any time since the creation of the world ceased to exist. Only now has it been called Christianity." In its deepest aspects, this Mystical Body subsists in the timelessness of Eternity, and for this reason some of its teachers declare that its central ceremonial brings its members into a timeless contact and experience of that Mystery which was expressed in earthly time and space through the life, death, and resurrection of Jesus Christ.

We may thus define the *Egregore*. It is the resultant, in the Inner Worlds, of the united concepts, emotions, and symbolic words and actions of the followers of the particular cult or faith, throughout the whole of its history. Just as we have an *Egregore* for every religious faith, so have we a Magical *Egregore* for what we may term the Planetary Tradition of the Earth. But within this all-embracing group-thought-form (which, it must be remembered, exists as a living entity on the Inner Planes) there are differentiations. The first differentiation is into two main traditions, the Eastern and the Western. Though basically at one, the methods of these two traditions are adapted to the conditions of the races of the East and West respectively. On philosophic levels, and in their higher degrees, the two traditions unite to form the Planetary Tradition, but in their lower aspects, and in their methods of training, there is considerable divergence.

There is no reason why the Western magician should not study the philosophy and principles evolved by his Eastern brother, but when it comes to the practical work, there is danger in what may be called "magical mis-mating." All magical work should be done within the *Egregore* of the appropriate tradition.

Although we have stated that the relevant tradition should be followed, this does *not* mean that we must only use such traditional forms as have been handed down to us. Some such traditional forms have of late years been given out publicly, but a careful examination will show that quite a lot of the detailed work is, in point of fact, unnecessary. Here again, we see that secondary attributions have often been mistaken for primary ones. However, since they have been so used, they will work in the right hands; but we may, if we will, construct our home-made rituals, basing them upon the primary principles, and by them we may succeed when the initiate of a genuine magical school, though using the traditional ritual and ceremonial, may fail ignominiously through his lack of realisation of the principles involved.

If our home-made ritual is built up on the lines of the true principles of the *Egregore* of our tradition, then by a process of induction we may draw power from that tradition, and become linked with it. Now behind every magical school, behind the Eastern and Western Traditions, and again behind the Planetary Tradition, there are people, men and women of all grades of development, and these people, who are the Stewards or Guardians of their respective Mysteries, are only too glad to work with and through any earnest student who is working along their line. It therefore happens that an individual group of magical workers is drawn into psychic and spiritual contact with the Guardians of the Mysteries. From thenceforward it becomes a centre through which they may work.

Such a great privilege brings with it increasing responsibilities, but also increased opportunity for work in the service of the Elder Brothers of humanity.

Each country has its own group of "Watchers" and the normal magical evolution of any member of that country is within the sphere of that group. But to every man his own master. Some there are, who are Easterns in Western bodies, of whom the late Annie Besant was one, but they are the exception rather than the rule.

Chapter VII

VISUALISATION AND AUDITION

FOR successful magical work it is absolutely essential that the operator should be able to build up mental images, since, as we have seen, the forces of the Astral Light are directed and controlled by such mental images. It is therefore evident that the would-be magician must gain proficiency in this image-building if he is to do any effective work.

There are several points to be remembered when one is beginning to train the mind along these lines. One, and most probably the most important of them all, is that the mind strongly opposes any attempt to train it, and will resort to the strangest of tricks in order to prevent its owner in any way attempting to do so. These psychological tricks vary from a simple forgetting to do the exercise to a very definite feeling of headache, palpitation and general malaise. The mind judges, and usually quite correctly, that any adverse physical symptons will alarm us and so tend to make us drop our training. The reason for this trait of the mind is simply that the mind is a creature of habit, and once certain patterns have been established within it, it tends to work exclusively along those lines. Any new suggestions which tend to break up the existing state of things arouse strong subconscious opposition. But if the effort is persevered in, there comes a time when the new pattern is accepted and henceforth it will be as difficult for the person concerned to revert to the earlier pattern, as it was for him to adopt the later one.

How, then, may we best go to work in this training? Modern psychologists tell us that it is impossible to stop the flow of the conscious mental images in the waking consciousness, and still remain awake and conscious. But the Yogis say it *is* possible to be fully awake and at the same time to keep the mind perfectly blank. This for them is a matter of personal experience. In practice one finds it *is* possible to keep the mind clear of images, yet alert and ready to act. But in order to do this, the mind must be trained, and the statement of the psychologists omits this consideration.

For success in this, as in all magical work, it is essential that we keep ourselves firmly anchored on the objective levels, and this is best done by building images which are mental pictures of things around us, and only when considerable proficiency has been gained should abstract and purely mental concepts be visualised.

There are two different methods of mental form-building and each complements the other. So the path of true wisdom in these matters lies midway between. Both methods should be carefully and persistently worked with, and it will be found that they both have their justification, so that one is hindered by the absence of the other.

In one case the experimenter trains the mind to construct some image, not too simple, and such construction is carefully carried out. We may term this method the "Creation of Images." The reason why the image should not be too simple is that the mind requires variety and will soon tire of a simple picture, and tend to slip away from it.

In the second case, the mind is held by the will in a quiet and passive condition, and *the images are allowed to rise* in consciousness. This method may be termed the "Evocation of Images."

Now the impressions received from the five physical senses provide excellent material for the work, and by the very fact that they *are* derived from the physical plane, they tend to keep the mind in touch with the objective realities of physical life. Although we have only referred in the title to two of the five, the visual and audible images, the images from all the senses must be worked upon. The following exercises along the two lines already indicated will show how the training works, and any amount of similar exercises can be devised by the experimenter himself. It is well to remember that the pictures seen when we are just falling asleep, or when we are just awakening, are both of the "images rising" type known to psychologists as the "hypnopompic" and "hypnogogic" images.

When the two types of exercise have been practised for a little time, it will be found that there is a very real difference between them.

The development of the power of visualisation along the lines of the "image-arising" is greatly facilitated by the exercises here given, but it must be borne in mind that the relationship between the conscious and subconscious levels of the mind, when performing these exercises, must be that of the two principals in the Tarot card "the Lovers," i.e. one of happy co-operation; not an attempt to bully the subconscious into obedience.

In this connection the remarks of a writer on Alchemy are worth remembering. He says,* and he is speaking of one aspect of the subconscious, "She yields to nothing but love." In the Tarot card above mentioned the woman looks to the angel above, whilst

---

* *Coelum Terrae*, by Thomas Vaughan (pub. 1650).

the man, representing the conscious level of the mind, looks at the woman, perceiving in her, as in a mirror, the angel she perceives directly.

Some modern systems of concentration and visualisation do try to control the subconscious by force, but the results they obtain are negligible.

Since, however, the subconscious levels are affected by the unseen psychic and psychological tides of the universe (tides which work through the magnetic sphere of the earth) it will be found in practice that there are times when it is far easier to establish the necessary contact between the conscious and subconscious levels than at others, and every apprentice to the magical art should carefully note these times and draw up a chart of their fluctuations. Then by comparing his chart with objective data, he will find that the positions of the planets and the moon seem to be linked with certain phases of the subconscious life. If this work is done steadily and conscientiously, the "dry periods," when work with the images appears almost impossible, may be checked, and provided against. It is foolish to endeavour to swim against the tide (though sometimes this must be done deliberately in order to develop independence of action). "The wise man rules his stars; the fool obeys them." This is true, but in this, as in all occult work, discrimination is the first virtue. The real virtue is to know when and how to act or refrain from action, but for the beginner it is well if he observes the set of the tides and works accordingly. At a later date he can essay the deeper waters and swim against the tides if needs be.

The regular and conscientious performance of allowing the images to rise will tend to establish a channel by which many mental conflicts which were hitherto held in the unconscious, may come up into the daylight of the conscious mind. This is all to the good for it enables the self-consciousness to deal with such repressions, to break them down and to restore the locked-up psychic energy which ensouls them, back to the general river of energy, thus increasing the available force of the individual.

There is in magical work, an operation known as exorcism, whereby "evil" spirits are driven out of the individual or place infested by them. The Christian Church, in its older branches also practises such exorcism, as also do many spiritualists. But whether it be the magician or priest or leader of a spiritualist "rescue circle," one thing *must* be done if the exorcism is to be effective: the spirit to be exorcised must first be brought into material conditions as fully as possible. It is not possible to exorcise a spirit who isn't there! So evocation must always precede exorcism.

Now the practice of allowing the images to rise does mean that the repressed complexes, which are semi-independent mental groups, and may therefore be legitimately personified as "spirits," are evoked and begin to rise, and at first it seems likely that the waking consciousness may be drowned in the rising sub-conscious sea. At a later date such a submergence, but a *willed* submergence, of the "flyer," i.e. the waking consciousness, in the "sea" or sub-consciousness, must be attempted, but at the commencement of the exercise this must not be done as it usually leads to a form of trance which is not in itself productive of anything worth while.

Notes should be kept of the complexes which arise during the period when we are doing these exercises, and it must be remembered that as the psychic energy which was locked up in those complexes is released, there will be some pretty violent emotional fluctuations taking place in consciousness. This phase, which is a definite stage on the "path of self-knowledge," must always be expected and arrangements made to deal with it. It is the period when the "dross and scum" mentioned by the alchemists begins to rise to the surface.

But the apprentice must not think that, once this mental scum has ceased to rise, the purifying process is completed. There will always be a purging process as the self advances to higher levels, but the first purging is the most obvious, the later ones are far more subtle.

Here we come to one of the uses of the method of the "creation of images." If the mind has been trained to build definite images at will, then it can build up barriers which will prevent the unwanted intrusion of these uprising thoughts and emotions, and so keep the mental field clear for whatever may arise from the depths or descend from the heights of consciousness.

The two methods employ distinct and different mental powers. In the case of the "evocation of images" the mind is brought into a controlled state of passivity and the images arise on the blank mental screen.

In the "creation of images," such images are deliberately built up by the conscious mind. In the first case, what is required is a certain psychological knack of controlling the mind. In the second case, the steady application of the will and the visualising faculty is needed.

Let us now consider the first exercise in image-building. It is a very simple one, being "Kim's game" as recorded in the book *Kim*, by Rudyard Kipling. A number of articles are placed on a tray and covered by a cloth. Then the cloth is removed and the experimenter looks at the assorted objects for one minute. Then the tray is again covered, and the student writes down the description of as many of the articles as he can remember, and their position on the tray. This sounds so very simple, but in actual practice it is much more difficult than it appears.

This exercise very often reveals to the student some of the weak spots in his mental functioning. For instance, if he finds that certain articles are almost invariably forgotten when used in this exercise, he may be fairly certain that this is due to some psychological happening in his mind, and is not simply chance.

By using the object thus indicated as the starting point of a meditation, he may be able to draw up from the depths of the subconsciousness the particular thought-complex which is causing the trouble. When the repressed emotion locked up in this complex has been discharged, it will be found that the object connected therewith has ceased to be in any way different from the other articles used in the exercise.

When comparative efficiency has been reached with this exercise, the next may be commenced. Actually it may be started at the same time, if the apprentice magician has the necessary time to devote to it. Incidentally, these exercises may be attempted at any time which is convenient, but if a regular time can be set apart for them, so much the better. There is much to be said for using a definite time for the work, but under the conditions prevailing around the student it may well be impossible to do this. This should not be regarded as a great drawback, but the exercises should be carried out when it *is* possible to do them. The ingenuity of the apprentice can be used to adapt the exercises to his daily work. For instance, a storekeeper could make his work one long exercise in "Kim's game," and as proficiency is gained, he would become a better storekeeper.

The next exercise is somewhat different. It consists of gaining the peculiar knack of the re-focussing of perception, a cardinal mental power, and is performed thus:—"Transfer the vital effort from the optic nerve to the mental perception, or thought-seeing as distinct from the seeing with the eye. Let one form of apprehension glide on into the other. Produce the reality of the dream vision by positive will in the waking state . . . . "*

* Instructions given in *The Golden Dawn*, Vol. 4, page 16.

This was the instruction given in *The Golden Dawn* in connection with what are known as the *Tattva* visions, but purely as a mental exercise it is of the greatest value. Actually it is twofold, for it should also be practised "in reverse," i.e. efforts should be made to transfer a mental picture into apparent objectivity so that it may be seen, apparently, by the physical sense. Actually of course, it is not seen by the physical eye (except in certain rare cases) but it appears to be observed. The vision seen by a clairvoyant seer in a crystal or black mirror is an example of such a "projected" mental picture. It is well to remember that this is a *willed or voluntary projection,* since it is a characteristic of certain forms of psychopathology that such projections of mental pictures occur to the sufferer, but are *involuntary.* It is well, therefore, if the student always so arranges this particular exercise as to make it an entirely voluntary happening. *It should never be done except when he wills to do it, and this must never be when he is occupied with the ordinary mundane duties.* Also, and this too is important, he must carefully select the thought picture which he wishes to project, and must not allow (at least for this exercise) any chance mental picture to be used.

The present writer has found that one of the best ways of carrying out the first part of this exercise is to place the object in a good light on a monochrome surface, either dark or light, and use a paper or cardboard tube some eight inches long and two and a half inches inside diameter, through which to gaze at it, using the left and right eyes alternately. Or the tube may be made rectangular, so that both eyes may be used at the same time. Then, as the object is being steadily held in the field of vision, the eyes should be slightly thrown out of focus, as we sometimes do when we are "day-dreaming," and the visual picture now apparently brought mentally *within* the head. This is a psychological "trick" which is usually only acquired after a great deal of effort and failure. It is analogous to the knack of learning to balance when we first attempt to ride a bicycle. Once the knack has been gained, it will be found increasingly easy to bring this visual image into mental apprehension. A further development is to close the eyes—during the first attempts only slightly, then more fully in subsequent ones, until the final stage is reached when the student is able to see clearly inside his head, as it were, the picture of the object concerned, his eyes being closed in the meantime.

Once this has been accomplished, and practise has made it fairly easy, the complementary half should be essayed. The object chosen should be observed, and the perception transferred in the usual way to the subjective mental screen. Meanwhile a monochrome surface, such as a white disc on a black surround, or a black disc on a white surround, or a crystal or black concave mirror, should have been placed so that the student can use it as a screen upon which to project his mental picture.

He should now open his eyes sufficiently to see the disc or mirror (which should be in a dim light) whilst still holding the picture on the mental screen. Then by a quiet, calm effort of will he should project the picture outwardly onto the screen.

Again, there is a psychological knack to be gained, but once it *is* gained, and stabilised by subsequent practise, a very great step forward has been taken. It must again be emphasised that this projection should only be done deliberately at the will of the apprentice magician, *and any involuntary projections should be sternly resisted.*

When the knack has been gained, it is possible to project such a mental image so clearly that it is to all intents and purposes as though one were perceiving it with the physical eyes.

A further stage in this mental projection is one which is not often met with outside the occult lodges. It is possible, if the magician has the materialising type of body, or can employ a materialising medium, to cause such mental images to be clothed with ectoplasmic substance and become visible to the physical senses of all present.

Another way in which an apparent objectivity can be given to the projected images, is by a process of "telepathic radiation." Here the projected image, localised in one point of space, becomes what the psychic researchers term a "phantasmogenetic centre," and the simultaneous telepathic radiation by the magician induces what is known as a "collective hallucination" in those around. Again, this is not usually experienced outside the lodges, except apparently accidentally.

The technique of this latter method depends upon certain training which allows the conscious mind to be more closely linked with its subconscious levels. The magical feat known as the "Operation of Invisibility" is based on this technique, though, in some cases, something more enters into it, for the ectoplasmic substance can produce some very unusual effects. The present writer once took a photo of a high grade occultist. On developing the film, there was no trace of the figure of the person concerned, though all the chair in which he was sitting at the time showed quite clearly. It was just as though a photo had been taken of an empty chair. In the East there is a tradition of such "*akashic* shields" which can produce invisibility, and it may be that further research into the properties of the substance we know of as "ectoplasm" will bring new facts to light, bearing upon this subject. In the case of the purely mental operation of invisibility, it is to be remembered that we normally notice those things which either strike us forcibly, or in which we have some definite interest, or which are sufficiently isolated as to attract our attention. But a great deal of what we see is not noticed consciously at all, though, as hypnotic experiments prove, the memory is retained in the mind and can be brought up into consciousness.

If, therefore, the one who wishes to be unnoticed adapts such mannerisms, or alters any unusual appearance he may have, it is quite possible for him to pass in a crowd without being noticed by us. If, in addition, he has gained the knack of telepathic suggestion, then he affects those around him as the hypnotist affects his entranced subject, when he tells her that she will be unable to see another person who is in the room.*

The occultist, Dion Fortune, termed this particular occult operation "psychological hocus pocus," and so it can be. But just as "hocus pocus" is the ultra-protestant garbling of the Words of Consecration in the Roman Church, "*Hoc est Corpus Meum,*" . . . so the operation of invisibility is a misuse (as a general rule) of that mighty power within by means of which the trained magician may produce changes of consciousness in others. It will be remembered that we referred to the two types of magician, and here we have them at work. In all magical work these two types will be found, but trouble arises when one school of thought dwells exclusively upon one or other aspect. However, the physical materialisation of the image is much more uncommon than the collective mental, but it does take place.

So far we have been dealing with visual form building, but the training of the magician extends to *all* the senses. The technique we have here given for visual work, should be extended to cover all the other senses. In practice it will be found that the usual scale of success in these evokings will be headed by either visual or audible images, followed by taste, smell, and touch, in that order.

When training for audible image-making, the use of a gradually diminishing sound, such as the note of a tuning fork is a great help,

---

* The story given in St. Luke, Chap. V, 30, suggests that Jesus made use of such an operation of invisibility on occasion.

and the projection of the audible images is assisted by using the old gipsy trick of "listening to the sea" in the large sea-shells, so commonly used as ornaments in Victorian times. If we wish to provide a more modern "audible screen" upon which we may project our audible image, we may use a pair of headphones which are energised by an electric current so regulated as to give a steady "note" in the phones, and capable of being so adjusted as to allow of varying notes being used. This variation in the audible screen is the analogy in sound of the "Flashing Colours" used in the meditations based on the glyph of the Tree of Life. As with the visual work, so in the audible; *involuntary audible projections* must be absolutely left out. If they persist, a visit to a good psychologist (preferably one of the School of Jung) is indicated, together with an immediate cessation of all magical work.

It is no part of the magical training that one shall acquire new powers at the expense of one's sanity. It is for this reason that the genuine occult schools and orders insist that any "natural psychic" who wishes to join them, must close down his faculties until he has been thoroughly trained along the occult line; and experience has proved the necessity for this rule, which is found in both Eastern and Western traditions.

When doing the audible exercises, a very good method is the following, which has been used successfully by the present writer. It involves co-operation with a sympathetic helper, so under certain circumstances it may be out of court, but where it can be used it is very effective.

Let the helper, whose voice should be familiar to you, speak slowly in his normal voice, taking some piece of poetry or some general piece of reading. Using the same method as in the visual work, transfer perception to the mental levels. (After a minute. the helper should stop speaking and remain quiet).

When the shift of audible perception has become fairly easy, the reverse projection should be attempted, the shell or earphones brought into use, and the audible images projected until they appear objective.

A further stage, when this proficiency has been attained in some measure at least, is to "hear imaginatively" someone, whose voice is familiar to you, giving a lecture. The lecture must first be formulated by you, but at some one point you should cease to formulate and simply "listen" mentally; the subconscious will carry on the lecture, and you will simply listen to it. The final stage of this is when the audible images are projected and you hear the voice apparently objectively.* Again the warning: projection of the audible images MUST BE VOLUNTARY and under the control of the waking self.

This exercise is invaluable when the student essays the work of the "Chaldean method," where the Names of Power are "vibrated." When the mental training has been brought to a fair pitch of proficiency the visual and audible images arising will be capable of being used for purposes of communication between the conscious and superconscious levels of the student's nature, and will form the basis of the voluntary and controlled psychism which is required for the deeper ranges of the work.

The student from his own *ingenium* will be able to construct similar exercises for the other three senses.

It is important to relax thoroughly before attempting these exercises, and slow deep breathing should be employed in order to reduce the excessive speed of the mental action.

If these exercises are carried out methodically until proficiency is gained, the apprentice magician will be equipped for the next stage of his training.

---

* This gives a clue to the phenomena known to the spiritualists as "direct voice." The direct voice medium is of the physical or materialising type, and discarnate entities produce through him the same phenomena as those produced by the voluntary effort of the magician who has the natural materialising type of body.

Chapter VIII

WORDS OF POWER: THE MAGICAL USE OF SOUND

MOSTof us have memories of the many stories told us in our childhood wherein were certain words and phrases which were held to have magical power and significance. The "Open Sesame" of Ali Baba's treasure cave, the "Abracadabra" of the magician, and many more such magical phrases, all focussed our attention upon the possibilities latent within certain words and names. But we were not unique in this. In all ages, and in all parts of the world, the idea that names and words had magical power has been held.

More particularly in the East this subject has been made the object of deep study and research, though our own Western Scriptures show that the same idea was held by the people from whom much of our Christian teaching was primarily derived. It was an ancient Mystery teaching that "God spake, and the worlds became," and this idea underlines both the teaching of the Alexandrian Jew, Philo, and that of the author of the magnificent prologue to the Gospel of St. John.

In the Old Testament we read of the Creator giving a name to the first man, and then that first man giving a name to the first woman. We read also that the animals were brought before Adam and by whatsoever name he called them, that was their name. (The present writer, as a child, regarded this naming feat of Adam as something in the nature of a major miracle! To invent names for all living animals seemed to call for supernatural imagination.)

Later we read of Abram, whose name was changed to Abraham, and we learn, too, of the wrestling of Jacob with the Angel at the ford, "Except thou tell me thy Name, I will not let thee go," and we are told that because he had so wrestled with the Angel of the Presence, his name was changed to Israel ("Striver with God").

Later comes the account of the Theophany in the Burning Bush, when Moses was given the Name of his God. This Name which is translated in the Authorised Version as I Am That I Am, is, in the Hebrew, *Ehieh Asher Ehieh*, which Moffat translates as I Will Be What I Will Be, and this seems a far better rendering of the Hebrew; I have been told by a Hebrew scholar that it could be even more truly translated as I Am The Ever-Becoming.

But the sacred Name *par excellence* amongst the Hebrews was the Tetragrammaton, or Four Lettered Name. So sacred was it held to be, that a substitute Name, Adonai (My Lord) was used. In Christian usage, the Tetragrammaton has been turned into the name Jehovah, but, in point of fact, this particular form seems to have been either invented or copied from some unknown source by Tyndale, in whose translation of the Bible it appears for the first time.

Some may here protest that the books of the Old Testament are simply the record of the ethical and philosophical progress of a wandering Bedouin tribe, as it enlarged its concepts from the god who walked in the garden in the cool of the day, as any other eastern chief might do, to the magnificent conception of the post-exilic prophet "Thus saith the High and Holy One Who inhabiteth Eternity, Whose Name is Holy." A progress, moreover, which brought it as a nation to a monotheism not apparent in any contemporary nation. This, of course, is true, but there are other angles of approach, the normal Christian view that the Hebrews were being *guided by the Eternal* into larger concepts is one such angle, and there is another which is of greater relevance to the subject of Words of Power. The ancient Rabbis said that the Torah: the Law, was the Body, but the Qabalah was the spirit of their religion. So the record of the history of the Hebrews, interwoven as it is with the folklore of the race and the racial memories of Abraham's descendants, is but the outer appearance. Within this outer appearance was, and is, concealed that towering metaphysical system which we know of as the Qabalah. As the word implies, the teaching of the Qabalah was transmitted "from mouth to ear" until about the 12th century, when certain of its teachings were published in book form.

These Qabalistic books formed the basis of the great systems of magic which sprang up in the West in the Middle Ages, and in these magical systems Names and Words of Power played a very great part. As we shall see at a later point, the Names of Power of the Qabalah form a very interesting group of magical sound-forms.

In the folklore of many nations and races, the use of Words of Power, of "charms" and "spells" is to be found, but in the East there has been built up a massive system of philosophy, based upon and constantly checked by a mass of experimental data.

This system is usually referred to as "Mantra Yoga," and its fullest exposition is to be found in the Tantric work known as *The Garland of Letters*.

The Christian Church in its pilgrimage through the ages has

accumulated much which has reference to our subject. By the term "Christian Church" is meant not only the more orthodox and "respectable" streams of its being, the great Catholic Churches of the Eastern and Western Obediences together with the various Reformed and Nonconforming Churches, but also some of the many heretical sects which have "hived off" from the main stream of Christian tradition. The Gnostics of the early Church formed a group of such sects, and their teachings have for many centuries been regarded as heretical and evil. In some of its aspects the Gnostic teaching certainly justifies such condemnation though modern scholarship has done much to rehabilitate some of the most prominent teachers of the Gnosis.

But quite apart from their specific theological views, the Gnostics placed very great stress upon the efficacy of names and sounds. By the name, declared some of them, Jesus worked His miracles, a name which He had stolen from the Holy of Holies of the temple. By the mystery of the name, declared another writer, was man's regeneration and deification effected, and in his knowledge of his own true name, lay his true peace.

Coming down to more recent times we find a floating tradition of a language "spoken in Paradise" the sound of which gave mastery over nature. Some curious communications received by the Elizabethan occultist and astrologer, Dr. John Dee gave fragments of what was called "The Enochian Tongue," and as Casaubon has shown, it was no mere gibberish, but possessed grammatical form and syntax.

In the latter part of the eighteenth century there arose in Poland a curious Qabalistic sect known as the "Chassidim." Some of its members were known as "the wonder-working rabbis," and these wonder-workers made great use of the Sacred Names. The leader of the Chassidim was Rabbi Israel Baal Shem Tov, "The Master of the Divine Name." In some of the circles of the Chassidim the language of Paradise was heard, and by its use the rabbis worked wonders and showed signs.

The revival of the Western occult tradition through the Order of the Golden Dawn and its offshoot *Stella Matutina* made use of both the Enochian language and the Qabalistic Words of Power, and, indeed, for the construction and use of the Telesmatic Images such words are essential.

Today, in countless ways the glamour of the Words of Power and the Magical Names still persists for many millions of people, and in the new political groupings which are emerging upon the world-stage we are witnessing the actual birth of such words and names which will in the years to come be charged with magical power over the minds and hearts of men.

Before we commence to study what we may term the more "occult" aspects of sound, it is as well to spend some time in considering the subject from the purely physical point of view. We may define it as a series of vibrations set up in matter. These vibrations are not all audible to the human ear, which can only receive within certain fairly definite limits. An empiric test of the range of human audition may be made by trying to hear the high-pitched cry of the bat, at one end of the scale, and the deep note of the diapason pipe of a large organ. It will be found that to many people, the bat's cry is inaudible, and many more will confess that they do not *hear*, but rather they *feel* the vibration of the diapason pipe. There is another proof of the limited range of human hearing in the curious "supersonic whistle" sometimes used as a dog-whistle. The sound given out by this whistle is far beyond the range of human perception, but immediately attracts the attention of all dogs within its radius.

Sound does not only travel through air, but also is transmitted through water, earth, and all material substances, and the contours of the ocean floor and the depths of mineral lodes in the earth have both been investigated by the reflection of sound waves. It is important to remember that although we *hear* sound by means of specialised sense-organs, we are actually bathed in a sea of sound all our lives. The intensity of sound is measured in terms of a standard unit, the "decibell," and it has been found that there is what may be described as a danger-point in the amount of sound to which human beings may safely be subjected. In actual practice it is found that the conditions of some of our large industrial cities come very near this danger line as do also some factory conditions. In studying the occult effects of sound, this must always be remembered. We are apt to limit its effects upon us solely to our auditory consciousness, but a little thought will make us aware that of course the sound which strikes upon our eardrums is only a small part of the actual sound vibration, and it is this greater part which is striking both upon one's body and upon the surrounding surfaces. This is, of course, well recognised when we are dealing with "acoustics" in connection with the sound-reflecting properties of public halls, churches, etc., but is liable to be overlooked when dealing with sound from the purely "occult" point of view.

In the latter part of last century, Mrs. Watts-Dunton Hughes invented a curious little instrument known as the "Eidophone." It was really an adaptation of what are known as "Chladni's Figures," an experiment in which a violin bow was drawn gently along the edge of a plate of glass covered with fine sand. The vibrations set up by the bow caused the sand to take up definite patterns. The Eidophone consisted of a cylinder over the open end of which was stretched a rubber diaphragm. Into the side of the cylinder was built a metal trumpet which served as a concentrator of sound. Upon the rubber diaphragm was sprinkled the fine spore-dust of the common "puff-ball" (*Lycopodium*). When anyone spoke or sang into the instrument, the lycopodium powder formed itself into intricate patterns, and these patterns were constant for any given sound or note. By lowering a prepared paper onto the surface of the diaphragm, a permanent record of the sound-form could be obtained, but of course, it is obvious that the actual sound vibration is three-dimensional. In recent times one American Rosicrucian organisation has perfected an instrument by means of which such three-dimensional sound forms may be viewed.

Some of the sound-form patterns are wonderfully intricate and they show how the sound vibrations affect surrounding matter. The long-continued sounding of one particular note tends to set up a sympathetic vibration or resonance in all the surrounding matter, and this sympathetic vibration may have queer effects. It is recorded that on one occasion, when a military band was playing beneath the walls of an old ruin, they played a piece which was apparently based upon the dominant "note" of the wall, which collapsed upon them! For this reason, soldiers, when marching over a light bridge are ordered to "break step," i.e. to walk out-of-step and unrhythmically, in order to avoid setting up a vibrational "swing" in the bridge structure. In the light of these things, the story of the fall of Jericho as recorded in the Bible may be profitably studied.

The converse side of this is to be seen in the stimulating effect upon wearied men of a stirring military march tune, and this brings us to another point. We have so far been studying the effects of sympathetic vibration upon material structures, but its power extends much further. It has tremendous effect upon the mind and the emotion, and not all of this effect is produced in the surface consciousness.

Chapter IX

THE WORDS AND NAMES IN MAGICAL WORKING

IN the Magical Workings, it has been found that in order efficiently to use the Words and Names of Power, certain methods must be used. The value of the Words and Names depends upon two things. The first is their own intrinsic power as vibratory forms of energy which by their correspondence with certain superphysical forms of force can act as the means whereby the forces of the Inner Planes may affect the physical levels. The other is the psychic "charge" which is stored up in the "thought-forms" which are linked with them.

In considering the first point, we may make it more clear by asking the question "If a gramophone record of a Word of Power were played in an empty room, would it produce any result, or is the effect of such a word simply dependent upon the associations in the minds of those who have been conditioned to it?"

The Swedish seer, Swedenborg, taught that the different planes of the universe were each separate from the other; were "discrete," not "continuous." Certain "occult" teaching at the present day seems to contradict this, but from both the arcane tradition and from personal experience many believe the Swedenborgian teaching to be correct. But, although the planes are separate manifestations, so that, for instance, those on the astral plane cannot *normally* perceive physical matter, and those on the physical plane cannot *normally* perceive astral matter, there are two definite points of contact between the planes. The first of these is what in the philosophy of the Qabalah is known as the *Mezla*, the divine spiritual influence which is the impelling cause behind the activities of all the manifested universe, and which by its presence binds all the diversities into a unity. This Divine Life pervading all things does therefore link all the planes together, and therefore to that extent they *are* continuous. Since the vibration-ratios of the Words and Names have their basis in the ultimate archetypal life, then if they are sounded forth, they will link the planes. Apart from this, also, the elemental life-wave which is even now pouring into this universe constitutes what may be described as the "life-side" of matter. All matter is, in its degree, living matter; there is no such thing as "dead" matter in the material sense of the word. All creation is alive, it is the luminous living garment of the Eternal. This again the Chaldean Oracles declare.

So our gramophone record, if played in an empty room, will cause certain things to happen. The physical matter of the walls of the room will be set into sympathetic vibration, and its living or "etheric" aspect will begin to act as a channel of energy between the inner and outer planes. But because the type of consciousness which is the vital principle of physical matter is of an extremely simple and primitive type, the simple vibration of the word or name will not produce much of a positive nature, unless something else, some other factor, is brought into play. This other factor is *organized consciousness*, and more especially *concentrated self-consciousness*. If the vibration of the word or name is imposed upon someone who has, by the active use of his self-conscious will, attuned himself to the energies of which the word is an expression, then such a one is a true mediator between the planes, and the power of the higher is brought through into the lower by his activities. If now, several people work together in the same way, then they form a united link between the planes; a link which is not merely the mathematical sum of their minds, but which is far greater than that. So two or three gathered together may well transmit more power than ten or twenty persons who are each working individually. It is for this reason that all the great religions have developed a corporate aspect. In fact, in Christianity this concept of the corporate nature of the Church is an integral part of its philosophy.

If, moreover, the word be vibrated by the group, the results will be correspondingly greater than if they are merely being sounded in the presence of such listeners. But this matter of "vibrating" a Name of Power is somewhat difficult to explain and even more difficult to teach. It is a psychological "trick" somewhat akin to that whereby, quite suddenly, the beginner on the bicycle suddenly finds himself balancing the machine and actually riding.

The only way in which the practice of vibrating the names can be indicated is to say that the voice must be made as vibrant as is possible, and this is best done by deliberately lowering the key of the voice and at the same time endeavouring to hold in the mind, as clearly as possible, the idea or group of ideas which are associated with the particular name or Word of Power. An interesting exercise in this vibration of the names is to vibrate the name in the palm of the hand, or from the solar plexus, or from the forehead. This at first sight seems an absurdity, but with steady practise the student suddenly finds himself able to locate the vibratory power in the hand or elsewhere. When this has taken place, it becomes easy to extend the practice to any other part of the body, and this can have a very beneficial effect upon the health of the part so "vibrated."

Now there are four kinds of vibration which we may use for our Words of Power. They are rhythm, pitch, vowel sounds and consonantal sounds. The first two can be produced on musical instruments, the other two by the voice. To induce emotional states, rhythm is the greatest of them all, and this rhythm can be regular or irregular. Syncopation is an example of rhythm-and-break which has an enormous value in the evocation of certain emotional states. There are sounds which affect the subconsciousness, even though the conscious mind may not like them at all. They are the mental analogues to the condiments of the dinner-table acting as emotional irritants and stimulants. It is evident, however, that like the condiments, they should only be taken in small doses.

There are certain factors in ceremonial magic which make for success. One, which has been dealt with elsewhere, is incense; the other is "chanting." Now there are chants many, and in the religious field one which has always been a very great help in corporate worship is the so-called "Gregorian." Its peculiar bar-less beat is extraordinarily efficacious in magical work. Now the ideal magical chant must appeal to the subconsciousness, and part of this subconsciousness is very primitive. Hence, the chant needs reiteration. But the reiteration of the same musical phrase can be very boring to the conscious mind, and for this reason the chant must be strongly rhythmical and its reiteration must be made to rise and fall by *change of key*.

We are accustomed in the Western world to music which is constructed round the pitch commonly known as "concert pitch," and it is to this that the ordinary piano is tuned. But the music of the *mantra* is half a tone lower, the so-called "primitive" pitch, and rises and falls in quarter-tones.

To anyone hearing this *mantric* music for the first time, it usually brings a feeling of exasperation, especially as the full singing voice is not used, but it is a matter of practical experience that the magical chanting when done at the ordinary pitch and with the ordinary singing voice is practically ineffective.

Before we leave the subject of Words and Names of Power, there is another aspect of the use of vibrations which we can consider with profit. This is the use of our own personal name for certain occult and magical work. By the personal name we do not necessarily mean the name which our fond parents bestowed upon

us as a result of an endeavour to incorporate as many of the family
names as possible in ours, nor yet the name which they took from
their favourite novel! One knows how soon, when school-days
commence, we receive what we call a "nick-name," and it is this
which is the personal name, since it is usually the result of subconscious perception on the part of our fellow-pupils, and fits
our personality quite well. Sometimes, of course, our baptismal
name seems to be found to fit our personality, and we never seem
to get a "nick-name." In this case, the baptismal name *is* the personal name.

The poet Tennyson, in private conversation used to refer to an
experience he had when, repeating aloud his own personal name;
he suddenly passed into a curious trance in which he became aware
of some greater aspect of himself. He used this experience as the
basis for the poem "The Ancient Sage." In this poem he makes the
Sage say : —

> And more than once, my son, As I sat all alone,
> Revolving in myself the word that is the symbol of myself;
> The mortal limit of the self was loosed and passed into the
>   Nameless,
> As a cloud melts into heaven.

The Sage goes on to say that he found himself with a body of
a different order, and with a consciousness which far transcended
his waking mind. This experience, one type of the so-called "astral
projection," has been recorded by many occultists, and the use of
the personal name for this purpose is definitely taught in certain
occult schools.

Chapter X

THE FLASHING COLOURS

I N practical magical work, the Qabalistically trained magician
makes great use of the technical device known as "The Flashing
Colours." But the rationale of the technique has been little understood even by those who have successfully employed it. It may be
said that there are several keys to the use of the flashing colours,
and only one of these is dealt with here.

It is, of course, not essential for the magician to understand the
mental and psychic machinery he is using, but when it is possible
to obtain such an understanding, it enables him to use the method
to greater advantage. It is for this reason that a brief consideration
of the technique of the flashing colours has been included here. It
will be clear to the reader that colour is of primary importance in
the magical work, and, in fact is one of its chief keys. Briefly, the
magician employs colour as a means of "tuning-in" to the various
forces with which he is dealing. We have said in another part of
this book that the magician is in the same position as regards his
art, as the violinist is in regard to his music. Both have to make
their own "notes," psychic or musical, and in the case of the magician, the psychic tuning-in is based upon a methodical building up
of symbols, colours and sounds all linked together by certain mental
and emotional concepts. Each Sephirah on the Tree of Life, and
each of the twenty-two Paths which connect the Sephiroth, is
coloured according to a traditional system. This system, which has
been handed down in the esoteric schools through many generations
of students is, as we have already said, partly based on actual
correspondence between the colour, sound and symbol, and the
actual nature of that aspect of the universe and the soul of man
which is being dealt with. But there are many such attributions
which are arbitrary, and which do not have any factual relationship
with the aspect concerned. Nevertheless, if the constant use of them
over the generations has built them into the psychic structure of
the magical *Egregore*, then such a magical correspondence will have
been established. This applies to the whole of the magical art. To
give out the principle involved in the use of the colour scales is
exceedingly difficult, but perhaps the consideration of the ordinary
musical scale may be helpful. If we study the action of the ordinary
piano, we find a large number of wires of increasingly finer diameter, and these wires, when struck, give out sounds varying from

Station on Tree	Atziluth	Briah	Yetzirah	Assiah
KETHER	BRILLIANCE	PURE WHITE BRILLIANCE	PURE WHITE BRILLIANCE	WHITE GOLD-FLECKED
CHOKMAH	PURE, SOFT BLUE	GREY	PEARL-GREY IRIDISCENT	WHITE RED, BLUE & YELLOW FLECKS
BINAH	CRIMSON	BLACK	DARK BROWN	GREY PINK FLECKS
GEDULAH (Chesed)	DEEP VIOLET	DEEP BLUE	DEEP PURPLE	DEEP AZURE YELLOW FLECKS
GEBURAH (Pachad)	ORANGE	SCARLET RED	BRIGHT SCARLET	RED BLACK FLECKS
TIPHARETH	CLEAR ROSE-PINK	YELLOW	RICH SALMON PINK	GOLDEN AMBER
NETZACH	AMBER	EMERALD	BRIGHT YELLOWISH GREEN	OLIVE GOLD FLECKS
HOD	VIOLET PURPLE	ORANGE	RUSSET RED	YELLOWISH BLACK WHITE FLECKS
YESOD	INDIGO	VIOLET	DARK PURPLE	CITRINE AZURE FLECKS
MALKUTH	YELLOW	CITRINE OLIVE RUSSET BLACK	CITRINE OLIVE RUSSET BLACK GOLD FLECK	BLACK RAYED YELLOW

THE COLOUR SCALES

THE PRINCIPLE OF THE FLASHING COLOURS

a very deep-sounding note at one end of the keyboard, to a very high shrill note at the other. In between, we have several eightfold divisions. If, for the sake of the argument, we have four such divisions, then we may name them A, B, C and D. Now we may number each thus:—A1, 2, 3, 4, 5, 6, 7, B1, 2, 3, 4, 5, 6, 7, C1, 2, 3, 4, 5, 6, 7, D1, 2, 3, 4, 5, 6, 7. Then B is the end of the series A—B, and the beginning of series B—C, and C is the end of the series B—C and the beginning of series C—D.

Or to use the terms of the Qabalah, B is the *Malkuth* of A—B, and the *Kether* of B—C. Whereas in music we have an eightfold scale, in the Qabalistic system we have a tenfold scale, but the principle is the same. In musical practice we have taken a certain section of the gamut of vibrations which lie around us, audible section, and have established a certain arbitrary musical code upon it. In magical practice we have taken that vibrational range, all of it, and have established thereon a similar code of interpretation. The magical notation is to be found in the "Tree of Life" and its associated correspondences and the relationships involved are indicated by the flashing colours.

Some of the colour attributions seem to be very arbitrary, and have been over-complicated by some of the leaders of the modern esoteric schools. There are actually four colour-scales in connection with the Tree of Life. These are known as the King, Queen, Emperor and Empress Scales.

When we consider the complexity of the scheme of four complete Trees with their appropriate colour scales, we may be excused if we feel that the subject has been unduly complicated. But although for most purposes we can use the first two colour scales only, we must not forget that more advanced work will necessitate the use of the other two. However, for ordinary work the first two scales, the "King" and "Queen" scales will be sufficient, and they have been included herein.

It is important to remember that these scales are tuning-in devices, and before they can be of any great use to us, we must build them into our consciousness.

This building-in is dual. There is first the definite visualisation and conscious building up of the colours concerned, together with a conscious presentation of the philosophical concept which is represented by the Sephirah with which we are dealing. Reference to Dion Fortune's *Mystical Qabalah* and Regardies *Tree of Life* will give the particular philosophical concepts required. But when the colour connected with a certain Sephirah has been built into the consciousness and linked with its appropriate concept, we have done only half the work. This complete visual and philosophical "constellation" or associated thought-group must now be passed through the dividing veil, or rather the threshold of the subconscious must be raised until the thought-group can be taken up by it. This is the "willed co-operation" of which we will speak in the chapter on "The Subconscious," and this willed co-operation or auto-hypnosis is accomplished by the use of the technical device of the flashing colours.

What do we mean by a "flashing colour"? The usual authorities give a quasi-mystical explanation which, although true is no real explanation, merely a "blind," which puts the frivolous off the scent. Not that the frivolous could employ the technique of the flashing colours to any real purpose; they have not the application and perseverence required!

They may essay the use of the flashing colours, with the most curious results, but the essence of the matter eludes them. So we may quite openly describe the use of the flashing colours as a technical Qabalistic method of auto-hypnosis. This auto-hypnosis is produced by the utilisation of a simple optical effect. As we have noted in our remarks on the *Tattvic* tides, if one gazes for any length of time at a coloured disc or other figure, and then looks away at any white screen one sees thereon the outline of the figure one has been gazing at, but in the *complementary* colour. Thus, if we have been gazing at a red disc, we shall see the complementary image of the disc on the white screen, but its colour will be a vivid *green* which is the complementary colour of red.

If now we construct a red disc whose surface is cut in facets or outlined in diamond shapes, and in the centre of each red facet we insert a brilliant green point, then we have a device which can prove very effective in bringing about this "willed co-operation" between the conscious and subconscious levels.

As we gaze quietly at it, *centring our attention upon the red "field,"* there comes a time when the muscles of the eye relax slightly, and its focus alters. Then immediately the complementary green flashes up, and at the same time the complementary red of the green "charges" flashes up, and the result is that the disc appears to be alive with brilliant flashes of red and green. Quiet and prolonged gaze at this "flashing tablet" will induce a condition wherein we are tuned in to the particular psychic energy in both ourselves and in the objective planes which is represented by the "field" colour red.

So the flashing tablet is a true contacting device which has the advantage of having a definite physical plane basis, and being therefore a more stable link than a purely mental image.

In constructing such a flashing tablet it is necessary to get clearly fixed in the mind the fact that the *ground* colour is the key colour with which we are working. The "charge" colour placed on the ground is the complementary. Thus in our example, the colour *red* is the one we are working with, as we wish in this case to contact the energies of the Sephirah *Geburah* on the Tree.

It is important to note that for meditative work alone, we can use the second colour-scale, so that our work remains subjective. This is very important, especially in the early stages of training. To make contact suddenly with the objective energies concerned can be very startling, to say the least.

Chapter XI

THE VESTMENTS

AS we have seen, when we considered the colour scales, the various levels of the Unseen are symbolised each by their own colour. Though in some cases these symbols may be arbitrary and bear little initial correspondence to the plane they symbolise, yet if they have been in use long enough, they will have been built into the *Egregore* and will therefore be effective in keying the student to that particular level. If they are truly in correspondence with the plane concerned, their power will be proportionately greater. In this matter there exists a great need for a thorough revision of much of the magical tradition. One of the weak points of the Order of the Golden Dawn was its excessive eclecticism. It tried to include far too much, and some very doubtful attributions crept into use. Though through use these attributions do act as channels of power, a good deal would be gained if they were, by process of neglect and the cultivation of the true correspondence, allowed to slip back into disuse.

But the use of the colours is fundamental. They are to be found throughout the whole magical scheme, and the use of the Flashing Colours is foundation work.

As the colours key us to certain forces, it follows that the use of vestments of the appropriate colour will help us to link up with those forces. That is the simple rationale of the vestments. Since the Western Tradition has been strongly influenced by the Greek, Hebrew and Egyptian traditions on the one hand and the mediæval Catholic Church on the other, it will be found that the robes worn in the magical fraternities reflect one or other of these sources. Many of them are magnificent pieces of work, but it is necessary for the student to remember that their value does not depend merely upon their magnificence. Plain robes of the appropriate colour are every bit as effective as the most exotic designs!

Apart from their value as "colour-suggestions," they serve a very useful purpose; they screen off the personality of the operator, and so make for impersonality.

This is of very great importance, especially when magical work is being done by a group comprising both sexes. In some lodges, cowls or hoods are used, and this gives even greater impersonality.

The robes have another interesting effect. They act as a very strong auto-suggestion, which has the power of keying the mind to the operation in hand. Merely to vest oneself in the robes of one's grade automatically quickens the emotional link which we have with our group or fraternity. This is a great help in the first part of a magical rite, when we are concerned with the operation of the "Preparation of the Place of Working."

From another angle, the robes are of use. During the many magical operations undertaken through the years, the robes become "charged" with a certain etheric energy or "magnetism," and though the fairly frequent cleaning processes, which are necessary, though not always carried out, will disperse some of this magnetism, they soon become charged up again. In this state they play a part in the interplay of etheric forces which occurs in the Magical Lodge.

A word of warning. When you have once used your magical robe, *never under any conditions,* thereafter use it for any purely secular purpose; never parade it before others even in private, and never, never follow the example of one lady, an actress of note and a prominent member of the Hermetic Order of the Golden Dawn, who attended a fancy-dress ball clad in the robes of her grade in the order!*

---

* The present writer once broke this rule—and on entering his lodge some days later, was greatly surprised to receive a thorough "telling-off" from the ruler of his degree, whose clairvoyant faculty had evidently made him aware of the incident which had happened several miles away, and of which he could not normally have been aware. It was a salutary lesson!

Chapter XII

THE SUBCONSCIOUS

A certain knowledge of psychology is necessary if the apprentice magician is to make the most use of his art, but this psychological knowledge must always be "held lightly." What a short time ago was termed "The New Psychology" has developed so swiftly that it now suffers from *embarasse de richesse* and the beginner finds it most difficult to follow intelligently the intellectual mazes of the Freudian, Jungian and Adlerian Schools of Psychology, to mention only the primary schools. The many schools depending upon these three, but expressing themselves from differing angles, need not be mentioned here, since their general teaching is the same.

What are the simple outlines? This question is most difficult to answer, since any simplification is bound to omit points which seem to many to be of primary importance.

What we will here attempt is not a simplification of modern psychological theories, but rather a restatement in psychological terms of the magical teaching concerning the mind of man; or rather, to be more exact, the soul of man.

The first point to be considered is the nature of the soul, and here the magical schools declare with one voice, that man is a Spark of the Eternal Flame, a "god" in the making. This is the true man, the "Indweller of Light," as the old Gnostics termed him.

This immortal Self, for reasons which lie outside our present terms of reference, is making contact with, and manifesting in, the material worlds of physical and super-physical matter.

The instrument by means of which this contact and manifestation is maintained, is known as the "personality," and it is indeed, as the etymology of the word suggests, a *persona* or mask through which the true self works.

So we come to the statement ascribed to the old Greek initiates "I am a child of earth, but my Race is from the Starry Heavens."

The personality we may term "the lower self." Now the mind of man* is the point of contact between these two aspects of himself, and we therefore find that part of his mind is conditioned by, and linked to, his immortal Self, whilst the other part is linked to, and conditioned by, his material consciousness. Now the material consciousness is largely built up through the perceptions of the material

---

* The word "man" is derived from the Sanscrit *Manas* which means, "the thinker."

senses and more particularly through the perceptions of the five physical senses. This aspect of the mind is usually referred to as "the lower" mind, and together with the emotional aspect of our natures, it makes up what the Qabalists term the *Ruach* or "Reasonable Soul." This *Ruach* is the instrument of the Higher Self, its mask or *persona*, and it is here that what has sometimes been called the "false ego" is centred. This false "I", which seems to the ordinary person to *be* himself, is in reality an illusion in so far as it is thought to be the true Ego.

Below the *Ruach* or Reasonable Soul, we come to the *Nephesh* or Animal Soul, and this can be equated psychologically with the subconscious. Perhaps the Jungian term "Personal Unconscious" is a more correct term.

All the aspects of man centre in and are expressed through the *Guph* or physical body, and here it must be remembered that as psycho-somatic medicine has pointed out, there is no separate physical body, it is one aspect of the living whole, and is in very truth the Temple of the Holy Ghost.

Now the subconsciousness is related most closely to that system of nerves known as the "sympathetic system," and it is this sympathetic or involuntary nerve system which carries on the multitudinous activities of the physical organism—the processes of digestion and elimination, the beating of the heart, the respiratory action and the complex activities of the glands. All these, which now are automatic or subconscious activities, were at one time conscious actions. Their particular form of activity has been stereotyped through aeons of evolution, and now operates without the aid or knowledge of the conscious self.

It is possible, however, to bring this automatic control back under conscious control, though it is not always wise so to do. But when this is done, then it is possible to consciously control many of the purely involuntary mechanisms of the body, and even, under certain circumstances, to affect the purely automatic functioning which is the basic level of the physical somatic life. We have said that such conscious control is not always advisable. This is true, for the clumsy probing of the conscious mind may easily upset the delicate mental and physical mechanisms. It is on record that Sir Francis Galton, the pioneer in Eugenics, experimented in gaining conscious control of his breathing. Having at last gained the power to shut off the automatic breathing impulse, and to remain without any effort of breathing, he found to his dismay that he had somehow lost the power of automatic breathing, and had to spend a very anxious day and night taking each breath consciously and with an effort of will, before the automatic function returned. Various yogis can be found in both East and West who can perform various psycho-physiological tricks, such as altering the heart-beat, stopping the breathing, or reversing peristaltic action at will. The techniques used vary according to the grade and status of such people, and are best left alone by the apprentice magician. There are other ways by which he may eventually come to this physical dominion over his body, and these ways are safer than the usual techniques.

But although we want neither an uncontrolled irruption of the subconscious into the normal consciousness, nor yet a clumsy interference by the conscious mind into the subconscious processes, it *is* desirable that we shall have some reliable method whereby we may be able to bring through into the waking consciousness the knowledge and the energies which are all around us awaiting our efforts. We have access to forces and energies beyond our normal ken, if we will but open the doors in the right way. Now here we come again to the saying of Bulwer-Lytton's Rosicrucian Adept, Mejnour, "Man's first initiation is in trance." This will be indignantly denied by many of the so-called "positive" people. In their estimation, trance is retrograde and entirely undesirable. With certain reservations we may agree with this facile generalisation, but the reservations cover quite a lot of country! In a period of over forty years of practical occult, psychic and magical work one has obtained certain data on this point.

We agree that the induction of the purely involuntary negative trance state under no protective conditions at all is both undesirable and psychologically dangerous to the normal individual, though *some* race-types can safely practise it.

In the purely negative trance, the doors of the subconscious are thrown open and a general jail-delivery of subconscious thoughts and energies pours out into the conscious self. Such an irruption can be most harmful.

But there are several degrees of trance, ranging from the passive, involuntary trance of pathological dissociation, through the negative, but willed trance of many spiritualist mediums, to the voluntary positive power of trance projection, wherein the personality, consciously and deliberately, temporarily vacates his body.

But even in the pathological trance of dissociation, there need be no danger if it is dealt with aright, and in the cases of the other varieties of trance, the establishment of certain protective conditions will obviate any risk. The present writer has had the opportunity

of observing very many people, of greatly varying types of mentality, working with the trance-state under varying conditions. Some
of these people were definitely the worse for their experiences, but
they formed a very small minority. The real trouble with the negative forms of trance is that they either open up the subconscious in
a very haphazard and wholesale way, or else they allow of the
uncontrolled emergence of various psychological and psychic patho-
logies which were already present but held down below the subliminal threshold.

Without going into the technical points involved, it may be
stated that the negative trance state usually involves complete unconsciousness of the physical plane, and as a general rule of the
inner planes also. The thread of consciousness is broken at the
point of departure, and again at the point of return. In the ascending
degrees of trance, up to the most positive form, the thread of consciousness begins to remain without a break, and in some cases a
curious dual consciousness develops. In this dual consciousness, the
psychic is more or less fully aware of the physical plane surroundings, whilst at the same time he is fully conscious and active on
the Inner Planes. In this particular field an ounce of practice is
worth a ton of theory, and the present writer can assure his readers
that trance, *per se*, is not *necessarily* dangerous. At the same time
it is true that *under certain conditions* the voluntary or involuntary
induction of trance is undesirable, and may even be dangerous.
Under these conditions it is advisable for the 'prentice magician to
aim at the positive end of the psychic range.

It is also to be remembered that at a certain point in his development it will be necessary for the flyer to be deliberately plunged
into the sea. "The flyer" is an old alchemical term for the conscious
self, and the "sea" is their name for the Unconscious. But until the
conscious self is properly integrated or knit together, a premature
immersion in the psychic sea of the Unconscious is not advisable.

Short of the deeper trance conditions, however, there are distinct
advantages in a willed co-operation between the conscious and subconscious parts of our mind, and these have been used in the
magical technique. The process is one of "auto-hypnosis." This
term in itself will, in all probability, cause some of our "ultra-
positive" critics to frown, but let us hasten to say that this particular
form of auto-hypnosis is most carefully controlled and directed, and
is at all times fully under the dominion of the conscious will.

Having reassured the fearful, let us proceed. The principle used
is that known as the "conditioned reflex." A typical conditioned

reflex is the watering at the mouth of a dog when it sees food. Here the reflex is physical. In the case of the magician, the reflex is mental and emotional. Briefly, a visual, audible or other sensory symbol is passed into the subconscious mind, and this evokes a response in accordance with the type of symbol used. If this symbol is one of, or is mentally associated with, one or other of the archetypal images in the depths of the Unconscious, then the response may be very strong, and care has to be taken to see that the up-welling energies evoked by the symbol are run into safe channels. If the magician is working with the Qabalistic glyph of the Tree of Life, then he will be working with such channels already provided.

In order to pass a symbol into the subconsciousness in such a way as to be able to evoke any particular response, it is first necessary to "sensitise" the subconscious, or raise its level nearer to the waking consciousness. This willed emergence, or outcropping, of the subconscious is imperative; unless it is done, the symbol does not "take," i.e. evoke an immediate response, and this is one of the primary keys of art magic. It is to be noted that the passing of the symbol into the subconscious must be an *effortless* act, to use an Irishism. Beyond the immediate clear-cut conscious "intention" to transmit the symbol, *no* further effort is required. Indeed any such further effort will frustrate the purpose in hand. A very good simile is that of the electric light switch. It requires only a small momentary physical exertion to press down the switch and so produce light. No matter how long we keep our finger pressed on the switch, we shall obtain no more light, neither will it be put out if we remove our finger entirely. Indeed, our undue pressure on the switch may cause it to be put out of action, and so produce just what we were trying to prevent.

So it is with magical work. But before the symbols can be the starting points of conditioned reflexes, it is necessary that the required conscious mental effort must have been used with them, and this is done through the training exercises which are to be found in all magical schools. The symbols must be built up by the image-building power of the mind, as described in the section of this book devoted to "Visualisation and Audition."

Then *conscious meditation* must be made upon the spiritual, mental and emotional aspects of the symbol, together with the energies connected with it. Here the Tables of Correspondences used in the qabalistic method prove their value. When *sufficient* work has been done with the conscious mind, the student learns how to pass the symbol through to the open and sensitised sub-consciousness.

The process is similar to that of learning to play the violin. The musical symbols on the score are mentally interpreted as musical sounds, and the appropriate string of the violin is "stopped" with the finger to produce the note required. Now the correct point to "stop" the string is acquired by the subconscious reflex, but for a long time the movement of the fingers must be consciously brought about, until the mental, emotional and physical reflexes have been properly "conditioned." Then we speak of automatic habit. It is fairly evident that any attempt to short-circuit this necessary conditioning work is doomed to failure, yet the writer has met many who did try to evade it in magical work. However, the reader may be assured that although the use of certain short-cuts may provide some spasmodic magical activity, such activity will be unregulated and out of conscious control.

Let us briefly recapitulate. Within the depths of the personal and collective Unconscious in each one of us lie the powers and energies which we essay to evoke into appearance in our conscious self in order to effect those "changes in consciousness" which, by our definition of magic, are our declared aim.

In order to do this, we employ the device of the "conditioned reflex," by passing certain symbols into the sensitised subconscious in such a way as to evoke the required forces into the waking self.

Since the personal subconsciousness is very largely a pictorial type, we use visual and other sensory symbols in preference to audible images, i.e. words. (Certain "Words of Power" are used not for their literal meaning, but for their vibration, and the conditioned images which have been built around them.)

The means whereby the subconsciousness is sensitised or brought nearer to the threshold of the waking self is the technical auto-hypnotic device known as the use of the "Flashing Colours." This is used in conjunction with the colour scales and correspondences on the Tree of Life.

Chapter XIII

THE INTERWOVEN LIGHT

IT is a common part of modern occult and psychic teaching that everyone is surrounded by an invisible atmosphere, usually termed the "aura" or the "auric egg," and it is very often thought of as a separate part of the human personality. It is actually the extension of the various bodies or sheaths of the spirit. In the physical it shows itself as the emanation from the etheric double which is itself the framework upon which the physical body is formed.

This etheric, or "health aura," as it is sometimes called, extends for a number of inches from the surface of the body, and it does show the state of the physical health of the man by the disposition of the substance composing it. It is in and through the etheric body and its radiating aura that the various psychic and "magnetic" forces work down on to the physical levels. For this reason the magical schools have developed a technique of etheric training and control, and this technique is of the greatest importance. One of the weaknesses of the modern occult students in the West, is to fight shy of this basic training, on the plea of its dangers. There *are* dangers in this etheric training, but only when instructions are disregarded. The same argument applies to the crossing of a busy London street; yet there *are* those who regularly perform this dangerous feat!

If the student wishes to become a successful practitioner of *ars magica*, then it is imperative that he undertakes this basic etheric training. Otherwise, he may develop a subjective psychic awareness, but magical power will not be his.

It is assumed that the student is in earnest, and is prepared to train his etheric body, and its auric emanation, so we will commence by giving him a word of warning.

This basic training, once it has been under way for a little time *becomes intensely boring*, and after the first few attempts (when the emotional stimulus of newness is present) it yields very little for quite a long time. This, in itself, is both a test of the student's power of application and also one of the barriers which automatically rise as training is continued.

Unless these barriers *are* surmounted, the magical power lies beyond the student's grasp, at any rate in its entirety. Spasmodic successes may come, but only by steady and disciplined effort can the true magical certainty and ability be gained.

In another chapter we used the simile of an electrical switch-board to illustrate the difference between the mere ceremonial magical actions, and the same actions when the magical power has been contacted and allowed to flash down into the physical levels.

This chapter deals with the method used to make this contact, but before going further it will be as well, perhaps, if we briefly treat of the role of the physical body in this work. The Manichean heresy, of the total depravity of physical matter and the physical body, is no part of the true magical doctrine, though at various times the magical schools have, like orthodox Christianity, become infected by it. In the Qabalistic scheme, the physical plane, like all other planes, is an expression of *Ain Soph*, the Eternal Infinite. Therefore, physical matter and the physical body are not merely expressions of the creative Will of the Logos, but actually *are* that Logos manifesting in this particular way.

So the old "logion," discovered at Oxyrhincus, speaks truly when it quotes the Logos as saying "Where two or three are to-gether, I am there, and where there is one only, he is with God. Raise the stone and thou shalt find Me, cleave the wood, and I am there."

So the physical body is a manifestation of the Eternal, and is rendered even more holy, if this were possible, by its use as the vehicle of consciousness of a living spark of the Eternal Flame.

Within every atom of matter which composes our physical body, there is a living point of the Eternal Light, with its accom-panying modes of expression on the various "planes."

Now as we have said before, there is a constant flux of physical substance within the physical body.

New substance is being taken in and incorporated into the bodily structure, and at the same time cell substance is being continually broken down and passed out of the physical system. During their stay in the body, however, the "vibration aspects" of these physical atoms and molecules are reacting upon our consciousness, tending to tune it automatically to their level. At the same time our own consciousness is acting upon them and tuning them to its vibration-rate. Man is indeed, as he is termed in one of the Rituals, "The Rescuer of Matter." Now when the magical contact has been made, the inpouring energy stimulates all the energy-activities of the various bodies, until it surges through the physical body itself. Here it intensifies and fans to greater vigour the lesser energies of the physical substance, and it is because of this that certain dietary rules have been evolved. But this does not necessarily mean that the magician must immediately adopt a vegetarian diet, or savagely ascetic mode of life. It does mean, however, that physical excess of all kinds is to be avoided, and during the performance of certain magical operations, abstinence from many forms of quite legitimate activity may be necessary.

As the inflowing energy begins to surge through the physical body, so it begins to eject from it that type of matter which is of a coarse order, and the result is that finer types of matter are built into the body, and these finer types of matter present less resistance to the inflowing formative energy.

Thus, by the action of the magical energy, the physical body is truly purified and becomes a better channel for the outflow of that energy. It is obvious, of course, that this purging process goes on in all the bodies, not only in the physical, but it has been thought desirable to emphasise the importance of the functioning of the physical body as a channel of the Universal Power.

When we come to use the technique which is now to be described, it is necessary to remember that we shall be dealing with *all* the bodies, or vehicles of consciousness, together with their extensions or auras. The combined auras may be conveniently referred to as "the sphere of sensation," and this term will be used throughout this chapter.

First, the "Qabalistic Cross," described in Appendix B should be traced, and the consecrated circle formulated as described. Then, having been practised until comparative skill has been obtained, the apprentice magician should proceed to the exercise of the interwoven Light, usually known as the Middle Pillar Exercise, and described in Appendix B.

As will be seen, this exercise of the interwoven Light is designed to set up certain currents of energy in the sphere of sensation, and to bring these forces through into the physical levels. The first two parts of the Middle Pillar exercise are designed to create in the auric "sphere of sensation" two great currents of energy. When these parts of the exercise have been mastered, the next step may be taken, and a circulatory current started in the aura, commencing at the feet in the Sephirah *Malkuth*. This should be visualised as a broad, bandage-like band of white light, and it should be wound mentally around the body as though one were wrapping a mummy in its swathing bands. It is important to note that the direction of the bandaging should be from the right to the left, i.e. the energy current should start from the part of the Sephirah *Malkuth* upon which the right foot is placed, and should move over to the left foot and pass behind it. This is given in the description of the exercise, but is repeated here because of its importance.

An important point is that once the Middle Pillar has been brought into active use, its activity will tend to induce a similar activity in the auras of those who are near to its user, and "near" is not confined to the physical plane proximity. Herein lies the key to certain types of "initiation," as well as to some of the phenomena of evangelical and mystical "conversion." He that hath ears to hear, let him hear.

If we seem to have touched far too briefly upon this basic magical procedure, this is of set purpose. The essentials have been given, and from them the further work unfolds. Get the principles firmly established, and the detailed application can be left to the magician's own ingenium.

It remains now to consider the source of the energy which is drawn through by the Middle Pillar technique. In that exercise we have visualised it as springing from the Sephirah *Malkuth* which, in the subjective Tree of Life, is located below the feet. But this Sephirah is a point of contact between our subjective self, and the Earth-Soul, as the Sephirah *Kether,* which is formulated above the head is a contact point with the Cosmic Unmanifest.

Although we draw the basic energy through these two points of contact, we also retain a considerable store of latent energy which is under the control of, and located in the subconscious mind. This store of latent energy can be brought into action either spontaneously, under the influence of the deeper emotions of the self, as in certain types of religious conversion, or deliberately by the use of the occult techniques. One method of Yoga, known as Kundalini Yoga brings these latent reserves of power into action by direct conscious action, but the Western systems usually work on the billiards principle of "cannoning off the cush" i.e. they use the consciously directed imagination to arouse the subconscious activity, and this, through the psychic mechanism which has been constructed by the Middle-Pillar exercise, taps the latent energies.

But in order to do this, the *Malkuth* centre must be isolated from its normal earth-contact, and identified with the storage-centre of subjective energy, which in Yoga is known as the *Muladhara*, and in the Qabalistic system is equated with the Sephirah *Yesod* of the Tree of Life.

There are many curious ideas concerning this question of isola-
tion from the Earth-Soul. Many who use their psychic faculties for
the purpose of divination for water or minerals, state that if they
wear rubber-soled shoes they find themselves cut off from the earth-
forces and unable to use their faculty. But it has been found by
practical experiments that this is a purely *mental* inhibition. If the
diviner thinks he is wearing rubber soled shoes, then he subconsciously inhibits his power. If, however, he thinks he is *not* wearing
such shoes (though actually he is) then the faculty works freely.
When in India, the present writer talked with Yogis who used a
small mat composed of the roots of certain grass. Upon this mat
they sat during meditation in order to cut themselves off from the
earth. Other yogis one met did not use such a mat, but claimed to
obtain the same result by mentally visualising such an insulating
barrier.

In the case of the diviners in Western countries, the probable
basis of their belief in the inhibitory powers of rubber-soled shoes,
is to be found in the use of rubber as an insulator in electrical
work.*

The yogi posture known as the "lotus-posture," or *padmasana*,
does identify the *Malkuth* centre below the feet with the *Yesod*
centre at the base of the spine, since in this posture the yogi sits
cross-legged and the two centres are thus brought together. This
is, however a difficult posture for the average European, and it is
quite possible for such a one to break some of the small bones of
the foot in his efforts to achieve it. To those who find it impossible
to adopt this posture the following may be found of use.

Sit on a comfortably padded surface such as a folded carpet
and adopt the cross-legged position; then slip a small cushion under-
neath the crossed ankles so as to raise them slightly. This works
quite well. One magician known to the writer habitually meditated
in this way whilst seated on a large high-backed chair. This enabled
him to keep his spine erect with the minimum of discomfort.

However, those who *can* sit in the *padmasana* should do so.
When the earth-centre of the aura is identified in this way with the
Yesod centre, then certain magnetic currents in the etheric body are
re-directed, and the latent magnetic reserves are made available.
Of course, a certain proportion of these reserves is always available
and active, being the normal body-energy which in the Eastern
teaching is known collectively as "the fires of the body." But with

---

* There are, however, certain purely electrical currents in the earth's surface
which are, of course, cut off by the use of insulators.

the release of some of the latent reserves, these fires are fanned into greater activity, and the person concerned becomes capable of feats which are not normally possible to him.

The *regular graded development of this power* to tap the reserves of energy results in the charging-up of the whole personality, and when such a one engages in the "magical" work, the lights will flash and the meter needles move on the magical switchboard as the cosmic energy surges through the channels provided for it. By using the *padmasana* or allied postures (in which the earth-contact is "shorted" out) during the meditative building up of the "magical personality," this latent energy will be linked with that magical personality and as one is evoked, so will the other appear. Again, there is more here than the bare statement suggests.

PART III

THE MAGICAL KEYS

Chapter XIV

MAGNETISM

AS we have said elsewhere, the term "magnetism" is an unfortunate one when we are considering the subtle force which is
one of the principle factors in magical work. The use of the word
comes from the experimental work of the followers of Dr. Mesmer,
and though they did attempt to make it clear that the subtle energy
which, according to their philosophy, permeated the whole universe
was *not* the phenomenon which the scientist terms "magnetism,"
the misuse of the word has persisted up to the present day. The
mesmerists termed this subtle force "animal magnetism" since, they
stated it was the power which accompanied physical magnetism,
but which was also found in all living things.

At a later date the German, Baron von Reichenbach, studied
the subject exhaustively, and his findings have much of value for
the practical magician. As far as it has been possible for the present
writer to check his results they appear to be correct, and as they
certainly enter into all magical work, it may be helpful if we give
here a general outline of them.

Briefly, von Reichenbach stated that there was a force which,
without being identifiable with them, yet seemed to underly the
physical forces of electricity, magnetism, light and heat. To this
force he gave the name of "Od."

Through his researches, he came to the conclusion that this
"odic force" was, as he put it, "the odic garment of the universe";
present everywhere, but manifesting most strongly in certain things.

Such things are the light radiations from the stars and the sun,
all crystalline bodies, "permanent magnets" and "electro-magnets,"
chemical action of all kinds, and most important of all, living vegetable, animal and human organisms.

In some magical lodges, a great deal of experimental work has
been done upon this particular subject, and we may here indicate
some of the conclusions reached. It must be remembered that thousands of experiments have been made and the results tabulated in
the lodge archives. Dr. Rhine and his followers are not the only,
or even the first, workers in this field!

All living animal forms appear to have two vertical definite
"poles," to use the magnetic term. The right side of the body is of
one polarity and the left side of the reverse odic polarity. There is
also an horizontal polarity; the upper part of the body being of

one polarity and the lower half of the opposite polarity. The same applies to living vegetable forms.

The vibrations of sound have the power of liberating the odic force, and combustion which is, of course, a form of chemical action, does the same.

All substances radiate their own quality of "odic" force, as do also all electrical manifestations. In connection with this latter, a very interesting series of experiments was made at the Theosophical Research Centre, using the clairvoyant faculty of one of the members: Mr. Geoffrey Hodson. It was found that he could correctly indicate when a current of electricity was flowing in a wire placed before him, the push-button controlling the current being actuated by someone in another room.

It is of interest to note that it was the sensations experienced by a Bishop of the Protestant Episcopal Church in America when even in total darkness he accidentally touched anything made of brass, which led to investigations by Prof. Buchanan and Dr. Denton into the phenomenon now known as "psychometry."

In certain magical work, use is made of the breath of the operator, and in the Catholic ritual used every year for the consecration of the "Holy Oils" the Bishop and his attendant priests breathe over the oils in the sign of the Cross. This particular use of the breath, apart from the symbolism as explained by theologians, is based upon the fact that the breath is strongly charged with the odic energy.

But the whole body radiates this energy, as we have seen, and the odic field of force around every person has received the name of the "health aura," since its appearance indicates to the trained seer the health conditions of the physical body.

Vital energy *of all types* is drawn into the etheric body and specialised for use therein. The surplus is radiated out and forms an energy field around the body. The late Dr. Kilner by the use of dicyanine screens observed and recorded the health indications given by the "etheric aura," as this field of living force is called.

It has been established that the "auric fields" of human beings tend to affect each other in various ways. Some auras unite easily with certain other auras, but are strongly repellent to others. Since such attraction and repulsion induces certain subconscious and conscious reactions, it is essential that the operators in a magical ceremonial should be magnetically in harmony, as the blending of their auras is one of the foundations upon which the ceremony rests.

It is of interest to note in this connection, that there are certain people whose auric energy seems to act as an "enzyme" or ferment, and in their presence even opposing auras seem temporarily to blend. Such people are invaluable in lodge working, since the lodge phenomena work through such a blended aura.

They are of the greatest value in spiritualistic "seances," when their presence will often turn what would have been a failure into a successful sitting. It has been noted, in this connection, that many of these human "enzymes" are of the auburn and red-headed types.

It is obvious that each individual brings his own unique potentialities into magical lodge and psychic circle alike, and the unfoldment of these powers, and their interaction with the powers of others in the lodge, not only opens up many possibilities, but also presents the lodge with new problems. It is true that the lodges have, through the centuries built up a fairly comprehensive body of knowledge by means of which they can meet such problems, but at the same time, since these powers are emerging under modern conditions, and new types of psychic make-up are coming into the lodges, there will always be forces and combinations of those forces which will tax the powers of the rulers thereof.

It is important to remember that the operation of any power or force in the human personality has its *subjective* side, and the subjective expression of "magnetism" is "emotion." For the purposes of the magician, magnetism and emotion are the same.

Stir the emotions, and the magnetic flow increases. Induce the magnetic flow, and emotions arise.

This is very apparent in the relationship between the sexes; indeed a certain debased form of the *tantrik* magic deliberately makes use of this for its own not very exalted purposes, and this not in the East alone!* Physical movements of a rhythmic type also tend to liberate magnetism, and certain forms of musical sound do the same.

To the clairvoyant vision, the psychic atmosphere of a dance-hall present a most interesting spectacle, particularly when certain forms of music of negroid origin are used.

It is clear that many people would seem to possess very little emotional force indeed. They appear to be, and often are, frigid both in their everyday life and in their sexual outlook. Psychologists know, however, that in many of these cases, the lack of emotional drive is the sign that the greater part of the emotional power of the

* It will be noticed that we refer to a debased form of *Tantrika*. This philosophic and occult system, has also its heights as well as its depths, a point often forgotten by many occult students.

personality has for some reason or other been locked up below the threshold of the conscious mind, and is therefore not available for conscious use. The methods of psycho-analysis disperse the repressed emotional forces, and allow them to rise freely into consciousness, there to be integrated into the normal emotional circuit. Such a release of suppressed energy quickly restores normality, and the abnormal frigidity of body and mind disappears.

In the magical lodge, this redirection of the emotional energies also takes place, partly due to the emotion-stirring ritual, and partly due to the inclusion of the individual in the general magnetic circulation of the lodge. Under the graded system of the Western lodges, as also under the *guru-chela* relationship existing in the East between the teacher and his pupil or apprentice, this redirection of the emotional energy and its accompanying magnetism takes place gradually and under control. When, however, one is working alone, or with only one or two fellow-workers, care has to be taken that the magnetic energy does not escape from control.

There is, as a matter of psychic observation, a constant circulation which goes on in the finer bodies of man, and this process is easily affected by the mind. This mental control is exercised involuntarily and pathologically in the cases of suppression and mental dissociation, but it is part of the magical training for the aspirant to gain the power of conscious control of the magnetic energies. If these energies are aroused or liberated or increased (all perfectly valid lines of action), their corresponding mental channels and physical expression must be so directed and adjusted that the turbulent stream of energy may be safely diverted into the fertilising irrigation channels instead of sweeping chaotically over all the mental and emotional field.

Such enlarged and controllable channels are provided by the magical ritual if it is properly carried out, and for this reason alone, ritual magic can be a safer and more efficient method than any amount of Freudian psycho-analysis.

As we have pointed out, the psycho-magnetic flow of energy can be controlled by the mind, and in this way the available magnetism may be increased not merely by the release of suppressed energies but by an increase in the actual intake of those energies. One of the methods, and when properly employed one of the best, is the exercise which we have described more fully elsewhere: the Key exercise of the Interwoven Light.

Now the personality of man receives energy from two sources, and one of these, "elemental energy", flows in through the etheric body. It is to be remembered that this magnetic force, though it has many effects upon the physical body, circulates in, and through, the etheric body. There are, of course, detectable electric currents in the physical body, but this still more subtle force is not part of the physical forces, though its operation may be determined by the position and action of the physical vehicle, since the etheric body and the physical are interlocked most closely. This is the basis of so many of the Yogic *asanas,* or postures; they determine the circuit in which the magnetic energies may flow.

It will have been noticed that we have used a special term "elemental energy" to describe this subtle force. This has been done for two reasons. It is the term used in the particular occult fraternity in which the present writer received much of his training, and by using the term one covers all the various names, magnetism, odic force, *prana,* etc.

There remain two points to be borne in mind by the magical apprentice. The first is that this elemental energy in one of its forms is the underlying "pre-matter" from which physical matter as we know it is condensed or "materialised." It therefore equates with the *prana* of the Hindu systems. Many western students, mislead by some of the popular presentations of the Eastern systems of yoga, limit the term *prana,* to that aspect of it which is utilised in the exercises of *pranayama,* or breathing-control.

But in the philosophy which underlies the yoga systems, the term *prana* is much more comprehensive. The earthly *prana,* which manifests in all the living beings and organisms found on earth, is a modification of the solar *prana,* which in its turn is a modification of the cosmic *prana* which is the undifferentiated cosmic matter termed *Prakriti.** This is mentioned here in order to maintain the correct perspective in the student's mind. In one of the cryptic texts of the *Sepher Yetzirah,* it is said that "The Tenth Path (*Malkuth*) causes an influence to emanate from the Prince of Countenances, the Angel of *Kether* (the highest point of the Tree of Life)." In other words, by our actions in earthly matter and pre-matter we are also acting on and reacting to the highest spiritual levels.

All magical work must be seen in this perspective if the magical apprentice is to become anything more than a mere "sorcerer," a meddler with occult forces. It is for this reason and as a potent reminder of it, that the magician, during his operations, wears upon

* This is more fully worked out in the Sanscrit work, the *Shivagama,* one chapter of which deals entirely with this energy and its modifications.

his breast what is known as the "lamen." This is a symbol which represents the spiritual aspect of the work in which he is engaged, and it is by virtue of this spiritual intention that he asserts dominance and control over the creatures of the elements.

To return to our consideration of the elemental energy. The key to its use is that it can be "tied," mentally, to the breath, which in itself is said to be an expression of the dual energy of the Eternal, the outbreathing and inbreathing of Brahm. The actual exercises are simple, and tedious! The ones which form the foundation of such control of *prana* are given in the next chapter, but, of course, there are many variants and specific adaptations of the basic exercises. Before the student attempts any of them, it is imperative that *he learns to do them without any strain*. This is the most important rule, and any infringement of it may lead to most unwelcome results.

In practical training, therefore, the apprentice magician learns to release the body mechanism from the convulsive grip of the conscious mind. This is done by the exercise known as the "relaxation exercise." This will be found in the next chapter.

Once control over the intake of the elemental energy has been obtained, such energy may be dealt with in various ways. It may be used within the student's own etheric and physical bodies, and very real self-healing may be brought about thereby. Or it may be directed outwardly on to people and things, producing very real effects thereby.

When considering its use in the physical and psychic bodies, it should always be remembered that it is quite possible, if the student is careless or pays no attention to instructions, to disorganise seriously the subconscious psychological workings of the body, and many students have found this out, to their cost. Undue concentration upon any one of the psychic centres or *chakras* should be avoided for this reason, if for none other. The great psychic centres lie close to, and directly influence the endocrine, or ductless, glands, which play such a great part in the chemistry of the body. To stimulate the centres in a balanced way is one thing; to disorganise the entire physical economy is quite another!

When the elemental energy is projected outward towards others or towards other objects, then it may be used for healing, for the spiritual illumination and initiation of those persons, or for hurt and deceptive illusion, according to the spiritual status and intention of the magician. These are, of course, the two poles of such activity.

In practical experience, most of the magicians with whom we

have come into contact seem to work somewhere between these two opposites, veering one way and the other as they react to their own inner nature.

Although, theoretically, the elemental energy can be projected without any physical action, i.e., by mental effort alone, it has been found in practice that this projection is far more thorough and efficient when certain gestures and signs are employed, and certain definite thought-forms built up. The "Signs and Sigils" with which we dealt in Section II of this book, are all designed to act as vehicles for the elemental energy, and may be so used.

It is important that the magician keep ever before him the key idea that though he may draw down spiritual power from the heights, he must, if he is to give that power full expression, draw up from the earth-soul that elemental force which, as it ascends within him, changes its nature of manifestation from crude sex energy, as it passes through the centre attributed by the Qabalists to *Yesod*, to a radiating and harmonising force as it passes through the centre of *Tiphareth*.

This harmonised energy may now be discharged into the mental forms which have been built, and will truly serve as an effective link between the spiritual forces invoked, and the thought-forms through which they manifest.

Most thought-forms partake of the nature of the sparks from the smith's anvil. These fly upwards for a foot or so, and are extinguished. So most of the thought-forms created by the average person never leave the aura of their creator. Only when they have already been charged and vitalised by the elemental energy have they sufficient power to go forth. And in this connection we would again repeat, emotion and magnetism go together. A long continued emotional "brooding-over" some problem will generate and charge some pretty effective thought-forms. Though such emotional brooding is usually employed in the wrong way, it can and *must* be used in a constructive spiritual way by the aspirant to the Magic of Light.

Chapter XV

THE *TATTVIC* TIDES

THERE are tides in the Unseen, and the success of our magical working depends very largely upon the set of those tides. They are of several kinds, and produce different results. We may roughly divide them into five: Stellar, Solar, Planetary, Lunar and Terrestial.

In actual work the influences of the stellar, solar and lunar tides work upon us through the magnetic sphere of the Earth, since it is in the sphere of the Earth that they produce their effect. We, being children of earth, as well as of the race of the Starry Heavens, respond to the varying tides of our mother-planet.

In the West, very little has been given out publicly concerning the Earth tides, but in the East, where the subject has been studied without any danger of the student being persecuted, a body of knowledge concerning these things has been built up. The tides are known as the *Tattvas,* and that unseen medium in which they flow is known as *Prana.* This is understood to be the state of matter which is the next stage above terrestial matter, and we may term it "etheric matter"; surrounding the Sun and in which move the earth and other planets. This we may understand to be the "free etheric substance," whilst *prana* surrounding our planet, as well as the others of this solar system, may be called the "bound ether," or magnetic sphere of our planet.

As the earth revolves on its axis, and also travels at the same time around the sun, centres of stress are set up in the magnetic sphere of the earth. During the day of any part of the earth's surface, that part sends out a positive current from *East to West.* So there is a steady current, or tide, in the magnetic sphere of the earth, flowing from East to West.

As the earth moves round the sun, a magnetic current passes from the north to the south during six months, and the reverse is the case for the remaining six months. These "seasonal" tides are also of great practical value. They are marked by the solstices and equinoxes and are classified as follows:—

The Tide of Destruction: December 23rd—March 21st.
The Tide of Sowing: March 21st—June 21st.
The Tide of Reaping: June 21st—September 23rd.
The Tide of Planning: September 23rd—December 23rd.
The corresponding aspects of these tides for the Southern hemi-

BLUE "AIR"

VAYU

YELLOW "EARTH"

PRITHEVI

INDIGO "ETHER"

AKASHA

RED "FIRE"

TEJAS

SILVER "WATER"

APAS

TEJAS OF APAS

sphere can be worked out by the reader. The above are given for
the Northern hemisphere. Of course, they are not so sharply defined;
they merge one into the other and the "cusps," where this merging
takes place, are of mixed influence. As the author of Ecclesiastes
says, "there is a time for sowing and a time for reaping, a time to
be born and a time to die, and for everything under the sun there
is a time."

This does not mean that the magical student must meticulously
"observe times and seasons," but it does mean that when working
as a magician, it is advisable to perform your operation when the
right tide is flowing.

The positive currents emanate from the northern centre, the
negative currents from the southern centre, and the eastern and
western channels of these currents are known as the *Pingalâ* (E)
and *Idâ* (W) of the planet. They have their counterparts in the
human body, in the positive and negative currents which flow
through the etheric counterpart of the spine.

Generally speaking, the limit of the *magnetic* sphere of this
planet is around the limits of the atmosphere, and within this sphere
of force, every atom of earth is a centre of action and reaction for
the *tattvic* tides.

Thus all that has been done upon the earth is herein recorded,
and by a process of induction, these terrestial records are imprinted
also on the *pranic* sphere of the Sun. All these records are under
the influence of the negative *tattvic* forces, whose controller is the
Moon. For this reason, on the Tree of Life, *Yesod* the Moon-sphere
is termed the "Treasure-House of Images."

The Lunar tides work in a rhythm of that lunar month, and are
roughly divided into two: the tides of the waxing moon, and the
tides of the waning moon. It is customary not to essay practical
occult works (unless it is imperative they should be done) during
the "waning phase of the moon." The last quarter or "dark of the
moon" is usually reserved in the occult circles for simple lectures,
and so on.

The planetary tides as we have seen, affect us through the magnetic sphere of the earth, but their influence is subject to great
alteration by the terrestial magnetic currents.

Now, the *tattvic* tide which swirls around our planet from East
to West is five-fold, and each of its components has its maximum
and minimum periods. The Element of *Akasha* is strongest at sunrise, then it merges into the element of *Vayu*. This in its turn merges

into *Tejas,* and this into *Apas,* and finally *Apas* merges into *Prithivi.*
Then the cycle is repeated.

Each *tattvic* tide is composite. For instance, in the first flow of
the tide at sunrise, *Akasha* is the dominant, but together with
Akasha are the four other aspects of the tide, and these build up
in power until, as the dominant phase of *Akasha* begins to weaken,
the phase of *Vayu* becomes dominant, to be followed by the others
in succession. So all the five *tattvic* currents are always flowing, but
their individual power varies in a rhythmic fashion. Now each
tattvic aspect produces certain conditions in the magnetic sphere of
the earth, and so will help or hinder the magician in his particular
work. A knowledge of what tide is flowing is therefore very helpful.

There are certain symbols used to denote the *tattvas,* and these
are: —

AKASHA—Ether	Indigo or Black
VAYU—Air	Blue
TEJAS—Fire	Red
APAS—Water	Silver
PRITHIVI—Earth	Yellow

These *tattvic* symbols are of very great use when the student is
working with the visualising exercises detailed in the preceding
section. They may be combined, i.e. the red triangle of *Tejas* may
be placed in the centre of the yellow square of *Prithivi,* and they
are undoubtedly splendid objects for the exercises.

They can also be used as "gates" into the Astral Light, as key
symbols which will open up to the student the corresponding level
of the astral.

Chapter XVI

THE BODY OF LIGHT

"THE Body of Light" is a technical term used in the Western esoteric schools to refer to what may be described as an artificial body or vehicle of consciousness which is used by the magician to project his consciousness from his physical body. In some Eastern schools, this body is known as the *Manumayakosha* which may be roughly translated as "the thought-created sheath or body of illusion." In other words it is a mentally-produced vehicle of consciousness which appears to be a replica of the body of the magician (though it *need not* take that form).

The particular psychic operation which has been popularised of late years in western occult circles, the so-called "projection of the astral body," is an example of the use of the Body of Light. At the same time it should be realised that in some cases, far more than a simple thought-form is projected. This brings us to the crux of the matter. Anyone with a good visualising power can build up a thought-form, and with training may succeed in transferring his personal consciousness thereto. But for the further stages of this operation, it is essential that there should be what may be described as a "splitting up" of the subtle inner bodies. Most people nowadays are familiar with the idea of "split-personality," but this is not what we mean in this connection. In order to make our meaning perfectly clear, it is necessary to touch briefly upon the vehicles or bodies possessed by man.

We are all aware that we possess a physical body, since it is perfectly evident to our waking consciousness. We fail, however, to realise the existence of the inner bodies, because cognition of them does not extend into the normal waking consciousness.

Nevertheless, the various inner bodies do exist. For our present purposes we will briefly deal with the three inner bodies which are normally employed in the practice of astral projection. These are the so-called "etheric double," the "astral body" and the "mental body." The etheric body is really the true physical body, since it is the matrix or mould into which flows the physical substance gained from food and drink. But as we know, this material substance is in a constant state of flux or movement, and in the course of a few years all atoms of matter which make up the physical body have been replaced by new atoms. So there is a constant intake of matter, its assimilation by the living cells of the body, and its later rejection

and discharge from the body. The individual cell lives are energised by the permanent (for this life) etheric body, and will therefore
build the new atoms into the old pattern. So our body retains its
distinctive appearance, though, as the years go by, the power of the
cell-life to build truly on the etheric pattern begins to lessen, and
false patterns are built in. An example of this sometimes occurs in
the nervous system where, instead of the true nerve-substance being
built up, the cell-life builds into the nerve that particular type of
substance known as "connective tissue." This is a very useful substance in its proper place, but when it is built up into a nerve it is
as though we replaced part of a wire which carries electricity, by a
length of rubber. The rubber, being a non-conductor of electricity
will prevent any current flowing, and in like manner, the connective
tissue which may be built up into parts of a nerve, does not transmit the nerve-current, and renders the nerve useless. Some forms
of deafness in aged people are due to this faulty rebuilding of the
aural nerves.

Now the etheric matrix or "double," normally remains in close
union with the physical body, and is only separated therefrom, and
then only partially, by certain drugs, general anæsthetics, mesmerism and hypnotism.

When the etheric is driven out of the physical body by any one
of these means, a certain amount of it remains with the physical,
and between the exteriorised etheric double and the part still remaining on the physical levels, there is what has been termed the
"silver cord." Should this cord be broken, then death has occured.

It is important to realise that although the etheric double is the
permanent mould of the physical, it is in itself "fluidic," i.e. it can
be split up into several more etheric duplicates of itself. The double
is, also, both the channel for the vital energies which keep the
physical body going, and the link between the physical brain and
the corresponding centres of consciousness of the inner bodies.

To remember, or "bring through" the recollection of an astral
plane activity, it is necessary to so work upon the etheric body, that
a certain amount of its substance vibrates in harmony with our
astral consciousness. When this has been done, then it is possible
to induce in the physical brain some memory of what has been
seen and done on the inner planes, though since inner plane experiences are not of the material order, it will be found almost impossible to bring through a full realisation of such experiences; the
essence will usually escape us. In the Western schools a system of

symbol-building is used to enable the magician to deal with the superphysical experiences.

The alteration of the vibration rate of part of the etheric double is sometimes known as the "splitting of the moon," since the etheric double is like our moon, a reflector of light received from another source. The exercise described in the section dealing with the "interwoven light" has the effect, among many others, of splitting the etheric, or, more precisely, adapting part of it to the vibration ratio of the astral body of the student.

The astral or "psychic" body is usually well developed in most people, and the astral senses (or rather sense) active. But because of a lack of contact between the physical brain and the astral centre of consciousness the perceptions of the psychic senses are not transmitted to the physical plane consciousness. What is known as psychic development makes such links of contact, and equally the magician's training is intended to build up such links between the consciousness on the outer and inner planes.

When, after the preliminary work with the interwoven light, the magician comes to the work of formulating and using the Body of Light, he will find that, although the technique is simple enough, there are several "critical points," where failure may ensue. But persistent practice will in the end produce the desired result. Indeed, it may be stated that *persistence* is one of the most important traits to be developed by the magician. Again and again will the endeavour to formulate the Body of Light be unsuccessful, but again and again must he try until, suddenly he one day finds that he is no longer in the inert physical body, which he sees resting on the bed or couch before him. Like Tennyson's "Ancient Sage," the mortal limit of the self has been loosed, and the student stands, fully conscious in the Body of Light.

This is a tremendous experience, and the present writer well remembers the time, now some forty years ago, when, under the guidance of his teacher, he first stood forth in the Body of Light, and gazed on his earthly form lying in deep trance on the couch. Whoever has this experience *knows* in a mode of absolute knowledge, that he is not the physical body with which he has for so long identified himself. It is possibly one of the greatest experiences which can happen to man, and perhaps the novelist, Lord Bulwer Lytton, was thinking of this in his book *Zanoni,* when he makes the Rosicrucian adept Mejnour remark, "Man's first initiation is in trance."

The transference of the consciousness from the physical body to the Body of Light results in the sleep of the physical, and this sleep may vary from so light a condition of unconsciousness that such a thing as a check in the circulation of the blood, due to a tight article of clothing, or a change in temperature, may bring back the projected consciousness into the physical body, to a state of cataleptic rigour, in which the whole body is stiff and rigid.

Normally, however, the "trance of projection" is not so deep as the cataleptic condition. It is interesting to note that in the deeper stages of trance there are well-defined changes in the chemical composition of the blood-stream. Many beginners are afraid that if they are successful in projecting the Body of Light, they may be "locked out" as it were, and unable to get back.* They need have no fear on this score. The difficulty, especially in the early stage, is to *keep out of the physical*!

We said that the etheric double, whenever it partially or wholly leaves the physical body, is connected with it by a connecting etheric link or "cord." This etheric "cable tow" is extremely sensitive to changes occurring in the physical body, and constantly tends to draw the extruded etheric substance back into the body. Such withdrawal is sometimes practically instantaneous. The writer has seen the body of a medium marked with very definite bruises when the extruded double, together with a certain amount of ectoplasmic substance had returned suddenly and violently to the physical body from which it came, this sudden return being because a sitter had suddenly grasped the materialised form.†

We have dwelt upon this point in order to reassure those who feel that to project out of the body is akin to jumping into deep water when you are unable to swim. You may get out, or you may not! In projection, however, such a danger is so remote that, for all practical purposes, it does not exist. A far more definite danger is that the practice may throw a strain upon the heart. (But *no one* should attempt practical magical work if they suffer from any organic disease of the heart. If such a sufferer wishes to become consciously aware of the astral world, let him develop the links between the astral and physical levels of his consciousness by the use of a "symbol-chain" when falling asleep, and again when waking. He may in this way attain without risk to his health, practical

---

* Cf. a story by H. G. Wells, "The Stolen Body," which deals with such a dilemma!

† This phenomenon of the infliction of injury upon the medium by injury inflicted on the extruded etheric form is known as "repercussion," and figures in much of the evidence in the trials of witches in medieval times.

knowledge and experience of the inner worlds.) How is the formulation and projection of the Body of Light accomplished? The first step is quite easy, the more so if the visualising exercises already described have been systematically used.

The student should be seated in such a position that he is free from any undue worry about his physical body. The less he receives in sensations telegraphed to his brain consciousness by the nerves of sensation, the better. Some European students attempt to sit in one or other of the various *asanas* or postures which are commonly used in the Orient. But, although, when they are mastered they can be most comfortable, they are usually anything but comfortable to the European type of body. Now since the student is endeavouring to take the consciousness *out* of the body, it seems rather foolish to adopt a position which will continually be calling the consciousness back into the body.

It is true that certain yoga postures do "short-circuit" and link together some of the magnetic currents of the body, but for the purpose of projection, intricate etheric postures are not necessary.

So let the posture be one of comfort. Quite a good one is sitting in an easy chair so arranged that the body leans slightly back from the perpendicular, and the back is kept straight.

Or the student can lie flat on his back on a couch or bed, but whatever position he is in, he must, when he commences this exercise, visualise his Body of Light as being in identically the same position.

Before attempting the actual projection, the Banishing Ritual of the Lesser Pentagram should be used.

Then, seated in his particular posture, the student should carefully visualise (subjectively) the shape of that form he desires to project.

Next he should externalise this mental image, and see it apparently objectively. The figure may be clothed as is the experimenter, or as his fancy dictates. A good image, so the present writer found out many years ago, is of a robed and hooded figure, the details of robe and figure being clearly pictured and projected.

When this has been done, the second stage in projection may be attempted. Here the experimenter is splitting the etheric and transferring the tenuous etheric, astral and mental substance to the thought-form which he has projected. Such transference can be achieved by the use of the exercise of the interwoven light, and the breathing exercises based upon it.

When the thought-image has been "charged" with energy in this way, the third stage may be started. The experimenter is now trying to transfer his waking consciousness into the form.

For this stage, the first step consists in making the Body of Light do certain things, move about, speak, etc., as though it was a puppet actuated by remote radio control. When the visualised form can be clearly kept in the mental vision and made to move easily, the final act of identification can be made. First of all, the mental "intention" to project consciousness into the form is made by a strong *momentary* effort of will. Do not keep on "willing"; the definite "intention" or act of will sets the appropriate etheric and astral forces in action.

The next step is to step forward in thought and enter the form which stands before you, and *immediately* make an imaginative effort to see and hear and feel from the standpoint of the figure. This is the crucial point in the operation, and as we have said the student may try many times before success is achieved. Usually, when one is at last successful, there is heard a curious sound, somewhat like a sharp metallic "click."

The student is now standing out of his physical body and is clothed in the Body of Light. At first he will clearly see the physical plane surroundings, all apparently self-luminous with a clear bluish light. His sleeping physical body lies before him, and a thin silvery cord of misty light connects him with it.

If, however, he wishes to go any distance from his physical body, he must, again by a momentary effort of will, send back some of the denser etheric substance in which he is now working. When this has been done, the Body of Light is less susceptible to physical plane disturbances of various kinds and it can be projected to much greater distances.

Always the student will, in the earlier stages at least, feel the pull of the silver cord, as it responds to the varying physical plane impressions coming in via the physical body, but with increasing dexterity, the tendency to move back into the physical will lessen.

During projection it is comparatively easy, if any "automatic-writing" ability has been developed, to concentrate mentally upon the physical brain, causing the hand to write automatically and so record the observations one is making. Or concentration may be made upon the throat and the physical voice will record the telepathic impressions being sent in from its owner. But these are later developments, as such concentration on the physical body tends to draw one back into it.

It is when the student first stands forth in the Body of Light that his troubles begin. For he is as a child newly born on the etheric

plane. The surging magnetic tides of the etheric earth will tend to
drift him aimlessly along, and his ill-controlled imagination will
switch him instantaneously from one set of conditions to another.
Here, too, he will find that what were but "symbols" on the physical
plane, are living things, and here will he find that many of the fixed
"laws of nature" concerning which he has so proudly spoken, are
reversed and work in a very different way.

It is necessary to have some clue to the astral maze, and this
clue is to be found in the use of the symbols associated with the
pivotal diagram of the Western Magical Schools, the "Tree of Life."
By using these symbols as "doors" through which one makes contact with the astral powers, it is possible for the student to bring
order and method into his astral wanderings, and thus avoid becoming one of those whom one occult teacher I knew referred to as
"astral tramps"!

The student should always remember that, in the words of
Marcus Aurelius, "we are never less alone than when we think we
are alone." There are guides and teachers who may not at first be
perceived, but who will make themselves known to him. Always he
should test such teachers by the moral and mental standards which
he has built by his series of meditations when he was engaged in
building his "magical personality."

These standards he will have embodied in certain symbolic
figures and gestures, and these he will use to test those who appear
in the astral and claim to guide and teach him.

Having left the physical and worked in the Body of Light, the
student must now return. For some time there will have been an
increasing pull from the physical, and he has only to yield voluntarily to this pull for him to be instantaneously "yanked" back into
the material body.

Such a rapid return tends to break the consciousness link
and also the memory chain which enables him to recollect his
astral experiences.

The return should therefore be deliberate. This is not easy at
first, as the pull of the physical is increased as one comes near it.

If the student has gone out by the way of the Pylon Door of
some train of associated symbols, then by that door he should return
until, in his Body of Light he stands once more gazing down upon
his sleeping physical organism.

The "intention" to return *slowly* into the physical should be
made, and the same projection of consciousness as that used in the
stepping-out should be made, but, of course, "in reverse."

When the "star of consciousness," with its associated astral memories, has been transferred into the physical, the student should visualise the Body of Light, in which he has been working, as standing before him.

He should then, by a steady effort of will, draw it back into himself. This should *never* be omitted. The form will subsist in his astro-mental sphere, and be more easily formulated and sent forth in the future. But to leave such a form, or forms, drifting idly around in ones psychic atmosphere is definitely unwise.

One curious point emerges here, a point with which the student will make practical acquaintance as time goes on. The Body of Light may show alarming signs of being itself an independent being, and will not respond to its formulator. When this occurs, the practice of projection should be preceded by a meditation on the principles used to build up the magical personality, and the errant Body of Light disciplined and controlled.* Never allow it to break away or become dominant. It is *your vahan, your* vehicle, and you should be its master, and it must be your servant.

---

* Of course, as we have said, *all* magical work, including the projection of the Body of Light, should be preceded by the assumption of the "magical personality."

Chapter XVII

THE MAGICAL PERSONALITY

THERE are several ways in which what we may term the "magical pressure" in the personality may be increased, and of these the "magical personality" is one of the most important. As the psychologists have proved through the study of those curious states of mind known as "alternating" or "split" personalities, our ordinary personality is a rather unstable thing, constructed haphazardly, and easily affected by outside conditions. It is possible for us to remould that personality, indeed at some time or other in our magical career we shall have to do this, but long before the permanent alteration is effected we can have commenced to build up an alternative personality which shall serve as an efficient instrument for our magical work. There are definite rules for the construction of such a magical personality, and if they are carefully observed, the result will be of the greatest help to the magician.

It must, however, be kept in mind that the personality-splitting, or "schizophrenic" tendency, has to be reckoned with in this work. We see a similar state of affairs in connection with certain actors and actresses who have to play some particular character in a play which enjoys a very long run. The stage character they have been portraying for so long seems to gain a certain kind of individual existence in their mind, and does at times appear to intrude into and supersede the normal waking consciousness. But this, of course, is what we do not want to happen in our magical work. In that work we must *always* be positive and dominant *masters* of the temple of our personality. This is one of the cardinal points in magical work. Although the personality must be held open to any inflow of power, light or wisdom from the deeper self within, it must be so built and trained that no involuntary alterations can take place in it. When we begin to build up the *magical* personality, therefore, we must so work that all involuntary manifestations of it are stopped at source. The magical personality must *never* be allowed to manifest suddenly unless the will and waking consciousness of the normal personality concur. So rule one is—*always build the magical personality positively, and never allow it to manifest without your definite personal agreement.*

In order to build up a balanced magical personality, construct it around the three basic aspects of life: Power, Love and Wisdom. Take each one of these in turn and use it as the central idea in your meditation. Here is a typical meditation on the power aspect.

"I am meditating on Power—with a capital P.—Why a capital?
—why, all manifestations of energy are individual expressions of
the one energy which lies behind them all—the flaming crater of
the volcano, the mountainous waves of the tempest-torn ocean, the
devastating fury of the hurricane, the roaring terror of the avalanche
—all are expressions of the primal energy. So, too, are the manifestations of power in the realms of life—the strength of the masto-
don, and the great saurians, the fury of the lion and the conquering
wills of those men and women who in their day and generation have
altered the destinies of the nations.

All these were but partial manifestations of that Strength which
guides Arcturus and his sons, which upholds all creation by the
might of Its Power.

And I, son of earth, feeble and ignorant, am also of the race
of the Starry Heavens, a spark of that Mighty Flame, and within
me also is that Power.

I aspire towards that radiant Source of all Power. O Thou, the
Eternal, Whose spark dwells within me, I strive to realise Thee
within myself. May Thy Power descend upon me and work through
me, that Thy Will may be done, and Thy Plan brought to its consummation within me. To the Greater, I submit."

This, of course, is but a rough draft of such a meditation, but
the idea will be seen. In the same way, similar meditations should
be made on the other two aspects—Love and Wisdom. In all these
meditations the aim should be a realisation of the unity of all the
manifestations of the particular aspect which is being considered,
followed by an aspiration towards union with that transcendent
Unity.

It is *most important* that the building up of the form-aspect of
the magical personality should not be commenced before these
three aspects of Life have been thoroughly meditated upon, and
some realisation of their nature gained. Now comes the next step.
This must be taken carefully, and all details fully worked out.
To build up a faulty magical personality is worse than useless; it
can cause quite serious trouble under certain circumstances. So the
apprentice magician should most carefully consider what he is doing, and patiently carry out the routine training.

We have already said that this artificial magical personality must
be fully under the control of the magician's will, and should not be
allowed to manifest in any way except when the conscious self so
wills it. Also, when the purpose for which it was summoned forth

has been fulfilled, it should be positively dismissed by the operator, and returned into the subconsciousness. These two points are of the highest importance, and anyone who attempts this exercise without having developed the power to control the manifestations of the magical personality is simply asking for trouble.

The exercise should be started by the operator selecting some object which is to be closely identified with the magical personality which is to be constructed. A ring is one of the best objects for this purpose. A symbol made of metal may be worn as a pendant over the heart, but since this is the position in which the magical breast plate or "Lamen" is worn, the ring is the better object of the two.

In the various "grimoires," or books of magical instruction, great stress is laid upon the "virginity" of the various articles used in the rites. This simply means that the object should be one that has not been used for any other purpose, and one that has therefore, no association links with other things and no "magnetic" charge which would link it with other influences. It is also laid down that the operator must make and consecrate his own magical instruments, and it is certainly a very good exercise for the operator to do this, as it implies a concentration upon the article which will be far greater than that which could be exerted upon a ready-made article. But since it is not so easy to make a ring, at least not easy for those who are not mechanically minded, a shop-bought ring certainly saves time.

If, however, the ring is bought at second-hand, it will in all probability be charged with influences from its past history, and will therefore be unsuitable for our purpose until it has been magnetically cleansed and charged.

In all cases, whether the object chosen is new or second-hand, it is recharged with the idea (held firmly in the operator's mind) that when this ring is put on the magical personality is assumed through that action, and when it is removed, then the magical personality is put off, and returned to the subconscious levels. Again it is repeated: the magical personality must never be assumed, except at the conscious command of the will, and for these training purposes, such assumption must be keyed to the deliberate action of putting on the magical ring.

The ring has been placed upon the finger, and the operator is now about to assume the magical personality. How is this done? Let him see himself as an actor assuming a certain character in a play. It is not necessary to visualise any particular form, but simply to think and feel himself to be that character. In the beginning of this exercise, he has three character parts to play, and his routine training should be so arranged that each of these characters is used in turn. At a later stage, the three are fused together into the one magical personality, but it is necessary to develop each aspect separately before attempting such a fusion.

Our apprentice-magician has already carried out his basic meditations on the three aspects of Life: Power, Love and Wisdom. Now he will take one of them and try to think and feel as if he were the physical embodiment of that aspect. It is more than probable that most people would choose the Power aspect for a start and this, of course, is very natural. But the *next time* the magical personality is assumed, the aspect chosen *must be* one of the complementary aspects of Love and Wisdom. This rule must never be broken or relaxed in any way, until the fusion of the three aspects of the magical personality is complete. Even then it will be found in practice that one or other of the aspects seems to predominate when the magical work is being done, and the integrated magical personality will be found to be temporarily "biassed" toward such an aspect, the aspect evoked being related to the type of work being done.

In the exercises, the apprentice should think, feel, speak and act *as if* he were the channel and expression of the aspect chosen. Since speech is important, it is advisable to carry out this exercise somewhere where there is freedom from interruption. A simple ritual should be devised by the operator, and this ritual should be performed with the idea that he is identified with the magical personality, that he *is* it, and every thought and feeling should be directed towards this one end.

A way in which this can be greatly intensified is to use the ring as an auto-hypnotic device by turning it bezel inwards, and quietly contemplating the symbol engraved thereon, at the same time affirming the intention of assuming the magical personality. Since at the present point of training the operator is not attempting contact with any other levels of being, but is using a purely psychological technique, the Qabalistic symbol of *Malkuth*, the Kingdom of Earth, is a very good one to use.*

Having assumed the magical personality, the student should now proceed to the controlled use of "phantasy," i.e. the image-building faculty which he uses when he is, as we say, "day-dreaming." He should picture mentally a number of characters engaged in

* See diagram of the Tree, page 36.

doing some particular thing, and from the standpoint of his magical personality, he should put himself into the phantasy and see and feel himself as one of the characters.

Thus, we will assume that the "Wisdom" facet of the magical personality has been adopted by the student. He builds up his phantasy, shall we say one in which a number of men and women in an office are apparently in a glorious confusion because of lack of method. The student in his magical personality steps down into the picture and brings order out of chaos, organises and systematises the work that is being done by the actors in his little mental play, and then retires from the picture, leaving the situation balanced and co-ordinated.

Should the Power facet of the magical personality have been assumed, then a situation is visualised in which power is seen to be absent, with resultant non-action. The student in his Power personality steps into the picture and applies power in a balanced form, thus energising the static conditions visualised in the mental picture.

Similarly with the Love facet. It must always be kept in mind that this is not only a *mental* exercise, it should bring in all the appropriate emotions, not only in the magical personality but also in the actors on the mental stage.

Once the technique has been mastered it will be found that, although, as will be seen, the magical personality is dismissed from consciousness and returned to its place in the subconscious, it will, nevertheless, continue to operate indirectly upon the normal consciousness. For this reason it is a very great help in the building up of the balanced earth-personality.

Again, the student is warned that the *direct* expression of the magical personality should *always* be under the full control of the waking consciousness, and its evocation and dismissal must always be voluntary.

At the commencement of the exercise, the magical personality should not be assumed for longer than ten minutes. At the end of that time the operator should visualise a silvery veil behind him, and mentally see the robed and hooded figure of the magical personality pass through it and disappear. The ring should be taken off and put away, and the operator should stamp once on the ground, thus asserting symbolically that he has returned to normal everyday consciousness. The success or otherwise of the exercise should be noted down in a diary kept for this purpose. The magical personality should then be dismissed from memory until the exercise is again due.

Once the technique has been learnt, and the magical personality stabilised, the time of the exercise may be lengthened, but by then the operator will have commenced some at least of the elementary magical rites, and will know how long the magical personality must be assumed for the work in hand.

It should be clearly understood that the magical personality must be used throughout any ritual operation, which is undertaken. It forms also the basis of the so-called "Body of Light" which is used in the magical operation of "astral projection" or, more accurately, the operation of "Rising on the Planes."

PART IV
MAGICAL RITES

Chapter XVIII

THE CONSTRUCTION AND USE OF FORMS

WE come now to what is sometimes known as the "invisible work" of the magical lodges. It *is* invisible to the physical senses, but very perceptible indeed to trained clairvoyant vision. Before we commence to examine it in detail, it will perhaps be as well if we outline the aim of such work. Briefly, for most of us, our minds are linked so closely with matter that they are to all intents and purposes fixed. Now the magical student has to learn how to detach the mind from its fixation in matter. Next, when this has been done, and the free-flowing mental energy is at his disposal, he has to learn how to control it. Then the power of matter can be used to help the mind, for if the mental energy is now attached to objects that do not belong to the world of sense, though derived from it, the subtle energy can be controlled and directed. So the reflections in the mind of the objects of the material world may be used as channels through which the forces may be directed.

Here we come to the use of "material action." If we mentally visualise the sign of the cross, we do indeed build up a thought image, but if we reinforce our mental picture by making the sign with our hand in the air before us as we build the picture, then the effect of the gesture is to cause the thought-form to become more clearly defined, quite apart from the "magnetic" stresses we may be causing. So, whenever we can, we link symbolic gesture with thought-form construction. As we shall see when we consider the signs and sigils, in certain thought-forms and signs there is a true "correspondence" with much deeper aspects of creation, and the association between the gesture and the thought-form is an organic one; they are the two aspects of an invisible reality.

Before attempting to build the Great Forms, the magical apprentice has to learn how to build up lesser forms, and acquires dexterity thereby.

The principle thought-forms built up in a magical lodge are "The Astral Temple" and the "God-forms," and these are built up most carefully according to a well-established system. In an old-established lodge, there will always be some of the "senior brethren" who are expert in this form construction, and their trained minds will form an invisible foundation into which the inexpert efforts of the "juniors" will be fitted. So, the telesmatic images, as they are termed, are built up by the seniors, but the "temple-form" is built up by all, each member working according to his knowledge and grade. Usually, the energy to be built up is indicated by a series of descriptive passages which are read aloud by one of the *brethren* before the actual ritual is started.

As we have seen, the colour-symbolism employed in magic is of cardinal importance, and the temple-form is built up in those colours, and their complementaries, which in the magical symbolism have been assigned to a particular type of manifested force. Thus, an operation of Venus will need a temple-form coloured in green and its complementaries, whilst an operation of Luna will call for a temple in mauve and silver, and the complementaries thereto.

When the magical work is being centred upon the individual consciousness of the magician, as in the "path-workings"* so called, then the imagery assigned to the particular path is built up later in the ceremony, but the "temple-form" will be that of the Sephirah at the head of the path chosen. For example, the 32nd path leads from *Malkuth* to *Yesod* on the Tree, and the temple would be built according to the imagery of *Yesod*.

It is well to remember here that the Sephiroth on the Tree of Life represent the points where the individual subjective consciousness makes contact with the objective energies of the spiritual universe around him. Again it must be reiterated that the whole of the Tree, the ten holy Sephiroth and their twenty-two connecting paths, can be used in the colour scales, and the effect will then be according to the scale used.

Here is an excerpt from some descriptive passages which are used in this way. It is part of a ritual designed to make contact with the Celtic forces and images in the racial mind:—

> Brethren, allow this vision to rise before you. We stand upon a high hill in the presence of the Holy Angel in whose care is the sleeping city below. His mighty figure towers above us and His blessing is upon us as we turn our faces westward and forward towards our goal.
>
> We are travelling alike in Time and Space, and as we proceed, there rise around us the scenes and conditions of primæval Britain; that Britain whose children we are.
>
> Beneath our feet is the close green turf of the ancient road, above us the Moon shines brilliantly in the star-studded indigo vault of the Heavens, and around us gradually appear the outlines of that Elder Britain wherein is contained the Sanctuary of our worship. This is the Britain of Arthur and Merlin, yea, and the Britain also of those who built this road, who reared these guiding mounds of earth, and first devised these dew-ponds which shine placidly before us in the

---

* In this use of the term "Path" we are omitting the ten "Paths" usually known collectively as the Sephiroth.

moonlight. They the Children of Atlantis, seeking in stern and rude conditions of Nature, relief from the degenerate luxury of their Home-land, established in this land a Centre of Light which through the ages has stood and shall stand until that day when the purposes of the Lord of the Aeon have been accomplished.

Around arise mighty forests . . . .

As we have said, this journey ends in the temple-form of the particular station on the Tree with whose forces we desire to work. The senior brethren present will have built up the temple-form in great detail, and the telepathic pressure of their trained minds will cause the crude efforts of some of the junior brethren to be modified sufficiently to enable them to be built into the "form" which has been constructed. Indeed at times it does happen that one of the lesser brethren finds that instead of his own personal images arising in response to the description of the vision-journey, a set of strange, yet potent images arise within his consciousness. This is due to his psychic rapport with one or other of the senior brethren, or with the temple-form they have built up.

The layout of the temple as described in the key-reading with its symbolic furniture, of which the physical plane temple is a replica, will build up an astral counterpart to the latter, and it is in this astral temple, built without hands, and in itself symbolising another temple, eternal in the heavens, that the invisible forces invoked and concentrated by the ritual will flow in their proper channels. The symbolic furniture of the lodge, which is "magnet-ised" by the presiding magus, becomes both a channel of the forces, and a series of indicators, by means of which we may know how those energies are operating at any given moment.

But indicators and channels alike are useless unless there is power present. Many people who have tried their 'prentice hand with magical ritual fail to realise this. They are like someone who stands before a switchboard which is crowded with indicators and switches.

They see the switches are " on," and they think the current is flowing. But the main switch is " off," and all the lesser switches are without power. Should the main switch be put " on," then immediately the switchboard is "live," the needles on the meters move to indicate the power, and the indicating lamps light up. Quite a definite change.

So it is with the magical lodge. The astral temple may have been built and linked with its physical counterpart, but before the astral energies can flow, the equivalent of the main switch must be operated, and its power passed through its correct channels to the lodge. This is done by the use of the Telesmatic Images, and in the very first part of the ritual, known as "The Preparation of the Place," some of these images with their appropriate signs are built up in order that all vagrant astral and etheric forces may be cleared from the temple.

One form of this preparation of the place may be seen in any Catholic Church at the commencement of the Mass, when the celebrant performs the "Asperges." He sprinkles "magnetised" or "Holy Water" around the altar and sanctuary and towards the congregation, holding in his mind the "intention" of purification, and reciting part of a Psalm "Thou shalt purge me with hyssop O Lord, and I shall be clean . . . . . "

This being done, he invokes the assistance of the "Angel of the Mass," that this Being may "guide, guard, visit, protect and cherish" those who have met together for worship. In the lodge rituals this preparation of the place is done by one of two methods. The first and most generally used in the lodges of the Lesser Mysteries is what is known as the Banishing Ritual of the Lesser Pentagram.

The actual Sign of the Pentagram or Five-pointed Star is one which has been used in magical work for many centuries, but the Ritual of the Pentagram seems to owe its origin to the synthetic genius of the Hermetic Order of the Golden Dawn, that magical system which is the fount from which most of the Western magical systems have been derived.

There are several ways of tracing the pentagram, and these are referred to the four elements. The Banishing Pentagram is the Pentagram of " Earth."

The ritual is described by Israel Regardie in his book *The Middle Pillar,* and the relevant part will be found in Appendix I at the end of this book.

The circumambulation around the lodge-room, which is part of this Banishing Ritual, has the effect of building up, in the astral temple, of what appears to clairvoyant vision to be a shimmering wall or barrier of swiftly-moving light. This seems to surround the whole of the lodge, and takes the shape of a half-sphere, whose highest point is directly over the altar; which, in the rituals, is placed in the centre of the lodge floor. Presumably the psychic wall is a full sphere, the other half being under the lodge floor. That this is the case, in some instances at least, was brought home to the writer in a very definite manner. In all magical work punctuality is of the utmost importance, and to ensure this, the doors of the building in

THE CONSTRUCTION AND USE OF FORMS

which the lodge (of which he was a member) was situated, were closed twenty minutes before the time fixed for the lodge meeting. By a mischance, he arrived late, and though he got in, he could not go up into the lodge room, but had to sit down below until the conclusion of the ritual.

Sitting quietly in the room immediately below the actual lodge-room, he suddenly became aware that the psychic atmosphere around had quite definitely altered, and the whole "feel" of the room was that of the purified astral conditions of the lodge-room itself.

The theosophical clairvoyant, Bishop C. W. Leadbeater, in his book *The Science of the Sacraments*, gives a similar description of the purified psychic atmosphere of the Church after certain ritual work has been done.

Sir Ronald Fraser, in his occult novel *Sun in Scorpio*, refers to this purified atmosphere as producing some degree of dizziness, or even slight nose-bleeding in those who enter it unprepared. The present writer can vouch for this happening, in some cases at least. It is within this atmosphere, which constitutes a veritable "forcing-house" of magical power, that the work of the lodge is done, and its effects upon the members thereof is to quicken into activity the latent powers which they all possess. This astro-etheric atmosphere is not always the same. It varies greatly in intensity, and no two ritual-workings are ever exactly alike, although the ceremonial in both cases may be the same.

The Banishing Ritual of the Lesser Pentagram is designed to be applied from a particular mental angle. If it is used blindly and without any knowledge of the principles which underlie it, then, although it works up to a point, it does not produce the maximum purification possible. It is a ritual which is designed to bring through certain forces into the psychic atmosphere of the lodge. These forces proceed from the Intelligences who direct those aspects of elemental life which are known in occultism as the four elements of Earth, Air, Fire and Water.

Only the very ignorant and naïve critics of Magic still believe that the occultists think of these "elements" as being the material earth, air, fire and water. They are actually the elemental energies which lie behind and express themselves through the physical plane elements. All manifestation is sacramental, the outward and visible sign being a channel of that spiritual power of which it is the expression in the phenomenal worlds.

So the basic "inertia" of the physical element, earth is the expression of an energy whose mode of manifestation it is. So it is with all the four elements of the magicians. They are the "self-relationships," if we may use such a term, through which the cosmic life is manifested in matter. In order to dispel any doubt, the esoteric schools refer to the occult "elements" as the Water of the Wise, the Earth of the Wise, the Air of the Wise, and the Fire of the Wise, thus tacitly pointing out the distinction between them and their physical plane expressions.

We have spoken of "directing intelligences." These are sometimes termed the "Kings of the Elements," sometimes "The Deva Lords," and those who have heard of the "Four Crowned Kings" will realise that the story reveals and yet conceals the mysteries of "Another Place."

These Kings of the Elements, then, are the directing Beings under whom comes the ocean of evolving life, and this evolving life is behind and working through the matter of this physical plane. Now the elemental life is not individual, as is ours. It is a *wave of life*, not *a group of lives*, even though individual wavelets on the crest of the wave appear to be individual and independent. This is but an appearance, not yet are the masks to be lit by the flame of the eternally proceeding Word, and to become living souls. Although possessed of the normal powers of their plane, powers which to us appear supernormal and "miraculous," it must never be forgotten that they are *below* man in spiritual evolution.

Any attempt to drive a bargain with them or to attempt to bribe or appease them in order that they may be induced to act on our behalf brings us on to their level, and results in our becoming their slaves, not their masters.

Nor may we adjure and curse them by the mighty Names to render obedience to us, for such use of the mighty Names can only be operated from the level of the personality, with all its faults and imperfections, and again will expose us to the risk of being dominated by the forces we invoke.

But, if we approach the elemental hosts having in our aura the signs of the Elemental Kings, then we come as light-bearers to the lesser lives; we are channels to them of the glory of their rulers, and our employment of them works along the plan which those Mighty Ones have for their evolving children.

But how may we become the servants and ambassadors of those Mighty Ones? Simply by rising in meditation to a realisation of their nature and spiritual degree. In so far as we do this, so those aspects of our personality which correspond to them, which are actually parts of them, will glow and evolve, and automatically we shall dominate the elemental beings, since we come in the names and the powers of their most potent rulers.

Let the would-be magician meditate upon this; let him endeavour to follow the hints thrown out in the various magical books, and as he begins to realise the true nature of the rulers, he will find that the elemental kingdoms become his servants. He will have seen a plan placed upon the tracing board, eternal in the Heavens, and in that plan he will have discerned his own place and opportunity, and will have surrendered himself to it. Then having nothing, but gaining all things, dying to the personal self that the true Self may be served, he will have become one with the rulers of the elementals, and in their name will he speak the Words of Power. Then the elemental host will obey him, for upon his brow will they behold the sigils of their kings.

This is the ideal which the would-be magician must hold ever before him, and though, of course, its perfection is not to be gained in an instant, it must always be held in his consciousness as in the name of the Eternal, he evokes the elemental hosts.

In the Pentagram Ritual, the four Arch-angels, Michael, Gabriel, Uriel and Raphael are invoked as the rulers respectively of Fire, Water, Earth and Air, and the telesmatic images should be built up in detail. With the success of the concentration and visualisation exercises such image-building should become easy for the apprentice magician. Although the telesmatic images of the Pentagram Ritual afford excellent objects for such visualisation practice, it is advised that the apprentice should gain his proficiency by using other images which have no immediate significance, and reserve his visualisation of the Archangelic images for the times when he begins to practise the use of the Pentagram Ritual.

Just as the aspirant to the Catholic priesthood performs the ceremony of the Mass again and again for practise, but without deliberately invoking the spiritual forces which are brought through thereby, so the magical aspirant should perform this ritual daily, attempting each time to build up the telesmatic images in all their detail and colouring, but being careful not to invoke the forces of which they will be channels at some future date.

Since the meditation above described will have begun, the work will proceed "from above to below"; as the spiritual realisation gained is brought through into the personality, and "from below upwards," as the visualising faculty builds up the forms through which the forces will work.

Finally, the time will come, unmistakeably made known to the student, when the forces at last flow through the forms. A routine exercise may have been commenced in the usual way. Then, quite suddenly, as the telesmatic images build up in the mental vision, there is a spasm of will which appears to be independent of the normal consciousness, and is almost a pain within the heart, the realisation of previous meditations are suddenly present in the mind, and as the words are vibrated there comes the sudden thrill of awe, the shiver of the personality as the higher powers flood through it. Then into the magical Names and Words there comes a majesty and a power, the voice "rings" with the true magical "note" and through the personality pours the power of the rulers, and the telesmatic images live and shine with the radiant life and light of Those whom they represent.

Thereafter will the student be able effectively to employ this ritual.

What has been written concerning the telesmatic images of the Pentagram Ritual, holds good for all the other images: the God-Forms, etc., used in the lodge and also in the construction of what are known as talismans, i.e. articles which have been "charged" with certain psychic energies, and have thus been linked up or "contacted" with the underlying spiritual forces of the macrocosm.

With talismans we will deal separately, since their production forms a very important part of practical magical work.

Chapter XIX

BUILDING A RITUAL

THE title of this chapter may be somewhat surprising to many students of magical work, since they have a fixed idea that one should only use those rituals which have been handed down from the past, and when such ancient rituals are used, not one single word should be altered. Although one should not alter a ritual without good reason, and though, as the "Chaldean Oracles" declare the "barbarous names" of evocation should not be changed, it remains that the practising magician often makes use of rituals constructed by himself. They meet an immediate need, and are quite as effective, in their own way, as the traditional rites. For the purpose of his training, the apprentice magician is also made to construct rituals dealing with the various forces with which he is working, and these rituals are carefully checked by his teacher. They are based upon the principles he has been given, and are an excellent test of his grasp of those principles.

So it has been decided to give the principles of such ritual construction in this book. If a rite is properly constructed then it can be of the greatest value to those who use it, but it is first of all necessary for the student to get a clear idea in his mind as to the *purpose* for which the ritual is required.

As we have seen in that part of this book which deals with the building of the magical personality, there are three main aspects under which the Inner Plane forces present themselves to us, and it is along the appropriate line that we must work.

It is therefore necessary that before we begin to construct a ritual we should, by careful meditation, get our reason for working this rite crystal-clear in our mind. This is not always easy, as associated secondary motives usually make themselves known, but with perseverance they can be resolved, and the main reason for our proposed working isolated in our mind.

In the Catholic Church, such special reasons for the celebration of the Mass are known as "Intentions," and in the magical work such an Intention is *absolutely necessary,* for the mind of the magician must be one-pointed if the invoked and evoked forces are to be wisely directed. The mind supplies the forms and channels through which the forces work, and the more definite the channel, the more control can be exercised over the forces flowing therein.

Having determined our Intention, the next step is to ascertain what beings and forces must be invoked or evoked for the work in hand, and the magical correspondences must then be checked up. In practical magical training, tables of correspondences are used as part of the routine exercises. The most important of these, as far as the Ten Stations of the Tree of Life are concerned, are given in Dion Fortune's *The Mystical Qabalah*. There are many other correspondences, but these are the primary ones. Since we are dealing with Western magic, it is the Qabalistic Tree of Life upon which we draw for our work.

Other systems, as we have seen, have other *mandalas*, or glyphs, which are equally effective for those who are working along these lines, but it is imperative that the magician should keep strictly to one system. This canot be too greatly emphasised. Though we may learn from the philosophies and techniques of other systems, we are inviting trouble if we mix the practical methods. We may adapt them for our purpose when, at a later date, we have the requisite knowledge, but this adaptation is work for the magus, not the neophyte.

From the tables of correspondences then, we may now select those we need. Here we are guided by our Intention, for this will clearly indicate the station of the Tree on which we shall work.

A point to be remembered here is that we are working within the Earth-Sphere, *Malkuth* on the Tree, nor in any direct sense do we transcend that station. If we invoke the divine forces of *Atziluth*, it is by a process of induction that they work upon the corresponding levels in the objective earth-sphere, and our own subjective sphere of sensation, stimulating into activity our own inner forces.

In passing, it may be noted that the power of a great teacher lies not in his teaching, which may be simply a re-presentation of existing teaching, nor is it due to his personal power over his followers. Rather it is a catalytic action, whereby what he is causes the inner nature of his followers to emerge from the depths, thus bringing their personal selves through the death of the lower self to a resurrection and a "rebirth in eternity."

Now in the depths of the earth-sphere there are the archaic images, which through all the millenia of man's existence have been the conditioning channels through which the universal life was mediated to the sons of men, and these images are the mundane expressions of the bright archetypal images through which the material world has been projected into materialisation.

The archaic images used will, as we have seen, depend upon

our Intention, and we will suppose that this is for "Illumination from our true Inner Self," our higher spiritual consciousness, that part of our nature which, according to Christian mysticism, is the "ground where God and man meet."

The station of the Tree, therefore is *Tiphareth*. We are now faced with the choice of three magical images: a child, a majestic king and a sacrificed god. We may use whichever of these three is most expressive of our Intention. Since this is illumination from our higher consciousness, then either the Child or the King will be appropriate.

For various reasons, some not unconnected with the tendency of the lower or "false ego" to identify the higher with itself rather than the reverse, the magical image of the Child is by far the better of the two for the beginner. It points out that the process of illumination is a gradual one, and this is something which must be realised by the beginner. In many books and articles on the subject of magic, the results obtainable by the trained magician after many years of practice are indicated as being within the grasp of the beginner.

Now in certain cases this may be to some extent correct. We come to the magical work bringing with us our natural talents, and in some people the magical capacity seems to be so near the surface that its awakening is both rapid and spectacular. But, in the majority of cases, the ecstatic heights of the Mountain of Illumination are not for the neophyte. In the traditional magical schools, those who show such spectacular promise are usually put through the routine training mill a great deal more thoroughly than their less-gifted brethren, in order that they may bring a *balanced* personality to the Great Work.

Since the Sephirah *Tiphareth* is also the station of the Sun, we find the colour scale to be golden amber for we desire to bring the higher consciousness through into the physical brain consciousness.

This colour must be somehow used in the furnishing of our place of operation or in the vestments we use. If we are not using vestments, then we must visualise the colour around ourselves as a vesture of golden light.

We come now to the God-Name, under the presidency of which the station of *Tiphareth* is placed. This name is *Tetragrammaton Aloah Va Daath*. This Name may be meditated on in the interpretation given in *The Mystical Qabalah*, "God made manifest in the sphere of the mind."

The archangel is Raphael, the healer; and, if we think of

"health" in its meaning of "wholeness," then we see how appropriate is the attribution of the archangel of healing to the sphere of harmonised balance.

The angels are the kings of the elements and here we are linking with those spiritual principles which manifest in our world as the elemental instincts. Concerning these we have already written.

The breast-jewel or lamen, is the Rose-Cross, and in the usual form this is a Latin cross with exfoliated arms, and in its centre a red rose of thirty-two petals, thus linking the symbol with the glyph of the Tree of Life.

The altar should be a double cube. This is the symbol of *Malkuth,* the Kingdom of Earth, whereas the symbol of *Tiphareth* is the cube. But as we are in intention bringing through the forces of *Tiphareth* into *Malkuth,* the altar of the double cube is quite appropriate.

Upon the altar should be set a light, symbolising the "Light that lighteth every man," which shines ever within the heart. Upon the altar, also, should be placed the volume of the sacred scriptures of ones own race, as a symbol that we are working not by our own personal desires but in obedience to the Law of the Eternal, whose children we are.

The covering of the altar should be white or gold, and this should also be the colour of our vestments.

The incense burning in our temple should be one of the Dionysiac perfumes; Cinnamon is ascribed to *Tiphareth.*

We must now commence to devise our ritual. We begin by "preparing the place of working." This means that we cleanse the etheric and astral atmosphere of our room by the use of a banishing ritual, such as the ritual of the Lesser Pentagram, which cleanses the room and at the same time erects a formidable barrier of psychic force, a barrier which prevents intrusion from the swarming astral lives which are attracted like moths to a flame, by our magical work.

Having cleansed the place of working (and, by the same token, having cleansed ourselves also by the performance of this rite) we now make our psychic contacts with our assistants, who are functioning as fellow-priests of the Mysteries. If we are working alone, then we make an interior psychic contact with those aspects of our own nature which would otherwise be represented by the assistants. This psychic contact is made by a series of questions and answers.

It is to be remembered that when we thus awaken and co-ordinate our forces, we are making contact with the telesmatic images which are linked with them, and through which they flow.

Having thus linked ourselves with the great deep within us, we now aspire to the Eternal. But we do this in the name and power of the great archangel of the sphere of *Shemesh*, the Sun, even Raphael the healer, vibrating his name and at the same time building up the telesmatic image which shall be the channel of his power.

Now we approach the climax of our operation. We build up the magical image of *Tiphareth*, in this case the image of the Child and affirm our Intention.

Then, holding our mind upon that image, we remain mentally poised, like a seagull floating apparently motionless in the gale. We know, when we see the gull thus motionless, that there is a very real effort being made, and only by that effort can it maintain its position in the face of the wind. So it is with this invocation of light. Upon the ritual, as upon a four-square foundation, we have erected a pyramid of thought and effort, and now, standing upon its truncated summit we reach forth into the divine aether and wait, poised thus in an ecstasy of aspiration.

Now it may be that we reach this point many times without any apparent result. Results there will be, however, for the repeated use of the ritual is building a power within us, and one day, as we aspire towards the Divine Child standing with the light of the Supernal Sun raying out around Him, there will come that burning force which surges through us, the mental scene will disappear and we shall find ourselves in the station of the Sun which rises with healing in its wings. Around us will flame the glory of that Sun, as we become for a moment identified with the Eternal Child, and on either side of us will flame the Wings of Glory. Then the forms of the mind will fade from view and a new mode of consciousness, different entirely from our normal consciousness, will dawn upon us, and for that brief moment we shall know as that spirit which is our True Self always knows.

But even before this, there will have been periods when, having reached out in aspiration in this way, some less phenomenal contact will have been consciously experienced.

Usually this will take the form of a curious clarity of the mind. The ordinary mental processes seem for the time to be curiously interpenetrated by another mode of consciousness which is felt to be working at an entirely different rate and manner; a mode of consciousness which apprehends directly, instead of having to follow a definite train of thought.

Of course, in the early days, such a new mode of consciousness is somewhat unreliable; we have not had enough experience of it;

but as it recurs, and becomes more frequent, then we begin to build up in the waking consciousness a set of symbolic images which will enable us to use it to the fullest advantage.

When, in our ritual work, we have reached the stage of invocation and have reached out to the Infinite, we must remember that we have to return to the physical level, we "cannot at the shrine remain." In fact, to so do would be to nullify the contact we have made, for it is essential that the illumination we receive should be brought through into the physical consciousness if it is to be of use to us.

Therefore we must return from the pyramid on the heights of Abiegnus, and descending that Mountain of Illumination pass through the Pylon Gate into physical sensory consciousness.

We, therefore, again formulating the magical image and vibrating the God-name, adore the Eternal through that symbol, and then, recalling the telesmatic image of the archangel of the sphere we thank him for his assistance.

Then in the names of the elemental kings we give the benediction of the Eternal to the elemental beings who have assisted us, and dismiss them to their own place. In more precise terms we may say that, having set up a series of stresses in the Astral Light, we now release those stresses.

We then withdraw our contacts with the assistants who have been our fellow-priests of the Mystery, or if we have been working alone, we draw back into latency in our sphere of sensation the telesmatic images we used to evoke the corresponding aspects of our inner nature.

We are now back on the physical plane, and we should now perform some physical action which will symbolise our return into the sphere of *Malkuth*.

One such device is to use a gavel or other instrument to make a knock or series of knocks. These, since we are asserting our return to *Malkuth*, may be in two groups of five, or five groups of two, thus formulating the number ten which is assigned to this station on the Tree.

These knocks or " *knells*," as they are sometimes termed, have an added virtue, since they do tend to awaken us from any slight dreaminess, and so bring us more fully into mundane awareness.

Only two things are left. It is important that, *immediately after* such a magical experiment, *a record be made*. If this is not done, the finer and more delicate aspects of the experience will tend to be forgotten.

Finally, the magician should remember his own motto and having known, dared, and willed, should keep silent. To gossip about his experiences is to draw upon him thought-currents which may seriously hinder his magical progress.

It will be found that in the construction of a rite, the majestic beat and rhythm of the Elizabethan English is of the greatest help, and this is particularly the case with the magnificent language of the Authorised Version of the Bible.

The use of the technical device of Commemoration, already described, should not be lost sight of in the construction of the rite.

It should be a simple matter for the apprentice magician to select suitable characters for such commemorative work in the sphere of *Tiphareth*.

Chapter XX

TALISMANIC MAGIC

FOR most people the word "talisman" conjures up a picture of "lucky charms", oriental amulets, and such like devices, whilst Protestants of the narrower type would also include St. Christopher medallions, scapulars, rosaries and crucifixes under the same heading.

But in point of fact, such things as "lucky pigs" or zodiacal birth-stones are poles apart from St. Christopher medallions, etc.; the whole idea behind them is different.

Since magical work very often involves the use of talismans, it is necessary that we should consider their fashioning, and understand the theory of their action. That they *do* act, is a matter beyond dispute, for those who have carefully studied the subject, though *all* do not act, neither are those that do equally effective.

There are two distinct lines of thought in connection with the use of talismans and curiously enough these two modes of approach are to be found in the two great sections of Christendom, the Roman Catholic Church and the Eastern Orthodox Churches.

The first line of thought which we will consider is what may be termed the material line. In general terms it may be stated as follows. Material substances are capable of being "charged" with certain super-material forces, under certain conditions. Some substances are better than others for this class of work. As life is immanent in all things, since all things are an expression of the One Life, the substances of the material plane are the expressions, or "accidents," of the true underlying reality or " substance."

As living forces of all grades are ever flowing through the world, and through all living things, it follows that these forces will be altered in intensity or nature by the action upon them of other living consciousnesses. So it is held, an object which is to be used as a talisman must first be "purified"; the mixed "magnetisms" it has picked up in its travels must be banished from it. Then by will and thought a fresh charge of living energy is poured into it, and this charge of energy is in some mysterious way stored in the material talisman. Anyone wearing the talisman will be affected by it, and tuned to its own "vibration" (to use the occult cliché); they will tend to feel, think and act, in accordance with the intention of the maker of the talisman. This we may term the "charge" theory, since it regards the physical talisman as a *storehouse* of superphysical power.

The other theory is that everything physical is linked by our "concept" of it with our minds, and with the Universal Mind in such a way that the relationship between the object perceived and the perceiver results in a normal mental relationship between the two.

If now, the object is perceived in the mind as being in other than the normal relationship with the perceiver, then it becomes a sacramental thing, "an outward and visible sign of an inward and spiritual grace." To affect this change of perception, the one making the talisman must lift up his heart and mind to the highest concept he can mentally reach, and there realise for a brief moment the particular virtue for which the talisman is being made. The talisman is now linked, through his mind, with the divine power it is being made to evoke, and because all minds are one at the deeper levels, then the object is linked in this extra relationship with its maker, the one for whom it is made, and with that aspect of the divine mind which is the root of the particular virtue which the talisman is designed to help.

There is another theory, quite a simple matter-of-fact idea, held by the Roman Church, or at least by some of its priests. We think it was the Roman Catholic writer, Monseignor R. H. Benson, who wrote, "When the Catholic Church blesses a bridge, and invokes an angel to guard it, she confidently expects that God will send down such an angel."

Now the magical theory actually covers all three of these theories, and it is a theory which has been checked and tested by clairvoyant seers over many years.

The magical ritual regards the physical base of the talisman as being in its own way an expression of the Immanent Life, but as also being contaminated by the mixed emanations from other lives, of all grades of consciousness. So, like his Catholic brother, he first "exorcises" the object.

That is to say, he drives out of the object the heterogenous "magnetisms" it has accumulated.

Then he re-charges it with his own "magnetism" and according to the work which it has to do, he links it with the appropriate grade of being on the inner levels. Again, like his Catholic brother, he invokes the help of an angel and again he is certain, from the observations of seers through the ages, that the angel invoked does manifest and is linked with the object.

His concept of angels is, however, somewhat different from the conventional winged and robed figures of Christian art. Those who may have read the late Charles William's novel *The Place of the Lion* will perhaps understand more clearly than it can be expressed here, the nature of those beings whom we term "angels."

In the Eastern religious systems they are termed *devas* or Shining Ones, and they are held to be the subordinate intelligences behind all natural phenomena. Many grades of these beings are recognised, ranging from great solar angels down through countless levels to the infinitesimal consciousnesses behind the life of the cells of the physical body, and beyond to the infra-microscopic electronic systems of the atoms.

All departments of life and activity in this planet and its attendant subjective spheres of consciousness are under the control of these beings who in their turn are, as it were, the living mirrors from which the plan of the logos is reflected into this earth.

In my former book,* in a chapter dealing with the magical images, this subject of the *deva*-lives was touched upon in connection with the technical device of "Commemoration." One was dealing there with the use of the living personality as a focussing point for the great magical images of the collective unconscious, and the deva side of things was not stressed.

Nevertheless it is true that the very substance of our emotional and mental bodies is part of the being of the *devas* and all our emotions and thoughts are to some extent affected by the consciousnesses of these beings. In the Christian Revelation we learn of the Seven Mighty Spirits before the Throne, and these mighty ones are the seven archangels of Judaic-Christian thought. Of these the four best known are Gabriel, Michael, Raphael, and Uriel. It will be noted that these four find their place in the Banishing Ritual of the Lesser Pentagram, and on the stations of the Tree of Life, all seven are duly classified.

In the Roman Church the saints are often called upon in this matter of "blessing" a particular object, and because the saint, both in his earth-life and now in the spiritual realm, is a channel for a certain aspect of the divine power, so the *deva*-agents of that phase of divine energy work through that saint, even as the hosts of the mighty Raphael, the healer archangel, work through all who are called by profession or vocation to the ministry of healing, doctors, nurses, psychic, occult and metaphysical healers alike; all are under the care of the archangel of healing.

* *Magic: Its Ritual, Power and Purpose* (Aquarian Press).

So when the magician is "charging" his talisman, he recites the names of those who in their earth-days were the channels of the divine force with which he desires to charge the object. His "naming them with intention" links him with their psycho-magnetic "trace" in the Astral Light, their exalted consciousnesses strike down with a momentary flash upon the consciousness of the magician, and the *deva*-life of the corresponding grade links up with the object in the appearance of the person so commemorated.

But since this has linked the object with the mind of this being, it has also linked it with the corresponding level of the collective unconscious, and through that with the divine archetypes in the mind of the Logos.

It will be seen that a talisman may be made which is simply a storage battery for some of the magnetic energy of the operator, or by his "intention," a thought-form charged with that energy may be linked with it; the appropriate *deva*-life may be evoked to bring such an energy to bear upon the user of the talisman, or the article having been purified by exorcism and charged with the operator's magnetism, the appropriate *deva*-life may be evoked through his deliberate linking-up through the magnetic trace in the Astral Light with one who was, and still is, a channel for that power. Such a commemorative linking puts the operator in touch through this being with the divine archetypes.

It will easily be seen which is the most effective of these methods, but naturally they are all three used as conditions appear to indicate.

The material used for the making of a talisman varies according to the nature of the force concerned. The Tree of Life gives the metals, jewels, etc., appropriate. For example, a talisman for inspiring martial power would be made of iron or steel, since this is the metal associated with Mars, whilst one for the helping of emotional stress might be made of copper, the metal of Venus. Parchment is a good retainer of "magnetism." So is olive oil. Water quickly absorbs it, but soon loses it. Clay absorbs and holds it for a long period. Silk and glass are both bad substances for talismans. In fact silk is often used to wrap up a completed talisman in order to preserve its "charge."

The best talisman is one which you make for yourself. However it often happens that because of the lack of the particular power in question you are unable to effectively manufacture one. In this case, recourse must be had to someone who can make it for you.

This will always be done for you without any charge being made, for the true magician is bound to exact no fee for such work.

In the last resort, remember the talisman is but a device to help you to full activity along its particular line. There should come a time when you can cheerfully discard it, since it will have served its purpose. Each talisman is personal to the one for whom it was made, and cannot therefore be given to someone else suffering from a similar trouble; the diagnosis may be quite different!

This is very important, since second-hand talismans do appear now and again, and their use can cause much trouble. "When in doubt, cast it out" is a good maxim when dealing with such a thing, but where this for any reason is not possible, the talisman concerned should be taken to a competent magician to be de-magnetised, or if the owner has the necessary knowledge he may do this himself.

When once a talisman has been charged, it is *ipso facto* linked with the one who has charged it, and it is necessary to break this psychic link if the operator does not wish to be so linked.

This is done by using a "locking" prayer, and by breaking, in the mind, the silvery thread which is visualised as the link between the operator and the talisman.

When a talisman has to be destroyed it is first de-magnetised. For various occult reasons, this is important.

A very important aspect of this technique of charging or magnetising physical objects is the consecration of objects and buildings to be centres of radiation of spiritual forces.

The writer recently attended the dedication service of a rebuilt Presbyterian-Congregational United Church building, and was amused to hear the minister who dedicated it say in his sermon "We of the Reformed Tradition know that in this dedication we have performed no magical action, have made no change in this building."

As a matter of psychic fact, the writer had observed clairvoyantly a very decided change in the psychic atmosphere therein!

Chapter XXI

THE WAY OF *MAGICAL* ATTAINMENT

IT is now time to look back upon that which we have written in this book, and give the reader some instruction in the sequence of training in the magical art.

It will have been noticed that this training is based entirely upon the personality of the would-be magician and this carries with it many important implications. In the early stages of our magical training, our motives are usually mixed, but from the beginning one motive must be present in our minds if we wish safely to tread the magical path. This motive we have already referred to. It is *the desire to know in order to serve,* and it must be the primary motive of our interest in magic. Other motives, such as intellectual curiosity, emotional appeal or aesthetic appreciation, may co-exist with this primary desire, and may each in their own way be catered for. But this motive of service must always come first.

It is important to realise that the service of the magician to his fellow-men takes two definite forms. It may, and does, help them by what the magician *does,* but also (and always) they are helped by *what he is.* For the human race is one, in its deeper levels, and when one man begins to think and work in a certain way, he affects the whole of the group-soul of the race to which he belongs. It is not primarily necessary that he should teach others either publicly or privately, though of course he usually does.

Neither is it essential that he should organize bodies pledged to certain political, religious or social problems, though, once again, many do so work by forming such bodies. But the simple fact that he is what he is, is sufficient to influence the deeper mind of the race, and so affect all those myriad individuals whose minds make up that racial mind. So through wisdom does the magician build his house of life, his personality, anew, and by understanding is it established.

It will be seen later, how this is brought about. At the moment we are stressing this essential point that the primary service which the magician renders to his fellows is that he becomes a stable centre through which the Hierarchies of Light may lift up humanity.

In conversation with a fellow-priest, the present writer was told that the difference between the magician and the priest was that in the one instance powers were exercised *by* the magician, whilst in the other, power was exercised *through* the priest. But this is really a false antithesis. Both priest and magician do certain things, and *through* both of them power is made manifest. The real difference lies elsewhere, and does not enter into our present discussion. It is sufficient to say here that the magician affects others both by that which he does and by that which he is.

Now that which he does is very important, for it is building up into his personality certain magical reaction-habits, and it is these which in the end are far more important than the outward cere- monial and ritual of the magical act.

For the adept-magician, though he may use the age-old cere- monies, does not *depend* upon them. The observances which were the outward visible symbols of inner states of emotion, mind and spirit, have, through the training he has undergone, been withdrawn into and made components of his inner consciousness. Then the preparation of the place is effected within the Ring-Pass-Not, the limiting boundary of his own aura, the angel of the operation is invoked therein, and the mystical temple is built in his mental sphere. Then into this temple not made with hands, there descends the divine *Shekinah*, the Glory of the Eternal, and She abides over the Seat of Justice between the Cherubim in the Holy of Holies of the magician's heart.

Long ago it was said by a great mystic who wrote under the name of Angelus Silesius:

> Though Christ a thousand times
> In Bethlehem be born,
> And not within thy heart,
> Thou art all forlorn.
> The Cross on Calvary
> Thou lookest to in vain,
> Except within thy heart
> It be set up again.

But, it will be said, this is mysticism; what has that to do with magic? The answer is, that in the high reaches of both magic and mysticism we come to a common ground; that light within which lighteth every man, the indwelling spirit, our true Self.

Both magic and mysticism here find their true *raison d'etre*, and because of this, all the great religions of the world combine, in vary- ing proportions, these two paths to the eternal.

We have stressed this truly religious nature of magic in order to make quite clear to the beginner that although in the beginning his interest in magic may be simply motivated by intellectual curiosity or emotional appeal, against the background of his desire to serve humanity, yet as he progresses he will find himself irresist- ibly brought to a point where the truly religious nature of his chosen path becomes clear.

In the beginning, however, it is important that he is trained to perform the external ceremonies in such a way that on their own plane they are as perfect as it is possible to make them. Those who have read magical fiction will no doubt have read of the dire results following upon an ill-drawn pentagram, or the wrong pronunciation of a name.

Though the occult reasons for such unfortunate happenings are cogent enough, the real point at issue is that the outward ceremony should be perfect on its own plane.

In the yoga systems of the East there are three main paths; *Raja* yoga, *Bhakti* yoga, and *Gnani* yoga, the paths of Power, Love, and Wisdom respectively, but there are secondary preparatory yogas such as *Hatha* yoga which prepare the aspirant in readiness for the time when he will commence to tread his chosen path.

So, in the magical act, there is a definite path of preparation, and part of this is devoted to the training of the personality *on the physical plane and through the physical body,* and this is begun by the physical plane ceremonial training.

How many people realise that the "primordial language" of mime still speaks through our subconscious actions, gestures, mannerisms, etc., and is so communicated to those who are with us? But this is a very real factor in ceremonial; in fact it has been said that a magical rite could be celebrated without ritual words if the signs appropriate are used, and this is no idle statement, as the present writer has become aware.

So our ceremonial actions must be correctly carried out, and every gesture, every movement, be done in such a way that the whole ceremony, as the Roman Catholic writer, R. H. Benson, once said, is offered as a jewel, perfect of its type. He was referring to Catholic ceremonial, but the principle applies to all magical ceremonial work.

The "spell of woven paces and waving hands" is not likely to be one hundred per cent. efficient, if at the same time, by our subconscious physical gestures, we are asserting the opposite point of view!

So the magician-to-be must practise correct movement, poise and balance of the physical body. This is not easy, particularly when he is working alone, but it is something which must be done.

Along this line of physical training lies also the care of the physical body. Always the aim should be to make the body the willing steed of the spirit. False asceticism has no place here. If things are eschewed, it is simply in obedience to "if this, then not that." Certain physical habits may have to be deleted *for the time*, in order that certain work may be done, but the magical bow must not always be kept taut. There is deep wisdom in the story of the devotee who sought to speak with St. John, and found him playing with a tame partridge. As he gazed with a certain scorn at the apostle's occupation, the venerable man inquired of him whether, being a soldier, he *always* kept his bow tight strung!

So it is with the physical. In magical work we require a well-trained, well-adjusted and harmoniously balanced physical body, and this we shall not obtain by any excessive or false asceticism. So the first exercises in the magical training are concerned with *willed* relaxation of the body, and the control of the breath. These are essential basic exercises. Here it is necessary to reiterate that all the work which the aspirant may undertake at a later date depends *entirely* (apart, of course, from any exceptional natural magical ability) upon the faithful practise of these basic exercises. This is a point of which we often lose sight. The early exercises are regarded as dull routine which can be done perfunctorily and then forgotten as the beginner moves on to more exciting work. In point of fact, these exercises provide the essential foundation upon which all else must ultimately depend. To omit them is as though one essayed the heights of the higher mathematics without any training in simple arithmetic!

When the aspirant comes to the use of the signs and words of power, it is equally important that he should not only make the signs and speak the words correctly, but also that he should have carried out a definite series of meditations upon the inner meaning of those signs and words. This meditation should not be a purely intellectual approach, but should include the *emotional* content also.

By this steady emotional and mental work, the signs and words become effective in the hands of the aspirant. Here the training of the visual and audible imagination finds its place. But it must be remembered that all such meditative training must be co-ordinated, and this is best done by having some general plan into which all the symbols fit, and which displays their various inter-relationships. Such ground-plans are, in the East, termed *mandalas,* and the standard and ideal *mandala* for the Western student is the mighty glyph of the universe and the soul of man: the "Tree of Life" of the Qabalah.

The doctrine of the Astral Light must be carefully studied, and for the time, at all events, it must be *accepted as a working theory*. Later experience will prove its truth and validity, but successful

THE WAY OF *MAGICAL* ATTAINMENT

magical results are unlikely if the work is done in the spirit of the atheist who is reported to have prayed "Lord—if there is a Lord—save my soul—if I have a soul."

A clear idea of the nature of the magical *Egregore*, or group-form, should be built up in the mind in order that the aspirant may understand what part he plays in the whole complex scheme, and thereby may know how closely he is guided and aided in his chosen work.

Returning now to the physical plane, the apsirant should begin to collect together his magical impedimenta; his robes, wand, ring, etc., and the furnishings of his magical oratory. Here the general rule is that he should make his own things, and not buy them ready-made. Of course with regard to certain things this is not possible, but wherever it can be done, it is a great help to the magician, since by making such things himself, the symbolic values attached to them are firmly fixed in the mind, and the whole becomes, as it were, an extension of his own personality.

Here a word of warning is indicated. Whatever is thus made for the magical work must be made as perfectly as possible within the range of the maker's skill. Nothing should be slip-shod in construction; neither should it be some commonplace article disguised, for the inevitable association links with its usual uses will prevent it being of service.

If a number of broom-handles be used to make a tall candle-stick, they should be bought for the purpose and so combined that they cease to have their individual character as broom-handles any more. All such things should also be dedicated to the work in which they will be used.

A simplicity and dignity of both the oratory and the magical appurtenances must be the ideal. A room "cluttered-up" by a host of symbolic "bits and pieces" can effectively bring to naught the magical work essayed therein. All the symbols, etc., must relate directly to the central idea of the work being done.

Now comes the key-work of the magical act, that which we have dealt with in section three (The Magical Keys). Upon the faithful performance of this work all else depends. First of all, the "magical personality" must be built, using for this work the power gained by the previous visual and audible exercises.

Then the exercises of the Interwoven Light must be commenced, and the training of the Body of Light put in hand. At the same time the cultivation of the basic "magnetic" energies should enable the aspirant to begin certain simple talismanic work.

The flashing colours should now be carefully experimented with, until the requisite subconscious "trick" of consciousness-shift is obtained at will.

As the aspirant gains in proficiency, he may begin to experiment in various ways with his newly developed magical power, remembering always that it must not be used against the will of those concerned, nor for any other purpose than service.

Apart from any experiments along these various lines, the aspirant should steadily work the ritual designed to bring him into conscious contact with his own Higher Self, the "Holy Guardian Angel" of the Qabalistic teaching. This should be the primary aim of all his magical work, and he cannot be an Adeptus Minor, in the true sense, until this essential contact has taken place. This, and this alone, should be the primary motive, the ever present ideal, and the continually repeated magical work should be its ceremonial embodiment.

All other magical work, interesting and instructive though it may be, and of definite training value to the aspirant, can become, if duly concentrated upon, a diversion from the path of the true magic.

In the great mystical traditions to be found in Buddhism, Hinduism and Christianity alike, preoccupation with secondary results is condemned, often in harsh terms. But the instinct is sound, such things can divert us from our true aim, though at the same time they can assist us thereto.

The present writer believes, from his own experiences in this realm, that many of the strictures of the Buddhist and Catholic mystics are somewhat too severe, and that there is a *via media*, a way between undue absorption in the lesser magic and the occult and psychic powers on the one hand, and the high austere flights of the soul as practised by such mystics as St. John of the Cross on the other.

The middle way has its virtues, and this has been sufficiently indicated herein.

When once the mystic union with the Higher Self has been obtained, *and stabilised*, which is another matter altogether, then, as the sage Abramelin says in his teachings to his son, "Now at this point I commence to restrict myself in writing, seeing that by the Grace of the Lord I have submitted and consigned you unto a Master so great . . . . "

The personal will, dedicated as it has been throughout the magical training, to the service of God and man, is now linked with the true will of its higher spirit Self.

This means that at least at times, and increasingly so, the magician is impelled and motivated from his own true spiritual nature,
and all the technical perfection of the personal self which has been
gained through the magical training is surrendered to the will of
the higher Self: then all the intricate machinery of conditioned
reflexes and subconscious capabilities lies under the control of that
reigning spiritual Self. The outer complexity has been taken inwards
and it is no longer necessary for the arousing of the inner powers.

So in the Great Mysteries, "the Abyss" is passed, and the personal man is "reborn in eternity."

How far this result is due to his own efforts, how far it is due
to the efforts of his spiritual Self and the mediation of the indwelling
Christ, is outside the scope of this book; but we may repeat the
Qabalistic statement that "It (*Malkuth*, the Kingdom) causes an
influence to emanate from the Prince of Countenances, the Angel
of *Kether*" (the highest Sephirah on the "Tree of Life").

Or we may quote Sir Oliver Lodge, "It is evident that there is
something very valuable in the personality."

So the end of the magical way is the surrender in loving service,
of the lesser personality and will to the indwelling spiritual Self,
that the will of the eternal may be done on earth "amid the legions
of the living."

This consummation will bring to the magician that true and
harmoniously balanced consciousness which is the true ideal towards which the whole creation is striving, that union with and
response to the divine Will. Of this union, the blessed souls in
Paradise spoke truly to Dante when they told him, "In His Will
is our Peace."

So may it be in the days to come with those of my readers who,
having set out on this magical journey, have, by the grace of the
Eternal, "obtained these things."

Chapter XXII

L'ENVOI

OUR labours are ended, and the work is done. Perhaps it may be of value if we briefly summarise what has been given.

First of all, our intention has been to write on the subject in such a way as to give the essentials of the magic art, and to give them in such a way that the sincere seeker might safely begin his labours in this field. At the same time, although we have not left out any essential principles, we have so written that only the really earnest seeker will realise the full value of the book.

Those who are familiar with the magical art, and more particularly those who are initiates of the various esoteric magical schools, may think that we have given out some things which should not have been given out. This is a valid criticism, though we have high authority for doing this; "There is nothing hidden that shall not be revealed."

Much of the prejudice against the subject arises from the foolish and unworthy secrecy maintained by many of the chiefs of the magical orders, a secrecy mainly designed to foster the self-aggrandisement of the people concerned.

For this reason we have endeavoured to give the magical essentials in such a way that the sincere aspirant may make a start with the matter. As he increases in proficiency, so his deeper understanding of the principles will reveal new depths of meaning, until, when he makes conscious contact with his true spiritual self, he finds the real teacher who will lead him into the paths of peace.

We have indicated that the *higher ranges* of magic are for the most part for those who are truly "born magicians," and we have stressed this point to avoid giving our readers an unduly optimistic view of the work required.

At the same time it should be borne in mind that much of what might be termed the "Minor Arcana" lies open to all in varying degrees.

Perseverance in this "lesser" magical field will prepare the aspirant for the greater work that lies ahead We may say that such minor magic is the magical equivalent of the "five-finger exercises" so painfully gone through by many of us in the past!

It may be as well if at this point we say that one of the essential principles of magic is that man is part of, and one with, Nature; that he is truly the microcosm of the macrocosm, the little universe in and part of the greater universe around him. Because of this, his action on all levels of being, physical, emotional, mental and supramental affects his environment, and this in its turn conditions his life in the physical.

Because of this mystical interplay between man and his environment, magic becomes possible, since by our definition magic is the art of producing changes in consciousness at will.

If we change our consciousness, then we act directly upon the inner worlds around us, and thus, ultimately, upon the objective world.

Here is one of the keys. In magical work, all is done, in actuality, by the action of the conscious mind upon the subconscious both personal and collective. The objective conscious mind provides the igniting spark which throws into motion the subconscious machinery, and it is the reaction between the personal unconscious and the universal unconscious that causes the manifestations of magic.

Thus we come to the use of technical devices, such as the Flashing Colours, the *Tattvic* exercises, and the visualising work, all designed to train the mind along certain lines, and to make it a matter of acquired skill to bring about a *"willed* dissociation" of consciousness, as a commencement of the work that eventually leads to the "willed *integration"* which is the goal of both magic and religion.

Throughout this book the cardinal principle has been to lead the aspirant to the realisation that true magic brings one into conscious union with the indwelling Self, the God within, and though the practice of the magical arts may stop at some point perhaps remote from this, yet in the end the aspirant will find an inner compulsion to complete the journey and find his true peace.

The general details which have not been included, owing to lack of space, will be found in the books dealt with in the Bibliography at the end. From these can be obtained the detailed rituals, but it should always be remembered that such rituals were built upon the principles here laid down. As we have said, it is within the power of the individual worker to build such rituals himself, and if they are built upon sound principles, they will work.

We have tried also to show the stages of psychological and ethical training required of the aspirant, and we have also indicated how all the outer complexity of ritual and ceremonial is in the end subsumed into the inner temple of the heart, and becomes part of the automatic mental machinery by the use of which the personality makes its contact with the divine nature.

Thus, as Iamblichus in *The Mysteries* truly says, "from supplication we are in a short time led to the object of supplication,
acquire its similitude from intimate converse, and gradually obtain
divine perfection."

If it is thought that this book is somewhat discursive and un-
co-ordinated, the writer cheerfully agrees that this does appear to
be the case. But it was done with intention, and underlying the
apparent lack of co-ordination there is a true plan upon which it
has been constructed.

This plan is, however, based upon the psychological laws governing the subconscious aspect of the mind.

We have written to *instruct* the *conscious* mind of the reader,
and to *influence* his subconscious following the methods of training
used in the schools of the Qabalah.

Finally we would say to the reader: a way is herein shown forth,
by which you may pass from darkness into the light, and this book,
however imperfectly, indicates the stages of that way, and is the
result of our own personal experience. We testify to that which we
have seen, and we speak that which we do know.

That this may also be true of some at least of those who read
herein is our sincere wish.

Appendix A

RELAXATION AND BREATHING EXERCISES

THE closely related exercises of conscious relaxation and controlled breathing are two of the basic elements in the training of the magician. Indeed, they are of value in ordinary life, quite apart from any specialised training, since they can be most helpful in building up and maintaining the physical body in a really healthy condition. Since the body acts upon the mental processes, such a healthy body will act most favourably upon the mind, and since the mind and emotions affect the glandular system of the body, there is set up a circle of beneficial influence which can be of the greatest value.

Let us consider the art of relaxation, for an art it really is, and one, moreover, that is practised only by a small minority of people. Many people think that relaxation is a very simple thing, "one just relaxes," and that is all. However, when the practice is undertaken seriously, one finds there is much more to it than that!

It is of interest to note one's reactions during a holiday spent quietly, say amid country surroundings. Usually three or four days elapse, and then one suddenly realises that somehow or other, one has "let go," and there is an unmistakable feeling of restfulness. Why should there be this period before one lets go? The answer is that all day and every day we have been tensing ourselves mentally, emotionally and physically against the feverish rush and clamour of modern life. Many people, in estimating the harmful effect of the terrific noise of our towns, fail to realise that, although our appreciation and registration of sound waves is by the medium of the ear, it is nevertheless true that the whole surface of our body is being continually assailed by the continuous impact of the sound vibrations around us, and it is this continuous bombardment which is a great factor in the establishment of a state of muscular tension in the body.

The first stage, therefore, in the relaxation exercise, will be commenced under conditions as free from outer noises as possible. Later, the exercise can be carried out under conditions of noise, etc., which would have spelt failure in the early days.

Start by sitting in a comfortable chair, or lying on the back on a couch or bed. It is as well to point out here that at one point of the exercise there may occur a strong muscular spasm, and this sudden tensing of the muscles very often leads the beginner to think that some psychic experience is at hand. Certain accounts of "astral projection" have helped to create this impression, but in the greater number of cases, the cause is purely physical, though the phenomena may, and often does, accompany certain forms of psychic activity.

Usually, however, it is due to a simple physical mechanism. If we stand erect and close our eyes, we find that our sense of location is brought about by the interaction of certain definite physical sensations. If we commence to lose balance, we at once perceive the compensatory action of certain of the body muscles, and we perceive also that the localised area of the foot from which we gain our balance shifts as our weight is re-distributed, and this causes us to bring other muscles into play to correct our balance.

If we are lying flat on our back on a bed, then we have the weight of the body pressing down upon the whole of the back of the head, the shoulders, the buttocks and the underside of the thighs and knees, down to the back of the heels. If this position is maintained without movement of the body for some time, there comes a point where the steady pressure upon the nerve-endings all over that part of the body sets up a paralysis of sensation.

We no longer feel the bed beneath us, for a fraction of a second we seem to be *"falling free."* Since uncontrolled falling is usually detrimental, our subconscious immediately tenses up the muscles in a powerful spasm in order that some effort may be made to keep fixed and safe. This is one of the usual mechanisms resorted to by the subconscious when the "kinesthetic sense," the sense of location, has been lost. It operates during "astral projection" for the same reason, but its occurrence is not, in itself, a sign of such psychic activity. This particular point has been dwelt on because of its liability to be misinterpreted.

Having seated ourselves comfortably in a chair, or stretched ourselves out on the bed or couch, we are ready to start. It is most important that no article of clothing should be tight or in any way uncomfortable. We are going to *relax* the physical, and do not wish to have constant messages coming from various parts of the body calling for some relief. Here it may be noted for those who prefer the on-the-back position, that the pillow used should support the neck as well as the back of the head.

If this is not the case, then the head is liable to be forced forward, and the breathing restricted. This we must avoid, and for this reason a little experimentation with pillows or cushions is helpful, until one finds the best height required.

We now direct our attention to the top of our head and see if the scalp muscles are relaxed or tensed. If the latter, and this is the usual thing, we deliberately relax them and pass down to the forehead. Here we shall usually find very definite tensing of the muscles, and these should now be relaxed. It will often be found that the accommodation muscles of the eyeballs have become involved in this muscular tension, and will have to be deliberately relaxed. This is not quite so easy as one might think, especially in the early stages. Now we come to the muscles of the face and mouth, and the same procedure is carried out. The muscles of the neck are considered and relaxed, and with them the relaxation of the head is complete.

Now, in case we should be inclined to congratulate ourselves upon our ability to relax, we turn our attention back to the top of the head, and in eight cases out of ten we shall find that we have unconsciously tensed up the scalp muscles again! So once again we start to relax consciously! Eventually we arrive at a point where we have definitely relaxed all the head, face and throat muscles, and can now move down the trunk and the arms to the legs and finally the feet.

By starting with the head muscles and gaining some control over them before going on further, we break up the exercise and improve our technique. By taking the arms and trunk as our next objective, and finishing with the legs and feet, we are doing the exercise in the most effective manner.

When once we have achieved full relaxation in each section of the body, we can work for full relaxation through the whole body as one unit.

The aid of a sympathetic friend may be enlisted to check one's success in the matter. When we have successfully relaxed, say, the right arm, we ask our friend to lift it up and let it drop down again. If our relaxation has been successful the arm will fall back as a "dead weight." A similar test may be made with the legs. Another rather more stringent test may be made by arranging with our friend to strike down at our hand or arm as it lies in the relaxed condition, but not of course to actually hit it.

If we are not completely relaxed, we shall find that there will be the usual involuntary "start," but if we are relaxed, then there will be no reaction at all. In point of fact, when relaxation has been complete, it very often takes a definite effort to take up the necessary muscular tensions again.

Someone has said that the effect of this relaxation exercise is that one "rests in the waters of peace," and this is a very apt description of it.

It must be remembered, however, that apart from this very helpful use of the exercise, it is essential to the magician in training as a vital preliminary to the breathing exercises which constitute the next step of training.

Much nonsense has been spoken and written concerning breathing exercises. They have been condemned as dangerous, they have been lauded as miraculous and they have been wrenched from the context of the systems to which they belong and have inevitably been misused.

We shall here consider one form of breathing exercise which is linked up with the practise of relaxation on the one hand and the intake of psychic energy and etheric vitality on the other, and which is, *if carried out as here described*, perfectly safe.

Here we must point out an important part of the exercise. It will be seen that the practitioner is required to "hold the breath" for a stated time.

Most people attempt to "hold the breath" by closing the throat and nasal passage by an effort of will. As far as these breathing exercises are concerned, such a method is DANGEROUS, and should *never be attempted*. It is because of this that many people run into trouble in this matter.

The correct method of retaining the breath is to breath in for the allotted period, using the chest muscles and the great diaphragm muscle which lies between the chest and the intestinal area, to expand the chest and so fill the lungs with air. The chest should now be *held expanded* and the diaphragm muscle *held down*. The lungs are full of air, and this is being retained. But, and this is the test, if the chest is tapped sharply the air is partly expelled; there is *no barrier* in the throat or mouth.

This way of retaining the breath does not throw any strain upon the lung tissue, which is one of the chief dangers of breathing exercises. If this procedure is correctly carried out, there is no danger at all so far as the physical level is concerned. Having made this point quite clear, we may proceed to consider the exercise itself. We may note in passing, however, that most people use only a fraction of the total lung-area at their disposal, and certain cases of neuroses use even less than the average. From this viewpoint alone, then, the practise of breathing exercises is beneficial.

The most useful of the breathing exercises for general use is what we may call the fourfold breath.

Let the student sit or lie in a relaxed condition and breathe in the following way: —

1. Inhale slowly, mentally counting one, two, three, four. Now hold the breath, counting one, two.

2. Exhale at the same speed, again counting one, two, three, four. Now hold the lungs without movement, counting one, two.

Repeat this cycle of operations for about five minutes, not longer, at the commencement of the practise. Later on the time may be extended.

It is important that until the student is thoroughly proficient in this basic technique of relaxation and fourfold breathing, he *should not attempt* the exercise of the circulating light, or the Middle Pillar technique.

In the following appendix these two exercises will be considered.

THE BANISHING RITUAL

THE "Banishing Ritual of the Lesser Pentagram" is that technical magical operation known as "The Preparation of the Place." It is used as a means of defining and purifying the area in which the magical work is to be done, and this we may term the "objective" aspect of the rite.

There is, however, a subjective aspect to the matter, since all the outer rite is an externalisation in symbolic form of the inner emotional, mental and spiritual purpose of the magician and his assistants. This dual nature of *all* magical rites needs to be kept in mind if the full benefit of the work is to be gained.

In the Banishing Ritual we have, first of all, what is known as the Qabalistic Cross. This is done as follows: —

(a) Touch the forehead with the right hand and say *Ateh*.

(b) Lower the hand to the breast and whilst touching it say *Malkuth*.

(c) Touch the right shoulder, saying *Ve Geburah*.

(d) Bring the hand across the body and touch the left shoulder, saying *Ve Gedulah*.

(e) Clasp the hands on the breast and say *Le Olahm Amen*.

If the glyph of the Tree of Life is studied, it will be seen that the names *Geburah* and *Gedulah* are the names of two of the opposing Sephiroth of the Tree. It will be seen that, looking at the diagram as a glyph of the universe, i.e. as it is shown, the Sephirah *Geburah* is on the left hand pillar, and the Sephirah *Gedulah* on the right hand pillar. This is correct for the macrocosmic Tree, but when we are using the glyph as a diagram of the microcosm within us, then we "back into the Tree," i.e., we visualise it as if we stood with our backs to it. The Sephirah *Geburah* now comes near our right shoulder, and *Gedulah* is found on our left. It is this microcosmic Tree that we are using in this rite.

In an earlier section we considered the question of the esoteric use of sound vibrations, so it will suffice here if we refer the reader to that section in order that he may understand how to vibrate the words of the Cross Ritual. It must be understood that the ordinary speaking voice is not of use in this connection.

When we raise the hand above the head and lower it to touch the forehead, we are dealing with the symbolic expression of the highest spiritual nature within us; that radiant Being known to many

occult schools as the "Genius." By virtue of the psychic correspondences between that Being and the psychic centre situated in
the aura above the head, we draw down into our auric sphere the
radiant light-force.

Now the shaft of light which, in our visual imagination we have
pictured as coming down with our hand as we moved it down to
the forehead, is taken down towards the feet as we bring down the
hand to the solar plexus and vibrate the word *Malkuth.* This action
has now formulated a line of white light extending from above the
head down to the feet.

Now we touch the right shoulder and vibrate *Geburah.* From
this we move the hand over to the left shoulder, at the same time
visualising a line of white light-force as emanating from our right
shoulder and being drawn across to our left. Thus is formed in the
aura the Cross of Light. This cross should be strongly visualised
as we bring the hands together on the breast in the attitude of
prayer.

Although the cross has been formulated in the personal aura,
an attempt should be made, whenever it is so built up, to increase
its size, to visualise it *and* oneself as becoming huge and towering
in height. This is in itself a powerful suggestion that can help to
release the cramped personality from some of its self-imposed limitations, and so tend towards the ultimate union between the starry
Dweller of Eternity, who is our own true and deeper self, and our
limited and self-imprisoned personal self.

When the cross has been formulated as described, we commence
the next part of the work. Still facing East, as we did when we
began the Qabalistic Cross, we raise the right hand from a point
on our left side about midway between the hip and the knee. We
then move the right arm up to a point above the head, and bring
it down again to the corresponding point at our right side. It will
be seen that we have described an inverted "V". Now move the
right hand to a point slightly above the left shoulder, then to a
similar point above the right shoulder, and then from that point
bring it down diagonally to the point from which the figure was
started. Again, each movement of the hand must be seen mentally
to draw a line of white light-force, so that when we have completed
the movement, there glows in the air before us (mentally perceived)
a pentagram of white light. This pentagram must now be charged
with energy, and this is done by moving the hand rapidly to the
centre of the figure with a sharp stabbing motion, at the same time
vibrating the name *Yod-Heh-Vau-Heh.*

Turning to the South, with our outstretched hand drawing a line of light, we again build up a pentagram of light, this time vibrating *Ah-Doh-Ni*.

Then turning to the West, the pentagram is formulated again and the name *Eh-He-Heh* is vibrated. Now we turn to the North, vibrating *Ah-Gla* and finally we return to the East, where we stand with arms outstretched in the form of the cross as we formulate the Telesmatic Images in our visual imagination.

It will be remembered that we have formed four energy-charged thought-forms by the figures we have built at the four cardinal points of the compass. These forms we are now going to use as the focal points of the protecting barrier we have built, and we therefore build up behind them the telesmatic images of the four great archangels. As the forces of the universe are in the last resort living forces, emanations of the Universal Mind, so we may think of these telesmatic images as the psychic means whereby we are able to make contact with the living and intelligent forces which are personified in the great archangels. The *form* we build is a symbolic thought-form, but the life which fills it is the life of the great cosmic Being which we draw through that part of our nature which is in correspondence with Him, or, to be more accurate, which is a part of Him. As the old initiates declared "there is no part of me which is not of the gods."

So, facing East, we say "Before me Raphael, (Ra-fay-el) and formulate a mighty figure in a yellow robe in which shimmers the complementary mauve. As the East is the station of Air, we should mentally feel a gentle breeze coming from around the figure.

Now we say "Behind me Gabriel" (Ga-bree-el). The figure we build behind us in the Station of Water, the West, is robed in blue with orange complementary tones, and a crystal cup of blue water will be visualised as being held aloft by the figure. Water should be sensed as flowing from behind this figure.

Now we say "On my right hand Michael (Me-kay-el) and the telesmatic figure glows in robes of red, with vivid green overtones. A great sword of steel is uplifted in its hand and a radiant heat should be sensed as proceeding from it.

Finally "On my left hand Uriel" (Auriel). Here the figure will be robed in a parti-coloured robe in which citrine, olive, russet and black are intermingled. Around it should be visualised fertile ground (for this is the station of Earth) with grasses and wheat springing out around.

Now we conclude with the words "For around me flame the pentagrams, and above me shines the six-rayed star," and again formulate the Qabalistic Cross.

It will be obvious that much hard work will have to be put into the development of the visualising faculty if these Telesmatic Images are to be properly built and contacted with the living forces they symbolically represent.

Here is Labour—but it is basic work, and without it the Work may not be done.

Appendix C

THE EXERCISES OF THE MIDDLE PILLAR

THE exercise we are about to consider is in itself one of the most effective means of arousing within oneself the basic magical power without which ceremonial becomes simply a psychological method of approach to the powers of the Unconscious. Though, of course, the psychological method is of the greatest importance, it is only when it is supplemented by the magical energy brought into play through such an exercise as that of the middle pillar that the full range of the magical art may be experienced.

It is the contention of the present writer, and he is not alone in this, that if the magical fraternities and orders were to train their members from the commencement of their lodge training, in the practise of this exercise, they would greatly gain thereby.

For the philosophical and theoretical considerations of this exercise, the reader is referred to the bibliography given in the last part of this book. Here it will be sufficient if we give just an outline of the theory, and then describe the practice in detail.

Briefly the magical theory behind the middle pillar exercise is that by appropriate action upon the individual psychic machinery of the human personality, certain of its aspects may be aroused into activity, and this in its turn will cause external, objective energy to be drawn through into the "sphere of sensation" or "auric field" of the personality, thus charging it with vitality of a very powerful kind. This inflowing force may be used and directed as the magician wills, to effect those changes in consciousness, of himself or others, which we have stated to be the object of all true magical work.

The magical schools teach that there exist in the psychic body certain centres of activity, and these centres are located in the same general positions as the *chakras* of the eastern systems. We say, the same *general* positions, since there are certain variations from the theosophical classification. These do not, however, affect the results obtained and for this reason it is not our intention to enter into any comparison between the two systems.

It is sufficient for our purpose that the student should visualise himself as standing with his back to the diagram of the Tree of Life. The right-hand pillar will then be on his left hand, and the left-hand pillar on his right. The middle pillar, comprising the Sephiroth *Kether, Daath, Tiphareth, Yesod* and *Malkuth* will then be equated with his spinal column and feet.

Now let him visualise an inch or so above the crown of his head, a glowing whirling sphere of brilliant white light, and let him endeavour to realise that here is the upwelling fountain of the divine life within him. He should now "vibrate" the name Eheieh (Eh-he-yeh). Let him now picture a ray of brilliance shining down to the nape of his neck, where it shines out as a luminous sphere. Here the name to be vibrated is Jehovah Elohim (Ye-hoh-vo E-loh-heem).

Let the ray of light be now seen mentally as it strikes down to the centre of *Tiphareth*, located over the region of the physical heart, i.e. a little above the solar plexus. Here the name is Jehovah Aloah-Va-Daath (Ye-hoh-voh E-loah-va-daath).

Now the ray of light descends to the centre of *Yesod*, which is located over the generative organs, and the name Shaddai-El-Chai, (Sha-dai-el-kai) is sounded. Lastly the ray descends to the feet, where it ends in the centre of *Malkuth*. The name here is Adonai-Ha-Aretz (Ah-doh-nai-ha-aretz).

This completes the exercise. At first it suffices if the student passes fairly quickly down the body, merely formulating the spheres of the centres and vibrating the names. Later, as he becomes more proficient in the visualisation of the stations and the light-ray, he must begin to pause in contemplation at each station, meditating on the particular powers and activities attributed to it.

When this technique has been fully mastered, the student should begin to visualise the stations in their appropriate colour. *Kether*, the centre above the head is seen as a white brilliance, *Daath*, as a lavender coloured sphere, *Tiphareth*, as golden-yellow, *Yesod*, as purple, and *Malkuth* as dark olive green, or jet black.

It is not sufficient, however, that the student simply awaken the middle pillar centres in this way. It is necessary that the energies so drawn into the psychic field should be put into circulation, and this is done by the exercise of the Interwoven Light. Part of this, the "formula of circumambulation" as it is termed, we have already described in the chapter entitled "The Interwoven Light."

When the middle pillar technique has been thoroughly grasped, and the exercise mastered, the energies which are now being brought into the psychic organism may be directed by the visualising faculty in the following manner.

Having performed the exercise, and reached the station of *Malkuth*, the magician should bring his attention back to the station of *Kether*, above the head. Now the flaming white brilliance is willed and mentally seen to descend to the left shoulder, right down through the left side to the left foot. Here it passes through the sphere of *Malkuth*, enters the right foot, travels up the right side of the body to the right shoulder, and so back to *Kether*. This is the first phase of the exercise, and should be practised until proficiency is gained.

Now the second part can be commenced. Again the attention is directed to *Kether*. Then the white brilliance is visualised as coming down from that centre in front of the face and down the front of the body and legs to the toes. From these it travels along the soles of the feet, back up the calves and the back of the thighs, up over the spine and the back of the head to the station *Kether*.

It will be found helpful if the breathing is synchronised with this visualisation, the exhalation being performed as the visualised power travels downward, and the inhalation being done as the power travels upwards.

The third part of the exercise has already been described in the chapter on the Interwoven Light.

There are, of course, other exercises in connection with the middle pillar, but they do not need mention here, since they belong to the more advanced levels of magical training.

He who perseveres until he has mastered the basic exercises will learn, from one source or another, of the more advanced exercises. The student is never entirely without instruction.

The present writer would urge all his readers who desire seriously to practise the magical art, to train themselves thoroughly in this technique of the middle pillar. It is the key to practical magic.

BIBLIOGRAPHY

IT has been suggested to the writer that it would be of great assistance to students of magic if, instead of a simple list of books on
the subject, he gave a brief commentary on those which were likely
to be most useful to the reader.

We start, therefore, with some works by two of the foremost
writers on magical subjects, Israel Regardie and Dion Fortune.
The three books *The Garden of Pomegranates, The Tree of Life*
and *The Middle Pillar,* all by Regardie, are invaluable and all earnest students are indebted to him for these books alone. Another of
his works, *The Art of True Healing,* although small, is splendid
value. Having worked in the magical Order of the "Stella
Matutina," Regardie decided, for reasons which he gives, to publish
the secret rituals of the Order. This step has led to a considerable
amount of bitterness on both sides, but whether one agrees with his
action or not, there is no doubt that the four volumes of *The
Golden Dawn,* published in 1940, are veritable mines of information.

Dion Fortune has to her credit what is possibly the finest book
of Qabalistic exegesis ever written—*The Mystical Qabalah.* Other
books of hers in this connection are *The Esoteric Orders and their
Work, The Training and Work of an Initiate, The Esoteric Philosophy of Love and Marriage, Sane Occultism and Psychic Self-
Defence,* all published or to be published by The Aquarian Press.

Psychic Self-Defence is particularly recommended by the present
writer, who knew fairly intimately many of the people mentioned
therein.

Coming now to the standard writers on Magic, the two books
The History of Magic and *Transcendental Magic,* by Eliphas Levi,
are the source from which many modern writers have built up their
own expositions of magic. They are valuable not because of their
factual statements but rather for the stimulus they can give the en-
quiring mind.

Translations by A. E. Waite of these two books are published
by Riders.

Two of the early Theosophical books dealing with our subject
are *Natures Finer Forces,* by Rama Prasad, and *Magic: Black and
White,* by Dr. Franz Hartman. A book dealing with the occult
aspects of Christian ceremonial, *The Science of the Sacraments,* by
the Right Rev. C. W. Leadbeater, of the Liberal Catholic Church,
is published by the Theosophical Publishing House. Madame

Blavatsky's monumental work *Isis Unveiled*, is well worth studying, although the present writer agrees with Maeterlinck that it is "like a builder's yard"; it contains enough raw material for the building of innumerable mental edifices!

Two source books which must not be overlooked are *Sepher Yetzirah*, by Dr. Wynn Westcott, and *The Qabalah Unveiled*, by S. L. Magregor Mathers. These two men were, together with Brodie Innes, a Scotch "Writer to The Signet," the founders of the "Magical Order of the Golden Dawn." This is the parent stock from which many of the modern occult orders have stemmed. A word of warning here. These two books should not be attempted until the beginner has acquired quite a solid foundation of knowledge. He will then be able to read them with advantage.

Three books by Sir John Woodroffe (Arthur Avalon) are invaluable for giving a clear idea of the Hindu Tantric systems. These three are the *The Serpent Power*, *Shakti and Shakta*, and *The World as Power*.

A fine work on Egyptian magic is *The Occult Arts of Ancient Egypt*, by Bernard Bromage (Aquarian Press).

A book which throws much light on certain magical practices is *The Projection of the Astral Body*, by Muldoon and Carrington (Riders), and another which deals with magic from the Theosophical angle is *The Ritual of Higher Magic*, by Furze Morrish.

Mention is often made of the wonderful symbolic system known as the Tarot. The present writer considers the book by Paul Foster Case, *The Tarot* (Macoy Pub. Co.), to be the best published account of this very wonderful system.

Finally, there is the book *Magic: its Ritual, Power and Purpose*, by the present writer (Aquarian Press).

This is really an introductory study of the subject, leading up to the more detailed exposition of this present writing. For this reason, quite apart from any pecuniary interest in royalties, it is recommended that it be obtained and studied by the serious student.

Having dealt with the chief works on magic we will proceed to note some works dealing with the psychological basis of magic. Before we do this, however, we must return to our first list of books on magic. It will be seen that *none* of the writings of that strange being Aleister Crowley have been listed herein. This is because, whatever the value of his teaching may be, and there is much of real value therein, his literary style is so uneven, descending from sublime heights to depths of grossness, that he is no guide for the beginner in these matters. Advanced students may find much

that is illuminating in his works, but they will then be able to deal
selectively with his teachings.

Coming now to the books which throw light from the psychological angle upon our subject, the foremost are *The Secret of the
Golden Flower*, by Wilhelm and Jung, *The Integration of the
Personality* and *The Psychology of the Unconscious*, both by Dr.
Jung. *Suggestion and Auto-Suggestion*, by Baudoin, and *Hypnotism*,
by Dr. Moll give some idea of the working of the subconscious
mind, whilst Dr. Mary Harding's book *Women's Mysteries* is full
of real information on feminine psychology. A book which attempts
to bring together the East and the West is Dr. Geraldine Coster's
Yoga and Western Psychology.

Two works dealing with the psychic faculties are *Man's Latent
Powers*, by Phoebe Payne, and *Paranormal Cognition* by Dr. L. J.
Bendit. Both these books are published by Faber.

Some very interesting books dealing with the ceremonial of the
Masonic Order are *The Meaning of Masonry*, and *The Masonic
Initiation*, both by Bro. W. Wilmshurst, and *Freemasonry and the
Ancient Gods*, by Bro. J. S. M. Ward.

On the subject of *Magnetism*, the following works are worth
attention. *Letters on Od and Magnetism*, by Reichenbach (Hutchin-
sons), *Animal Magnetism*, by Gregory, *Vital Magnetic Healing*,
by Adelaide Gardner (T.P.H.), *Magnetism and Magic*, by Baron
de Sennevoy (Allen & Unwin), *The Rationale of Mesmerism*, by
A. P. Sinnett, and *The Human Atmosphere*, by Dr. Walter Kilner.

It is the belief of the present writer that much can be gained
from fictional representations of magical work, and for that reason
the following books have been included. They are of various grades
of value, but the discerning reader will be able to see who is writing
with the authority of knowledge concerning these things.

DION FORTUNE—

> *The Demon Lover; Secrets of Dr. Tavener; The Winged
> Bull; The Goat-foot God; The Sea Priestess; Moon Magic:
> The Memoirs of a Mistress of that Art.*

BRODIE INNES—

> *The Devil's Mistress; For the Soul of a Witch; Old as the
> World.*

SIR RONALD FRASER—

> *Sun in Scorpio; Glimpses of the Sun; Circular Tour; Fiery
> Gates; Bird Under Glass.*

MARJORIE LAWRENCE—
> *No. 7 Queer Street.*

ALGERNON BLACKWOOD—
> *John Silence; Julius Le Vallon; The Bright Messenger.*

DENNIS WHEATLEY—
> *The Devil Rides Out; Strange Conflict.*

J. M. A. MILLS—
> *Tomb of the Dark Ones; Lords of the Earth; There Will Your Heart Be.*

JOAN GRANT—
> *Winged Pharaoh; Eyes of Horus; Lord of the Horizon.*

L. ADAMS BECK—
> *House of Fulfilment.*

TALBOT MUNDY—
> *Black Light; Om.*

BULWER LYTTON—
> *Zanoni; A Strange Story.*

H. RIDER HAGGARD—
> *Wisdom's Daughter; Queen of the Dawn; Morning Star; The World's Desire.*

W. B. Yeats, the Irish poet and dramatist, was one of the early members of the magical Order of the Golden Dawn, and his autobiography *The Trembling of the Veil* is of considerable value.

Another of the early G. D. members was Arthur Edward Waite, and his autobiography, *Shadows of Life and Thought* is also of interest.

The Irish writer "A.E.", though not a member of the G.D., nevertheless was in touch with many of its initiates, and his book *The Candle of Vision* (Macmillan & Co.), is worth reading.

Ethel Archer, who was connected with the group which centred around Aleister Crowley, has written a very interesting story, *The Hieroglyph*, and another helpful piece of fiction is *High Magic's Aid*, by G. B. Gardner.

There are, of course, many other books on our subject, and lists of these will be found in some of those mentioned here.

Unfortunately many of these books are now out of print, and can only be obtained through the second-hand market.

POSTSCRIPT

I have written diffusely, leaving many loose ends of thought, and this for a very definite reason.

There is in the modern world far too much of the "tabloid" spirit – neat little digests of information made up into attractive mental packets for the use of those who wish to have a general knowledge of various subjects, without the trouble of really studying them.

Such a thing is highly dangerous, since it offers an ideal way in which the unscrupulous may put forward their own particular ideas without any mental resistance on the part of the victim. Such methods lead to the production of the mass mentality which can be such a deadly thing in the hands of the dictators – whether of the Right or the Left.

I have, therefore, not produced a "Digest of Magic", but have merely attempted to give my readers some glimpses – intriguing, or even exasperating – of the wonderful field of study which goes by the name of "Magic", and it is my hope that such glimpses will set them studying the works of those who are the recognised masters of the subject.

APPRENTICED TO MAGIC

—— & ——

MAGIC & THE QABALAH

In this special compilation volume, W.E. Butler's second two seminal works are reprinted with a new introduction by Dolores Ashcroft-Nowicki, cementing his reputation as 'The Grand Maistre of English Occultism'.

APPRENTICED TO MAGIC, designed to liberate the latent magical powers we all possess, takes the form of a series of personal instructions from a *guru* to his *chela*. The lessons are basic exercises in meditation and the training of one's visualizing power and includes information on mental exercises, magical rites and ceremonies, astral projection and the ancient Tree of Life.

MAGIC AND THE QABALAH is a stimulating examination of the QBL (literally 'from mouth to ear') and the significance of this unwritten tradition of esoteric knowledge over many centuries. The illuminating work provides much food for meditation and will be helpful in producing those changes of consciousness which are the goals of the magical art.

Together the two provide the reader with an exhilarating contact with the mind of an esoteric craftsman, an inestimable privilege for anyone who aspires to initiation into Western magical practice. And if his advice is read properly, meditated upon, and followed up, it will bring those who are ready to the Doors of the Mysteries.